IN DEFENSE OF
MUMIA

IN DEFENSE OF
MUMIA

Edited by

S.E. Anderson and Tony Medina

with Patricia A. Allen

Writers and Readers Publishing, Inc.

Writers and Readers Publishing, Inc.
P.O. Box 461, Village Station
New York, New York 10014

Editor: Patricia A. Allen
Cover and Book Design: Paul Gordon and Terrie Dunkelberger
Cover Art © 1996: Daniel Simmons

Library of Congress Cataloging-in-Publication Data
In Defense of Mumia / Edited by S.E. Anderson and Tony Medina.
     p. cm.
   ISBN 0-86316-099-9
   1. Abu-Jamal, Mumia -- Poetry. 2. Afro-Americans -- Legal Status,
laws, etc. -- Poetry. 3. Criminal justice, Administration of -- Poetry.
4. Race discrimination -- United States -- Poetry. 5. Afro-American
prisoners -- Poetry. 6. Death row -- United States -- Poetry.
7. Amercian poetry -- 20th century. 8. Abu-Jamal, Mumia. 9. Race
discrimination -- United States. 10. Afro-American prisoners.
I. Anderson, S.E. (Sam E.) II. Medina, Tony.
PS595.A215   1996
810.8'0351 -- dc20
                                        96-1927
                                         CIP

0 9 8 7 6 5 4 3 2 1

Manufactured in the United States of America

This book is dedicated to the memory of:

Conrad Lynn (1908 - 1995)– radical black attorney, Malcolm X's friend & lawyer, as well as defender of black activists and the oppressed

Bill Kunstler (1919 - 1995)– radical attorney always ready to defend the oppressed and to expose North America's hypocrisy

Andrew Salkey (1928 - 1995)– a teacher, novelist, broadcaster, anthologist, writer of children's books, poet and committed socialist

Toni Cade Bambara (1939 - 1995)– revolutionary Sista writer and teacher

Ken Saro-Wiwa (1941 - 1995)– Nigerian-Ogoni-antiimperialist writer and activist: *assassinated, along with eight other Ogoni comardes, by the Nigerian Military junta working for Shell Oil*

Contents

In Defense of Mumia

Preface:

Mumia Abu-Jamal *Walkin' in the Shadow of Death* .... *xv*

Acknowledgments .... *xix*

Introduction:

S.E. Anderson and **Tony Medina** *The Threat of Death Can Unite...
and Ignite!* 1

I. *Some things must burn* (The National Scene I)   **5**

Askia M. Touré *From the Projects of North Philly to the Pyramids
of Liberation* (prose poem) 6
Cornel West *'Free Mumia'?* (essay) 7
Richard Cammarieri *Domestic Policy* (poem) 8
Cornelius Eady *My Face* (poem) 10
Seth Tobocman *Freedom of the Press in Black and White* (cartoon)...... 11
Carolyn Peyser *Movin' On for Mumia* (poem) 26
Katha Pollitt *Subject to Debate* (essay) 27
Abdul Haqq *Death to Killer Cops* (poem) 29
Shariff Simmons *American Schizophrenia* (poem) 30
KRS-One *Free Mumia* (rap lyrics) 32
E.L. Doctorow *From Here to Death Row* (essay) 36
Manning Marable *Justice for Mumia Abu-Jamal* (essay) 38
Marvin X *Free Mumia Abu-Jamal* (poem) 39
Standing Deer *If They Were Going to Kill My Brother* (poem) 41
Keelyn Bradley *a battle hymn* (poem) 42
Tony Medina *Notes on a Hanging Judge* (poem) 43

II. *All the facts are lies* (The National Scene II)   **49**

Willie Perdomo *Dreaming, I Was Only Dreaming* (poem) 50
Toni Morrison *Racism and Fascism* (essay) 51
Kecia Élan Cole *Day-Glo Armageddon* (poem) 52
Xochipielli *L.A. law (and order)* (poem) 54
Saul Williams *Sha Clack Clack* (poem) 56
Danny Shot *My Money* (poem) 59
Lamont B. Steptoe *Begging for a Nightstick* (poem) 62

Lenard D. Moore *Rodney King* (poem) 63

Michael C. Ladd *The Bottom of the Storm* (poem) 64

Cornelius Eady *Rodney King Blues* (poem) 67

Maria Mazziotti Gillan *Coming of Age: Paterson* (poem) 68

Trinidad Sanchez, Jr. *America Is a Prison* (poem) 70

Allen Ginsberg *Ballad of the Skeletons* (poem) 71

Robert Farr *how's that?* (poem) 75

Paul Beatty *Old Yeller Dreams of Days When They Wasn't Just Whistlin' Dixie* (poem) 76

Pedro Pietri *DO NOT WALK ON THE GRASS UNTIL AFTER SMOKING IT* (poem) 78

June Jordan *Manifesto of the Rubber Gloves* (poem) 81

Naomi Long Madgett *Images* (poem) 86

Staci Rodriguez *where images are not sacred* (poem) 86

Julia Lopez *Colonialism on the Brain* (poem) 87

Jayne Cortez *What's Happening* (poem) 91

III. *Bringing the temple down* (MOVE)　　　　　　　　93

Lucille Clifton *move* (poem).. 94

Lucille Clifton *samson predicts from gaza the philadelphia fire* (poem) 95

MOVE *Why the MOVE Organization Supports Mumia Abu-Jamal* (essay) 95

Mumia Abu-Jamal *May 13th Still Burns!!!* (cartoon) 97

David Henderson *NOMAD ISLAND* (poem) 103

Ras Baraka *Why Mumia Must Live and Go Free* (poem) 104

Moe Seager *We Want Everything* (poem) 108

Rick Kearns *No Charges/Police Flashlight Ballet* (poem) 110

Gaston Neal *Mrs. Eleanor Bumpers, Age 69* (poem) 112

Marilyn Buck *One White Girl Ponders Strange Behavior* (poem) 113

Lamont B. Steptoe *Osage* (poem) 113

Lance Tooks *At 13th and Locust* (cartoon) 117

Kevin Powell *altar for four* (poem) 118

Mari Evans *Alabama Landscape* (poem) 120

IV. *Condemn death to death/This is no place to be* (Prisons)　　123

Amina Baraka *Dirge for the Lynched* (poem) 124

Safiya Henderson-Holmes *death row ain't* (poem) 125

Dennis Brutus *In the Courthouse* (poem) 126

John Edgar Wideman *Doing Time, Marking Race* (essay) 126

Piri Thomas *A First Night in El Sing Sing* (poem) 130

David Mills *All Things We Didn't Consider* (poem) 132

Abiodun Oyewole of The Last Poets *POLITICAL PRISONERS* (poem) 136

Rashidah Ishmaili *Missing Person—2* (poem) 137

Raul Salinas *News from San Quentin: August 21, 1971* (poem) 142

Jill Witherspoon Boyer *George Jackson* (poem) 143

Larvester Gaither *Conviction or a Fine? Are There Political Prisoners and P.O.W.s in the Good Ole U.S. of A.?* (essay) 144

Raymond R. Patterson *Words* (poem) 150

Susan Rosenberg *Shadow Life* (poem) 150

Lenina Morales Nadal *to the warrior with child* (poem) 151

Mumia Abu-Jamal *Bondage of Flesh (cartoon)* 153

Nat Hentoff *Death Condemned to Death in South Africa* (essay) 158

Samuel Allen *I Saw the Executioner* (poem) 161

Gwendolyn Brooks *To the Prisoners* (poem) 162

Peter Linebaugh *Qui Vive?: The Farce of the Death Penalty* (essay) 163

Eliot Katz *Lessons from an Uneasy Chair* (poem) 169

Tracie Morris *The Old Days* (poem) 169

Gregory Benton *A Deception of Justice* (cartoon) 171

Theodore A. Harris *The Housing Authority* (poem) 172

Patricia J. Williams *The Executioner's Automat* (essay) 172

Sally O'Brien *Interview with Mumia Abu-Jamal* 180

Bahíyyih Maroon *Fire Keeper* (poem) 192

V. *Look who watches* (The International Scene) **195**

Ngũgĩ wa Thiong'o *Prison Without Trial* (essay) 196

Daisy Zamora *Message to the Poets* (poem) 198

Jesus Papoleto Meléndez *A San Diego/Southern African Night* (poem) 199

Nancy Mercado *On My Return from Puerto Rico to the U.S.* (poem) 210

Ian Williams *Non-swinging Europe* (essay) 212

Rosemari Mealy *Cuba–In Defense of Mumia* (essay) 214

Margaret Randall *A WORD, BOSNIA* (poem) 218

Frank M. Chipasula *We Must Crush the Parasite* (poem) 219

Ammiel Alcalay *A Stitch in Time* (essay) 220

Martín Espada *The Meaning of the Shovel* (poem) 223

Jorge Matos Valldejuli *From the Cordillera to the Altiplano* (poem) 224

Suheir Hammad *Patience* (poem) 226

Ngô Thanh Nhàn *Mumia–the Dragon and the Prison* (poem) 228

VI. *My eyes wide open* (Statements) **233**

Safiya Bukhari *COINTELPRO & Philly Cops Conspire to Kill Mumia* (essay) 234

William M. Kunstler *Death Row Writer Deserves New and Fair Trial* (letter) 235

Herb Boyd *An Award-winning Journalist Denounces NABJ* (letter) 236

Standing Deer *Fast for Survival* (statement) 238

Leonard Peltier *Statement in Solidarity with Mumia Abu-Jamal* 239

Federation of Cuban Women *To: The Coalition to Free Mumia Abu-Jamal* (letter) 241

Pan African Congress of Azania *Statement in Support of Mumia Abu-Jamal* 242

International Academics for Mumia Abu-Jamal *Statements* 243

Mumia Abu-Jamal *Letter to asha bandele* 246

Kalamu ya Salaam *my eyes wide open: an open letter to my executioner* (poem) 248

VII. *In the land of confiscated dreams* (Literary Expressions)   251

John Edgar Wideman *Ascent by Balloon from the Yard of Walnut Street Jail* (short story)...... 252

Eugene B. Redmond *Mumia's Air/Mumia's Rainbow* (prose poem) 256

Ted Wilson *Take It Again... this time from the top* (poem) 258

Fred Ho *The Climbers* (poem) 260

Brenda Walcott *Asylum* (poem) 262

Michael S.Weaver *Improvisation for Piano* (poem) 264

Steve Cannon *Mysteriousa–Who Be Do Be Do* (poem) 265

Clairesa Clay *Much Ado About Nothang?* (essay) 266

Zöe Angelsey *Commit to Continuity* (poem) 268

Victor Hernández Cruz *If You See Me in L.A. It's Because I'm Looking
for the Airport* (poem) 268

asha bandele *4:15 in the a.m.* (poem) 272

Lesley-Ann Brown *Listen* (poem) 277

Michael S. Weaver *A Black Man's Sonata* (poem) 279

Bethany Johnson *My Synopsis of the World Aspects of a Jejune Mind* (poem) 280

Amiri Baraka *I AM* (poem) 281

Raymond R. Patterson *A Black Thought* (poem) 286

Cheryl Boyce Taylor *House of the Un Natural World* (poem) 286

Eunice Knight-Bowen *One Wing* (poem) 288

Stuart McCarrell *Paul Robeson* (poem) 289

Becky Billips *Move!* (essay) 289

Susan Rosenberg *Some Ragings on AIDS* (story) 290

Pamela Sneed *Rapunzel* (short story)... 292

Hettie Jones *Going to Jail* (short story) 293

Raymond M. Brown *Epistle from Hell: A Review of* Live from Death Row 293

Jelani W. Cobb *Review of* Live from Death Row 296

Jerome Washington *Stories from the Yard* (stories) 299

VIII. *Breaking Prayers* *(Towards Tomorrow)*   **303**

Dudley Randall *Roses and Revolutions* (poem) 304
Assata Shakur *Let Us Carry Our Tradition to Freedom!* (essay) 304
Melba Joyce Boyd *Breaking Prayers* (poem) 305
Piri Thomas *A Dialogue with Society* (poem) 308
Dennis Brutus *Sequence for Mumia Abu-Jamal* (poem) 310
Amiri Baraka *For Mumia: Revolutionary Culture at the Side of the People* (essay) 312
Arthur Amaker *After the March* (poem) 315
Olori *In Praise of Spirit* (poem) 316
Linda Wasson *Truth, can we save you before it's too late?* (poem)...................... 317
Graham Rayman *Cyber–Organizing for Mumia–The Progressive Use of the Worldwide Web* (essay) 320
Angela Jackson *Fannie (of Fannie Lou Hamer)* (poem)...................... 322
Nzadi Zimele Keita *pass the word* (poem)...................... 323
Sandra María Esteves *Till the Cows Come Home* (poem)...................... 324
Sandra María Esteves *Who Says I Can't* (poem) 325
Vicki Garvin *Step Up the Offensive Today for Victory* (essay)...................... 326
Sonia Sanchez *For Sweet Honey* (poem)...................... 328
Mike Farrell *Why I Joined Mumia's Ranks* (essay)...................... 330
Naomi Long Madgett *Tree of Heaven* (poem)...................... 331
Louis Reyes Rivera *the blacklit face of Mumia* (poem)...................... 331
Jan Carew *If We Let Him Go Quietly We, Too, Will Bleed* (poem) 334
Lamer Belle Steptoe *Mumia* (poem)...................... 336

Afterword:
S.E. Anderson and **Tony Medina** **337**

Contributors **339**

Credits **364**

In Defense of Mumia

Mac McGill	*ii*
Mac McGill	5
Mac McGill	34
John Abner	47
Tom Feelings	49
Wangeshi Mutu	83
Mac McGill	93
Mel Edwards	123
Shawn Alexander	128
Theodore A. Harris	138
Shawn Alexander	182
John Abner	193
George "Geo" Smtih	195
Renaldo Imani Davidson	213
Sandra María Estevez	217
Eric Drooker	233
Jaun Sánchez	237
Diana Hernandez	240
Deborah Pohl	245
Kraig Blue	249
Mac McGill	251
Diedra Harris-Kelley	273
John Abner	332

Contrary to popular belief, conventional wisdom would have one believe that it is insane to resist this, the mightiest of empires... . But what history really shows is that today's empire is tomorrow's ashes, that nothing lasts forever, and that to not resist is to acquiesce in your own oppression. The greatest form of sanity that anyone can exercise is to resist that force that is trying to repress, oppress, and fight down the human spirit.

—Mumia Abu-Jamal

Sometimes they have to kill us because they cannot break our spirit.

— John Trudell

Preface

Walkin' in the Shadow of Death
by Mumia Abu-Jamal ©1995

Hell is not the Dantean creation of eternal cacaphony, marked by the fevered screams of the tortured.

No.

Hell is quiet, still and chilled.

I know.

I live there.

It is a place of mind-robbing sameness, where days are pale echoes of the day before.

On a day like every preceding one, I was lost in concentration, my fingers flying in mindless abandon over typewriter keys, writing a motion for a pending pleading, until my consciousness split to monitor the nearing jangle of keys.

The jangle ceased.

A moment of silence.

A cleared throat.

"Uh, Jamal...would you step over to the door."

"What's up, man?"

"The, uh, lieutenant would like to see you."

Eyes meet, and in a flash, an odd admixture of sadness and duty reflect.

(Damn. Here it comes.)

"What's up, lieutenant?"

"Mr. Jamal, your death warrant has just been signed. We're gonna handcuff you and strip you down."

At least five guards, a sergeant and a lieutenant crowd the blue-tiled hallway, their nerves afire.

I turn to the baldheaded Buddhist Swami, with whom I spent most of this morning's library period, and ask him to gather my legal material.

"We'll take care of it," a guard answers.

My wrists are shackled.

I am escorted by a silent, uniformed mob to Phase II, an area on B pod, where men under death warrants are placed.

(Yo...this is Phase II!)

Six cells, shielded by plastic and steel cages, with small five-inch rectangular boxes fitted to the front door of each cell.

The boxes are 24-hour remote cameras which monitor each man's every movement.

The cells are bare except for a basin/toilet unit, a steel bed riveted to the right wall, a seat/desk arrangement and a property bin attached to the left wall.

The regulation strip search is conducted, leaving a naked man in a cold concrete cell.

Every item of clothing taken is not to be returned to the naked man, so guards, unprepared for this rare morning warrant, scurry to find Phase II clothing.

On institutional uniforms, a man's name and number are emblazoned.

Not so for Phase II uniforms, where, presumably, those with a date to die need no names.

"What's up, cuz?" asks 'Min, a tall, bald and bearded veteran of Phase II.

"What's up, 'Min? How you be, man?"

"Sheeit—Ya know how I be, cuz; I'm messed up!"

"Me and you both, huh?"

'Min is on his second death warrant and, as one of two men to have done so, is an authority among the five men caged on "the Faze."

The men make small talk among themselves, an attempt to chase the cold, constricting demons of fear away, as they clutch for the heart.

In an odd equation of death, the more talk equals more fear: [>t=>f].

Small talk amidst the awesome reality of impending death.

Approaching death, while waiting in an icebox.

The small talk diminishes into tiny talk and vanishes in the hush of quiet.

The omnipresent air blower rushes, its cool breath seemingly amplified by the stilled human voices.

Body sense whispers that hours have passed since my 9:45 a.m. notice of my new status.

I walk an empty cell, my footfalls an echo from the cold concrete walls.

(So, *this* is what an empty cell looks like!)

A rustle of "White Shirts" (or ranking guards) announces the arrival of news.

As expected, the "White Shirt" has come to "officially" inform me of what I, and all others in the block, knew.

"Jamal—your death warrant has been signed...."

He turns to a white piece of paper and reads:

> The Governor of the Commonwealth of Pennsylvania has signed your death warrant today, effective for the week of August 13, 1995.
>
> I have attached a copy of the warrant.
>
> The Department of Corrections has set the date of Thursday, August 17, 1995, to carry out this order at the state correctional institution at Rockview.

"Any questions?" the "White Shirt" asks, his blue eyes cool.

"I'd like to contact my family."

"Your block sergeant will take care of that," he announces, and with a sharp turn of his heels, he is gone after leaving a Xerox of the death warrant behind.

I look at it dumbly, seeing it, but not reading it.

'Min breaks me out of my reverie.

"Hey, Mu!"

"Yeah, 'Min—"

"Welcome to the club, baby!"

"Sheeit! Pardon me if I don't celebrate."

His high, nasal laughs careen off walls and plastic Plexiglas. I don't particularly feel much like yukkin' it up, but I remember how men talk to chase their fear, and before long, 'Min and I are talking—into the wee hours of the morning.

Walking into Memory

It has been over twelve years since I've walked into a county courtroom.

Twelve years since my banishment to the barren badlands of death row.

As I walk into this ancient, ornate, carpeted room, I notice the visages of long-dead jurists, their expressions cold and supercilious, all old White men, staring down from their framed perches on the wall but seeing nothing.

An expectant silence vibrates in the air, until a little boy shatters it.

"I love you, Grandpop!"

Laughter, and then, tentatively at first, until a little boy shatters it.

"I love you, Grandpop!"

Laughter, and then, tentatively at first, until building in confidence and crescendo, a round of applause breaks over the right side of the courtroom, long and sustained.

I am stunned by it, and when the thought strikes, I return the clenched-fist salute to many who offer this militant affirmation.

I sight my grandson, a reddish-brown dimpled munchkin who can barely see over the public rail, and tell him, "I love you too, son!," as a sweet smile bursts forth like spring sunshine.

He is nearing 4 and I have never touched him.

I have never seen him without a barrier between us.

Yet this child radiates a love so palpable one can swim in it, and all around him, people pulsate with a love, not of the flesh, but of the spirit.

Love—in a courtroom, a legal arena of death.

"Justice is just an emotional feeling, counselor," opines Senior Judge Albert F. Sabo as he denies a stay of execution sought by lead defense counsel Leonard I. Weinglass, "in the interest of justice."

I am reminded of a lawyer's tale of a trial before a judge who bellowed, "This isn't a court of justice! It's a court of law!"

In this courtroom, where I was sentenced to death, a sense of déjà vu oscillates with the ominous present, as Albert Sabo unleashes slur after slur at defense counsel.

"I don't know how you do it up in New York, counsel, but we don't do that in Philadelphia," he quips.

He hits several with contempt citations and orders one of my lawyers away from the bench, in handcuffs, to a jail cell.

Rachel Wolkenstein, Esq., had the temerity to dare question the jurist after one of his summary rulings of exclusion of documentary evidence. She dared do what defense lawyers are traditionally intimidated from doing in Sabo's courtroom—aggressively defending their clients.

In a moment of remembrance, I saw my trial lawyer hit with contempt for daring to follow his client's wishes, until a prosecutor begged Judge Sabo to reconsider.

In the midst of familial love is the undeniable presence of judicial hatred, for "justice is just an emotional feeling."

The Stay

After days of denying all defense motions, and denying subpoenas for over a third of the defense witnesses, Senior Judge Sabo, on the late morning of Aug. 7, 1995, did the unexpected.

The aging jurist, unbidden, issued a stay of execution.

The shock to the defense was electric.

The prosecution seemed unsurprised and subdued.

Shock radiates through the courtroom, and a scattered round of applause grows in response.

"Wait a while," interjects Sabo, his voice a mirror of irritation. "You might not wanna clap when ya hear what I'm sayin'...."

He then reads the full text of his order, which sets forth an "indefinite" stay, pending further appeals.

The unexpected nature of the ruling, coming as it did from a judge not known for such an act, left me guarded, awaiting the worm within the apple, so to speak.

I felt, like a wave on my back, the breath of relief from my children, grandchildren, the rest of my family and friends.

In all of our discussions, counsel didn't expect this decision from the opinionated jurist.

With 10 days of life remaining, the stay was admittedly welcome, from whatever source.

It does not mean, however, that I am no longer on death row.

It means the government still intends to kill me—just on another day.

By the stay, I am moved out of the lower depths of the state's hell, to a mid-range; from a dungeon, to a cage.

A cage located out in the boondocks, as far from Philadelphia as is possible and remain inside the stateline; a cage where men are held behind glass and steel; a cage where men await death.

•••

Acknowledgments

The making of the book was in itself a struggle and a journey. The struggle was not in finding an editor and publisher willing to take a chance on such a blatantly political project, for our editor, Patricia A. Allen, and our publisher, Glenn Thompson (both, imbued with political conscientiousness and integrity) jumped on the proposal without equivocation (like "two-toned birds of no hesitation," as Jayne Cortez would put it.) The great miracle and literary coup was to assemble the contributions and put the book together in four weeks time!... in the middle of August–when artists and academics are usually on vacation, no doubt! But there was always help from special, dedicated friends and comrades such as Lamont B. Steptoe, Nancy Mercado, and Jonathan Scott, who all assisted Medina in contacting the many writers across the country; and those who came in handy with other favors (particularly Kim Wade of Hunter College's Black Student Union for lending the fax and Max Bloch of *The Nation* for writing and faxing letters and granting permission to use a number of works); the staff at Writers and Readers: Paul Gordon, our designer; Ron David, for suggesting the title; Wilhelmina Harewood and Lisa Warburton, for help and patience to deal with our being in the way of their work; Patricia Allen, again, for all of your editorial assistance and courage and strength in putting up with us crazy poets; Karen Taylor, for reading and re-reading the text; and all the writers, artists, and activists who responded with enthusiasm to our request for work at such a short time.

Introduction

S.E. ANDERSON and TONY MEDINA

The Threat of Death Can Unite... and Ignite!

WHAT IF

*what if the day your life began was the day it ended, would you
think it was real, as real as a cold december morning on the 9th day
of the 12th month of your 27th year, would this be real, as real as a
car going the wrong way on a one-way street in the middle of the
dark in the middle of the cold, would you be in the twilight zone if
you come upon a car turned the wrong way on a one-way street in
the middle of that dark in the middle of that cold, and stopped to see
yourself, stopped to see your self, out in that cold up against that
hood, getting beat, getting beat, by some cop, would it be real if on
that night you saw your self, you saw yourself, your brother
appeared to take those blows, to take those blows against the hood of
that car turned the wrong way on a one-way street, and you ran to
his defense to take those blows, to take those blows against the hood
of that car turned the wrong way on a one-way street, and you ran
to his defense to take those blows, to take those blows to the chest,
the blood ringing in your ears, your eyes rolling back your ribs
sucking blows on a cold december morning in the darkness of a
philadelphia night and four bullets from a gun you never owned
wound up in the bloody cop's bleeding back, would you think you
were back in time would you think you were in the deep deep south in
johannesburg would it be real as real as the cops punching you in
your chest punching you in your wounds in the emergency room
would you think you were back in time would you think you were
huey newton in a hospital bed with lumps on your head your mouth*

*twisted shut would you think you were emmitt till layin up in a
wooden box while your mama cried cause she couldn't recognize her
boy cryin cause she can't recognize her boy*

– Tony Medina

This anthology of writings and artwork–by an array of international activists, writers, and
musicians–pays tribute to Mumia Abu-Jamal, a freedom fighter, a revolutionary journalist, a
father, a humble African man... a political prisoner threatened with execution by a truly
unjust criminal justice system.

Why Is Mumia Abu-Jamal Facing Execution?

As a print and radio journalist, Mumia Abu-Jamal was ever on the forefront of community
activism within the African American and Latino communities. Moonlighting as a cab dri-
ver, on the night of December 9, 1982, he witnessed a police officer beating an African
American male. Upon further inspection, he realized that this young victim was his brother.
Coming to his aid, Mumia was shot in the chest, and the police officer, Daniel Faulkner, was
shot and killed. Several eyewitnesses reported seeing another man shoot the policeman and
run from the scene. Through police intimidation and judicial incompetence and manipu-
lation, these eyewitnesses were never called to testify at Mumia's farcical trial. Because of his
radical political beliefs, and having been a former Black Panther, by mid-1982 Mumia Abu-
Jamal was sentenced to death. He was not allowed to choose his legal representation and was
allocated only $150 per witness for investigation.

He was not even allowed in the courtroom for most of the trial. Witnesses to the incident
were either intimidated by the Philadelphia police not to testify or told to lie about what they
actually saw in exchange for leniency. Some were coerced into lying on the stand for some
legal payoff (e.g., being allowed to drive a cab without a license for more than ten years or
eluding pending prostitution charges).

Only in recent months has the corporate (mainstream) media begun to reveal the institu-
tionalized racist brutality of the Philadelphia police department and the court system's overt
complicity with such bestiality. Mumia, who spearheaded the move to expose this (in
Philadelphia), is paying the price for telling the truth and unmasking the racist hypocrites.

  • In 1990, after eight years in prison, Mumia was represented by a competent legal team
willing to take his case all the way to the United States Supreme Court.

  • On June 2, 1995, Pennsylvania's Governor Tom Ridge signed the warrant for Mumia's
death by lethal injection, scheduled for August 17, 1995. But the groundswell of hundreds
of thousands of people demonstrating, phoning in, faxing, and internetting brought to

tremendous pressure on Judge Albert Sabo to grant an indefinite stay of execution.

• By September 15, 1995, Judge Sabo ruled that new evidence brought forth was not convincing enough to grant a new trial.

As we rush to publish this anthology, Mumia Abu-Jamal must now run the legal gauntlet of appealing to the higher courts of Pennsylvania and the federal government. Even as we prepare this text, the threat of death still looms over Mumia Abu-Jamal!

Thus far, Mumia's life has been spared because of the tremendous mobilization efforts of progressive and humane people here in the United States and throughout the world. All of this great national and international outpouring could not have happened without old-fashioned mobilization, political consciousness-raising, and the Internet's World Wide Web: **http://www.xs4all.nl/~tank/spg-l/mumia002.html**

The use of the Internet in getting the word out on Mumia demonstrates, somewhat ironically, the utilization of a technology originally intended for U.S. military purposes. Within an hour of the announcement of the Pennsylvania Governor's signing of the death warrant on June 2, 1995, Mumia Abu-Jamal's Defense Committee(s) across the world received the message and began mobilizing their forces. The use of the Internet and the computer's ability to search through a tremendous amount of data helps Mumia defenders to keep pace with the ever-changing machinations and fax and telephone numbers of Judge Sabo, Governor Ridge, Attorney General Janet Reno, and other officials.

The Anthology: Why and Who

In Defense of Mumia will help to keep the pressure on, to spread the word, and to send a strong, defiant message to the Pennsylvania criminal justice system and to the larger government as a whole; i.e., that the people, not only nationwide but worldwide, demand justice.

The writers, artists, and activists in this volume have been galvanized around the very real threat of the execution of Mumia Abu-Jamal and the concept of the death penalty itself. As a result of this solidarity and of the August 11, 1995, public poetry reading at the Schomburg Center for the Study of Black Culture, in Harlem, where 40 poets read [some of their contributions appear in this text, indicated by an asterisk ✳ after their names], we decided to document this historic movement with this book.

Among the over 140 writers, artists, and activists represented here are notable folk such as: Patricia J. Williams, Cornel West, Amiri Baraka, Manning Marable, Louis Reyes Rivera, Dennis Brutus, Piri Thomas, Jayne Cortez, Ernest Crichlow, Sonia Sanchez, Tom Feelings, Jan Carew, Allen Ginsberg, E.L. Doctorow, William Styron, Nat Hentoff, John Edgar Wideman, Gwendolyn Brooks, Margaret Randall, and Toni Morrison. Even Mumia has contributed representations from his political cartoon collection and some of his personal ruminations as well. Also included are younger, lesser-known writers and artists just starting out on their–as Ishmael Reed puts it–"Writin is fightin" journey.

Thus, this anthology also contains contributions from political prisoners languishing in U.S. prisons who have sacrificed and struggled through various levels of censorship and harassment to show their solidarity with Mumia–their comrade and brother. Many more wanted to contribute, but time and political censorship constrained us to these few political prisoners' voices singing revolutionary songs through these pages.

The contributors to this anthology may or may not see Mumia as innocent of the murder of Officer Faulkner, but they all condemn the unjust and racist nature of the Pennsylvania judicial system's handling of his initial trial and have selflessly donated their time and talent.

The royalties from this book will all be donated to the Mumia Abu-Jamal Legal Defense Fund.

•••

1. Some things must burn

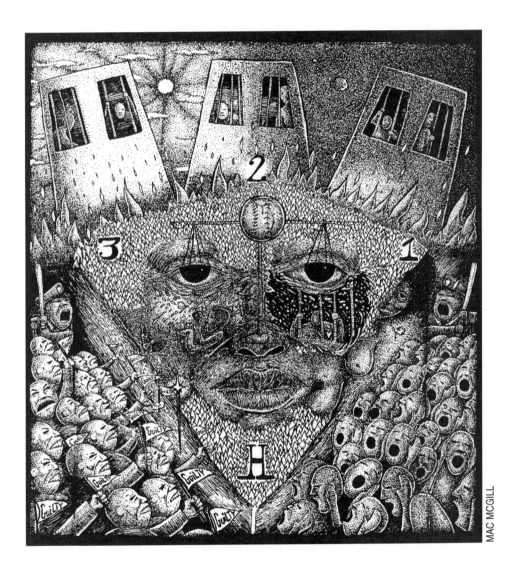

MAC MCGILL

(the national scene 1)

ASKIA M. TOURÉ

From the Projects of North Philly to the Pyramids of Liberation: A Griot's Tribute to Mumia!

Mumia Abu-Jamal. I'm speaking of a griot, a man dedicated to liberation, tested by bullets and batons, wielded by werewolves howling in asphalt jungles, neon graphitti flashing above sirens: hellcars manned by devils hunting myriad victims wearing our sepia faces. The Nameless the Homeless the Voiceless the Lost. Pariahs called poetically "The Wretched of the Earth" by radical chic Doctors Lawyers Social Workers and other suburban missionaries of benign White Supremacy in Marxist garb. Philly. Yes, I remember, Mumia. Philly, a deep, poisonous wound seared into my heart. Rizzo's Brothel. "The Big Bambino." Philly. Echoes of vast Black crowds marching on City Hall, from the North, meeting thousands marching from the west, thousands of angry, triumphant, defiant Blacks led by big Dave Richardson, Cecil Moore, Falaka Fattah, Saladin, Abba, Paul Washington, and thousands giving Voice to the Voiceless! (Big Dave has fallen this August; and us without banners or battalions to honor our leader. May his courageous spirit live on in these few poetic lines. Well done, Dave!) All of our youth, our fighting spirit embodied in a Black United Front, Mumia. Rizzo. George Fenzil, rabid police intelligence. Italian and Irish Mafia. And MOVE raging against oppression way out West. John Africa, shadowy philosopher, utopian, visionary; mentor of Louise, Chuckie, Jeanette, Delbert, underground in romantic dreams. And finally, you, Mumia; dredded and strong. North Philly. Projects. Tenements. Corner Boys. Dope Dealers. Mean Streets. Milton Streets. Lucien Blackwell. Black vendors fighting racist cops to work downtown streets. Black fists against red faces: City Council becomes a John Wayne Western, as John Streets tags Fran Rafferty with a mean left hook. Surprise! The Black and Puerto Rican masses unseat Rizzo! A new (colonial) mayor—George "Kingfish" Stevens—who takes "full responsibility" for Genocide: FBI-linked Police Intelligence bombing MOVE, killing men, women and children, burning down a vast section of affluent West Philly, without a whimper from our national Negro Leadership. Of course, there was one flaw, one important oversight: a dedicated freedomfighter turned journalist who couldn't be bought at any price...Mumia; it was inevitable, like Nat Turner and Slavery, like Dred Scott and the Supreme Court, like Crazy Horse and Custer: you couldn't back down and remain a griot. I heard your dynamic, magical voice on public radio, speaking of our precious heritage—Ghana, Mali and Songhai—and it changed my life forever! I was a revolutionary and a poet, but not a griot—until I heard your voice opening up our Ancestral World. Mumia; your Nat Turner, Marcus Garvey, Crazy Horse fighting spirit can never be conquered. You continue to challenge them even behind bars, from Hell's very depths! And, yes, the entire World hears and responds to your fiery Call. You are our Youth and Martial Spirit, our idealistic aspirations, revolutionary élan, our man/womanhood shining Black and feisty against the racist American Grain. Even our enemies recognize your special qualities and charisma; which is why they attempted to murder you on Marcus Garvey's birthday. They were attempting to kill a symbol, like Huey Newton sitting in the Afrikan king's chair, like Bros. John Carlos and

Tommy Smith raising Black Power fists on the victory stand at the Mexico Olympics, like Muhammad Ali, the People's Champ, refusing to step forward and join the Military in murdering Vietnamese; sons of Malcolm, symbols of our Afrikan Manhood.... And so, Brother Griot, we will continue to fight for you and our National Liberation, daily monthly yearly. Know This: Wherever our people stand up in Resistance and revolt against Oppression, You are there, fighting in spirit and truth. You Are Our Finest Example!

•••

CORNEL WEST
'Free Mumia'?

One sure sign of American democracy in decline is the undeniable decay of its two basic pillars: public education and the criminal justice system. Aristotle rightly argued in his classic "Politics" that without a vital "education of the citizens in the spirit of their constitution" and a widespread confidence in the courts where citizens could "seek redress on behalf of those who were wronged," no just society could survive and thrive.

The escalating levels of disillusionment and discouragement in much of Black America flow not simply from the mean-spirited politics of conservatives on Capitol Hill or the cold-hearted attacks on minimal efforts for racial fairness from the U.S. Supreme Court and California. A growing focus—especially among black youth—is the lethal connection between the decrepit public schools in chocolate cities and the treacherous abuse of justice in the legal system.

In short, law enforcement and prisons are major litmus tests to measure America's commitment to racial justice. And since America continues to sleepwalk through the nightmares of increasing unemployment, underemployment, dilapidated housing, inadequate health care, unavailable child care and civic erosion, we put an unbearable burden on the police and judges.

As we witnessed in Los Angeles three years ago, if the courts fail us, chaos often ensues. And as the cases of important political prisoners of the past and present—such as Geronimo Pratt in California and Mumia Abu-Jamal in Pennsylvania—move to the center of black consciousness, more social explosions loom large.

A political prisoner is both a fellow citizen who received an unfair trial and a powerful symbol for those of us who are convinced this unfairness partly results from their political beliefs—beliefs that highlight the criminal justice system as a structure of unfairness.

The case of Mumia Abu-Jamal, 41, is most pressing since Gov. Thomas Ridge signed his death warrant on June 1, 1995. The brutal killing of Officer Daniel Faulkner on December 9, 1981, was wrong and unjust. Whoever killed Faulkner deserves to be imprisoned. But only a fair trial will determine who that person is.

The bullets that caused Faulkner's death came from a .44-caliber gun, according to the medical examiner who removed them from his body. Abu-Jamal, a well-known journalist forced to drive a taxi as a result of his controversial work, was carrying a legally registered .38-caliber gun.

The trial was a farce. The chief grounds of the decision against Abu-Jamal were based on the testimony of a prostitute, brought from a Massachusetts jail cell to testify, who had a record of more than 35 arrests—and who was eager for immunity from arrest in return for her testimony. Four witnesses reported that the shooter fled; one of them described him as a large, heavy-set man about 6 feet 2 inches tall. Abu-Jamal, although 6 foot 1, weighed 170 pounds at the time of the crime.

I attended a hearing for Abu-Jamal on July 12, 1995, in Philadelphia. The atmosphere—including the judge's mockery and flippancy—was that of a Jim Crow court. For instance, at one point, the judge exclaimed roughly, "What's the rush? He's not being executed tomorrow; he's got a few more weeks." Abu-Jamal's family was in the front row.

Mumia Abu-Jamal is a former Black Panther, a supporter of the MOVE organization, the black radical Philadelphia group, a dreadlock-wearing, proud man whose prophetic pen and eloquent voice have challenged America to come to terms with the injustices in our past and present—as manifest in his book, *Live from Death Row.*

His superb lawyer, Leonard Weinglass, had planned to file a post-conviction review appeal in the Philadelphia Court of Common Pleas at City Hall three days before Ridge signed the death warrant. The planned date for execution was August 17, 1995—the 108th birthday of Marcus Garvey. Abu-Jamal deserves a new and fair trial.

Abu-Jamal's supporters include Alice Walker, E.L. Doctorow, Whoopi Goldberg, Ed Asner, Ossie Davis, Ruby Dee, Marla Gibbs, Henry Louis Gates, Jr., Nelson Mandela's African National Congress and millions of citizens of all colors. The fundamental issue is not simply the precious life of Mumia Abu-Jamal—in return for the precious life of Daniel Faulkner—or just another instance of the chronic breakdown of an unfair criminal justice system. This case also forces us to come to terms with how the failure of our two training grounds for citizenship—education and law—signify the disintegration of American democracy.

And as Malcolm X reminds us, black people—the historic victims of our democracy—disproportionately pay the price and bear the burden as the band plays on in Washington.

•••

RICHARD CAMMARIERI
Domestic Policy

I'm not crazy about it
but I am going to clean your house
your house affects me

it could take some time
there is water in your basement
roaches in your walls
and mice in your attic

there is smoke and stale and moldy
things in your kitchen

your living room is dead

your windows do not work
your appliances are irrelevant
the air is sour

there is confusion in your bedroom
your sheets are embarrassing
there is blood in your toilet
and something wet on the floor
I almost slipped on it

there are tarnished coins in the furniture
and soggy dollar bills stuck
on the mirrors

this is a nasty house

but I'll clean it

I may have to crush the walls
and rip off the roof
to get it right

I may need to call upon the whirlwind
and the flame
because some things cannot be washed away
some things must burn

but I will clean this house

you?
you must clean yourself

•••

CORNELIUS EADY
My Face

If you are caught
In my part of town
After dark,
You are not lost
You are abandoned.

All that the neighbors will tell
Your kin
Is that you should
Have known better.

All they will do
Is nod their heads.
They will feel sorry
For you,

But rules are rules,
And when you were
Of the right age
Someone pointed
A finger
In the wrong direction

And said
All they do
Is fuck and drink
All their good for
Ain't worth a shit.

You remember me now
To the police artists.
It wasn't really my face
That stared back that day,
But it was that look.

•••

FREEDOM OF THE PRESS IN BLACK AND WHITE

ART & STORY: **SETH TOBOCMAN** INKS: BARBARA LEE, S. TOBOCMAN, JOHN KIM
PHOTO REFERENCE: BARBARA LEE
INFO: Q.U.I.S.P., P.D.C., EQUAL JUSTICE, FIRST PUBLISHED IN WORLD WAR THREE.

MUMIA SPENT THE 1980s IN PRISON AWAITING EXECUTION.

MUMIA MUST BE SAVED!

BECAUSE OF THE STAY MUMIA NOW HAS TIME TO MAKE AP-
-PEALS. BUT IT IS STILL POSSIBLE HE WILL LOSE THE
APPEALS AND BE EXECUTED. ONLY A MASS MOVEMENT CAN
FORCE THE STATE TO GIVE HIM A NEW TRIAL, A FAIR TRIAL!
IF MUMIA DIES, NOTHING HAS CHANGED SINCE SLAVERY and FREEDOM of the
PRESS IS THE PRIVILEDGE OF THE FEW, NOT THE RIGHT OF THE MANY.
IF MUMIA DIES THEN THIS CAN HAPPEN TO ANYONE WHO CRITICISES THE
SYSTEM, PARTICULARLY IF THAT PERSON IS BLACK, FEMALE, GAY OR
POOR. BUT MUMIA IS STILL ALIVE   AND IF YOU GET OFF
YOUR ASS YOU CAN SAVE HIM.
TAKE THE PETITION ON THE OP-
-POSITE PAGE TO YOUR JOB, SCHOOL
OR COMMUNITY. WRITE MUMIA'S
NAME ON THE WALLS. PROTEST
NOW
BEFORE IT'S
TOO LATE.

To: ATTORNEY GENERAL JANET RENO
U.S. DEPARTMENT OF JUSTICE
10TH & CONSTITUTION AVE. N.W.
WASHINGTON D.C. 20530

MS. RENO,

WE SAY: SAVE THE LIFE OF MUMIA ABU JAMAL! THE DEATH PENALTY IS BARBARIC AND AN OUTRAGE AGAINST JUSTICE. MUMIA ABU JAMAL FACES DEATH BECAUSE OF HIS POLITICAL ACTS AND BELIEFS. MUMIA ABU JAMAL WAS MINISTER OF INFORMATION OF THE PHILADELPHIA CHAPTER OF THE BLACK PANTHER PARTY. HE BECAME A WELL KNOWN AND RESPECTED JOURNALIST AND HEAD OF THE PHILADELPHIA CHAPTER OF THE ASSOCIATION OF BLACK JOURNALISTS. HE WAS KNOWN AS A SUPPORTER OF THE MOVE ORGANIZATION. IN 1982 HE WAS FRAMED FOR THE KILLING OF A POLICEMAN. HE WAS SEN-TENCED TO DEATH FOR HIS POLITICAL BELIEFS SPECIFICALLY FOR STAT-MENTS HE MADE AS A BLACK PANTHER PARTY MEMBER 12 YEARS EARLIER.

HIS ORIGINAL TRIAL

SAVE MUMIA ABU JAMAL

NEW TRIAL

LIFE

WAS A SHAM! WE JOIN WITH PEOPLE ALL OVER THE WORLD IN DEMANDING A NEW TRIAL FOR MUMIA! HIS LIFE IS IN YOUR HANDS. WE HOLD YOU ACCOUNTABLE!

NAME	ADDRESS	SIGNATURE
1		
2		
3.		
4.		
5.		
6.		
7.		
8.		
9.		
10.		

DATE: _____

SEND ONE COPY TO RENO AND A 2ND COPY TO: EQUAL JUSTICE U.S.A., P.O. BOX 5206 HYATTSVILLE MD. 20782

CAROLYN PEYSER *
Movin' On for Mumia

this summer
they say
cutting it off
is
in fashion

wrapping it up or
greasing
it down
they hope hides
the bald spots

pulling out
just in time
they still think
will keep the tribes
tame

it's politics as usual
in this time
of fattened cows and
fed up lionesses
tigers & bears

left quietly
this country
lets leaders slip
past principle with
gaveling fears

and we know
our speaking out
never was
popular with
the big boys

---

* A contributor to the open-mike reading in support of Mumia Abu-Jamal at the Schomburg Center for the Study of Black Culture, in Harlem, on August 11, 1995.

they keep trying
to wave
flags
and draw
crowds

they forget we're
burned back
to long-watered
roots of our
discontent

but now we're
mobilized
we have
organized
phone-ringing
letter-writing
street-shouting
ass-whipping
work
to do

today it may
be life but
the dead
are
everywhere

•••

KATHA POLLITT
Subject to Debate

For thirteen years, Mumia Abu-Jamal sat on death row in Pennsylvania, and not too many people were interested outside the remnants of MOVE and the sectarian left. With some exceptions—the NAACP Legal Defense and Education Fund, the National Conference of Black Lawyers—the old-line civil rights organizations stayed away. So did those organizations' high-profile challengers: Louis Farrakhan, the Rev. Al Sharpton. When people, black and white, argued about whether the justice system targets blacks unfairly, the test cases were Mike Tyson and O.J. Simpson, multimillionaire celebrities defended by flocks of lawyers and accused of crimes against women; not so Mumia, whose case actually raises the relevant issues: a police vendetta, a biased judge, a political trial, a ferocious sentence for cop killing, which is a crime against the state.

At any moment in those thirteen years, the media could have shone their spotlights on Mumia. As a print and radio journalist, he was, after all, one of their own. But no reporter took up his case in the mainstream press, and when *All Things Considered* offered him a slot commenting on prison life, the Fraternal Order of Police pressured NPR into withdrawing it—a piece of genuine political censorship that evoked not a peep from the foes of "political correctness." The National Association of Black Journalists, of whose Philadelphia chapter he was once president, declined to take a stand on his trial or sentence, reluctantly calling only for "judicial review" (and then only on August 19, two days after he was originally scheduled for execution) and reserving its indignation for the prison official who denied journalists access to him. Death is one thing, the all-important pre-death interview another.

Still, thirteen years is a long time, and thanks to the tireless efforts of his small band of defenders, little by little Mumia picked up support: the longshoremen's union, locals of transportation workers, service workers, mail handlers, the Association of Black Police Officers, the United Church of Christ, the Quixote Center, Amnesty International. In Europe, where it is not so controversial to hold that racism infects the American judicial system, and where the death penalty has been abolished, there have been big demonstrations, un-reported in the mainstream U.S. press.

Given this history, it is beyond me how anyone can portray Mumia Abu-Jamal as the darling of the wine-and-cheese circuit, or lampoon his supporters as "radical chic," as Francis X. Clines did in the August 13, 1995 issue of *The New York Times*,"Week in Review." In a voice ripe with plummy jocularity, Clines lit into the signers of a recent full-page ad on Mumia's behalf by professing pity for Mumia's 3,009 "tongue-tied peers" on death row, who "can only wonder in silence, perchance grunting of their own innocence, but well ignored" while Mumia, "symbiosis of Muse and miscreant," attracts such "patrons" as Susan Sarandon, Spike Lee and Joyce Carol Oates. It's Leonard Bernstein and the Panthers all over again ("radical chic" having been invented by Tom Wolfe to describe Bernstein's famous party), or Jack Henry Abbott, or maybe Sacco and Vanzetti. If these examples strike you as rather different from one another and from Mumia—actually, the only one who illustrates Clines's point is Abbott, a dangerous murderer released from prison largely through the efforts of his literary mentor, Norman Mailer—you are clearly not cut out for big-time punditry.

Well, I can't speak for Jacques Derrida, but I signed that ad because I oppose the death penalty and am disquieted by the questions raised about the original trial. Literature and muses have nothing to do with it. I would sign a petition opposing the execution of Timothy McVeigh too—or any of the 3,009 convicted killers on death row, most of whom, guilty or innocent, articulate or "grunting"(!), have been on the receiving end of a judicial system biased against the black, the poor, the uneducated, and increasingly determined to kill as many of them as quickly as possible. That's not such a radical position, although I realize it's not a particularly chic one either.

Cline's charge that the pro-Mumia ad is a kind of elitist slap at other death-row inmates has a pseudo-clever ring of paradox to it. But isn't the mainstream media, which ignored Mumia for so long, that makes it politically necessary to harness famous names to a cause?

What prevents *The New York Times*, which opposes capital punishment, from bringing to public attention, day after day, the cases of those "tongue-tied" inmates Clines professes to care so much about? Answer: the same race and class biases that lead the paper to play up crimes with white upscale victims feature as a major news story the heroin-overdose death of a prosperous white West Sider and regard with anything but derision Arianna Huffington's metamorphosis from social-climbing New Age nut to the Madame Récamier of the Republican Party. Who mocks "conservative chic?"

Actually, what's interesting about the ad is how few signers fit the radical chic stereotype. Nadine Strossen? David Dinkins? Garry Wills? Pro-life, pro-moment-of-silence Maya Angelou, fan of Bill Clinton and Clarence Thomas? Sister Helen Prejean, who has spent years comforting death-row inmates and the families of their victims? "Radical chic," a term that connotes dilettantish frivolity, hardly describes E.L. Doctorow or Henry Louis Gates or Nadine Gordimer or William Styron or Salman Rushdie or even Abbot's angel, Norman Mailer. These people have been advocates for human rights and racial justice for the whole of their adult lives—something that can't be said of Tom Wolfe.

Could it be that what really upsets the *Times* isn't the Lenny Bernstein side of the equation but the Panther side? One way or another, the case of Mumia Abu-Jamal, himself a former Panther, has focused people all over the world on a kind of black politics we have been told for years is over, finished, dead. So maybe it isn't radical chic that bothers them but radicalism.

•••

ABDUL HAQQ
Death to Killer Cops

With time wickedly ticking
    in Pennsylvania
We must capture the clock
    to build a BOMB
To MOVE mountains
    for Mumia.
Volts Not Votes
    empower the oppressed
    against amerikkka.
So let this strong sound pound
    The air:
"Killer Cops Deserve
The Electric Chair!"
Fry! Die! Fly!
    brained bastards!
Make humanity happy.
We will share this

Thundering Thought
like food for the family,
and beauty.
Do cognitive kung-fu to
The hypocritical media hogs'
idea of death
for oppressed,
teenagers
& liberators.
Press the swine system
for Mumia's
life and freedom.
40 million fists
thrust-punch the sky
killer cops deserve to die!!!

•••

SHARIFF SIMMONS *

American Schizophrenia

I'll never charge
this false place
with making me
invisible
Like some thing
that can't be seen
in crowds
I'll never give
this miscreation that power
to make my being disappear
I choose to make myself valid
through those who see me clear
and never deal with the duality
of the captured state
and the colonized mind
For that
I feel blessed

I feel blessed 'cause I'm not the dumb
motherfucker
cheerin' on the hail of deadly steel

that takes one hundred and fifty thousand
lives like it ain't shit
while I'm getting dissed at work
I feel sharp
'cause I'm not the sucker
fallin' for the hookline and sinker
type o' bullshit
that covers the cool fire in your living room
telling you how humanitarian the carnivores be
when
in one breath
they starve millions of life forms
then claim
    they wish
        to feed
          the world
Like the traits of the schizophrenic
whose shit can't be cured
fueled by that insatiable
              capitalist
          nightmare
flashin' in the daily reports

"Today we fed a million Somalians in Africa,
then put an embargo on Cuba's ports."

Well, ain't that some shit!
Stealin' milk from a baby's mouth
'cause a country's politics don't fit
the script

The diagnosis is the psycho-mindsplit
brother
the type shit that breeds
        man eaters
           and
        kid killers
           and
        woman beaters
           and
mis-educated negroes
who wonder why Lani Guiniere
got dissed
and why the fast cities burn!

No
I'll never charge this false place with
making me invisible
for what I wish not to be
shall never give me hunger
when you lose
in the game
of America
and you slip into a
silent rage
turning a page

in a Crayola coloring book
in a padded
        Creedmor
         pilgrim
        or
bel room with a view
with a contagious
mental disease
you can catch
on any street
if you sleep
on the American Dream!

•••

KRS-ONE
Free Mumia

Everywhere I look there's another house negro
Talkin' about their people and how they should be equal
They're talkin' but their conversation ain't goin' nowhere
You can't diss hip-hop so don't you even go there
C. Dolores Tucker you wanna quote the scripture
Every time you hear "nigga" well listen up sista

I met up with this girl named Dolores a prankster
I said I MC she said you're a gangsta

But she was caught up/ she hit the floor like a breakdancer
Wrapped her up like the arms in a B-Boy stance
Recognize moms I'm one of your sons
I'm hip hop in the form of Channel Live and KRS-One
Representin' MCs across America
She said you the one who be causin' all that mass hysteria

Wisdom shall come out of the mouths of babes and suppling
But you blinded my cultural ignorance and steady judging
But judge not, lest ye may be judged
But the judgment ye judge shall surely be judged, you gets no love

She said I like it that's why I jock it
Then I said you're only on my back because I fill brothers' pockets
Got 'em drivin' Benzes, Jeeps, and Rolls Royces, attacking me will
Leave you with no voices the choice is yours not mine hang with me
I'll have you freestyling and bombing graffiti, we can cut it up like wax
Claiming I cause violence but America was violent before rap, fact

Warner, Elektra, Atlantic, gettin' W.E.A.
Instead of fightin' them why don't you go "Free Mumia"

Warner, Elektra, Atlantic, gettin' W.E.A.
Instead of fightin' them why don't you go "Free Mumia"

While recital I kick the vital like the final call
As I watch Babylon fall
I had to rush Limbaugh hit that pig with that ax
Toughy dips to the side walking can his head back (blup, blup, blup)
Because he sense of the usage of the metaphor
You can get the **** of my ****
Because it's you that brings the real hordcore
Expenditures be gettin' cut from the board

Why sure back before we were born they sold us out
Yeah J. Jackson we know what you're about
Youse a slave mason, not free mason

Before long the goddess Tiamont through hip hop you'll be facin'
Don't start me 'cause I be da lyricist at the 1999 millennium party
Held at Giza sayin' he's a fraud oh my goddess never in your life
Should you disrespect an artist, instead focus your attention
On astronomy, and the up and coming shift on the economy
If you can't do that then heed the final call Free Mumia Abu-Jamal

Hate to be so rough it could be the white owls
House niggaz are fulla crap like my Colin Powell
Kickin' vowels is how we relieve the tension
But should we start to bounce white people like suspension
You paint the pictures the black men on the corner
But tell me who blew up Oklahoma (the devil) the city
Ain't no pity for the beats it's Hakeem that voice from the east

Warner, Elektra, Atlantic, gettin' W.E.A.
Instead of fightin' them why don't you go "Free Mumia"

Warner, Elektra, Atlantic, gettin' W.E.A.
Instead of fightin' them why don't you go "Free Mumia"

It sounds like gunshots, but it could be the bark of a chicken
Definition is what you're missin' and listen to your children
Instead of dissin' 'em (word)
Senator Dole doesn't understand the younger
Like they be sayin' want to but we be sayin' wanna
They gettin' dumber every summer as they walk the road
Mainly because they cannot understand the code
In actuality there's so many based mentality always seems to represent
Minus 360% or degrees full circle dead from the purple
Raise up the sun I gots melanin so check it
Bag your nuts quick or get sick from being naked
Suspected was it the means for the end or just for you to drive a Benz
While you eat the big skins, heard you into mannequins
Is the trick to technology a revelation
Revelation, sensation, gives me inspiration a revolution
That's my solution there will be no sequels
I'm Audi 144, 000 with my people

From Caligula, to Hitler and now it's Schwarzenegger
A must for the violence use the science of their behavior
Who enslaves you (the devil), but the god of virtuosity
In other words created, could it be mental sodomy
Got my mind twistin' like the vains in Quantum leap
I sit in disbelief as he crawls underneath me
The rot caught back the glock 'cause I don't trust
The double R a volatile Babylon is dust (knowledge)

Warner, Elektra, Atlantic, gettin' W.E.A.
Instead of fightin' them why don't you go "Free Mumia"

Warner, Elektra, Atlantic, gettin' W.E.A.
Instead of fightin' them why don't you go "Free Mumia"

•••

E.L. DOCTOROW
From Here to Death Row

Just before 4 A.M. on Dec. 9, 1981, in a rough downtown neighborhood of Philadelphia, Police Officer Daniel Faulkner stopped a Volkswagen Beetle and arrested its driver, William Cook, for driving the wrong way down a one-way street. Expecting or experiencing trouble, Officer Faulkner radioed for assistance. When fellow police officers arrived, they found him lying in the street, shot in the back and the face. A few feet away, slumped in his own pool of blood, was Mr. Cook's brother, a freelance journalist and black activist named Mumia Abu-Jamal (born Wesley Cook).

Mr. Jamal, who moonlighted as a cab driver, later said that he had been driving by and, seeing a police officer hitting his brother, stopped his cab and rushed to his defense. His licensed .38 caliber pistol, which he had bought after having been robbed twice, was found at the scene.

Officer Faulkner died at Jefferson University Hospital an hour after the shooting. Mr. Jamal underwent surgery, a bullet from the officer's revolver having struck his chest and lodged near his spine.

Protesting his innocence, Mumia Abu-Jamal was charged with first-degree murder and brought to trial in early 1982. The prosecution maintained that he had come up behind the officer and shot him in the back, that the fallen officer had returned fire and that Mr. Jamal, though wounded, had stood over Officer Faulkner and fired the fatal shot into his face. Prosecutors produced two eyewitnesses who identified Mr. Jamal as the gunman and a third, whose identification was less certain. They also offered ballistic evidence that the bullet removed from the officer was of the high-velocity type in Mr. Jamal's pistol. Two other witnesses testified they heard Mr. Jamal confess to the shooting at the hospital.

Because he could not afford a lawyer, he chose to represent himself. The presiding judge, Albert Sabo, complained that Mr. Jamal was taking too long interviewing the jurors and replaced him with a court-appointed lawyer, who by his own statement was reluctant to take the case. Mr. Jamal objected and was eventually put out of the courtroom, the first of several exclusions that, all told, would absent him from large portions of the trial.

Another problem Mr. Jamal faced was his younger brother's inability or unwillingness to testify on his behalf. Mr. Jamal's lawyers said William Cook had a history of drug problems and was terrified of police retribution. (He is now believed to be homeless and has not been seen in a year.)

On July 2, 1982, Mumia Abu-Jamal was convicted of first-degree murder and sentenced to death by Judge Sabo. Now, after 14 years on death row, his appeals rejected, Mr. Jamal is scheduled to be executed at 10 o'clock on the night of August 17.

Yet his death warrant, signed by the new Governor of Pennsylvania, Tom Ridge, comes just as substantive doubts about the prosecution's case have been raised by Mr. Jamal's current lawyers, possibly his first competent legal representation. (They serve for minimal fees, paid largely by contributions raised by various defense committees that have formed over the years.)

In papers filed in June the lawyers asked that Judge Sabo—who, according to the NAACP Legal Defense and Education Fund, has handed down more than twice as many death sentences as any judge in the country—recuse himself from the case. They asked for a stay of execution and a new trial. This week, Judge Sabo refused to recuse himself or sign the stay.

A review of the lawyers' petition suggests that the evidence upon which Mr. Jamal was convicted does not hold up under examination. Of the two eyewitnesses who positively identified Mr. Jamal as the gunman, one was a prostitute with several charges pending against her and the other was a cab driver on probation for a felony arson conviction.

No other witnesses saw the prostitute at the scene. One witness told the defense that she arrived after the incident and asked bystanders what had happened. Nevertheless, she claimed in court she had seen Mr. Jamal wielding a gun. (Subsequently, charges against her were not prosecuted.)

The cab driver's testimony corroborated the prostitute's, but in a deposition taken on the night of the crime he said something else entirely—that the gunman was not the 170-pound Mr. Jamal but a heavyset man of well over 200 pounds who had fled the scene.

Four other witnesses who were never put on the stand, including one woman whose apartment overlooked the intersection, also reported seeing a man running away. Yet no police inquiries regarding another possible gunman were ever made.

An examination of the ballistic evidence reveals that no effort was made by the police to determine if Mr. Jamal's pistol had been fired that night. Moreover, the Police Department's own medical examiner concluded that the officer's fatal head wound was made by a .44 caliber bullet. Mr. Jamal's pistol was a .38 caliber.

The two witnesses who had been in the hospital waiting room with Mr. Jamal, and who testified that he shouted defiantly that he had shot Officer Faulkner, turned out to be the officer's former partner and best friend and a hospital security guard who was also a friend. The partner's log report of that night mentioned no confession. Neither did he report a confession in a statement he volunteered the following week. In fact, neither he nor the security guard said anything about a confession until months later—after Mr. Jamal filed a complaint that he was abused by the police while he was in the hospital.

Furthermore, another officer who was with Mr. Jamal from the time he was driven from the murder scene to the time the doctors started treating him wrote in his log report immediately after the episode that "the Negro male made no statements." This officer was given vacation leave at the time of the trial and never testified.

The prosecution's claim that Mr. Jamal was shot while standing over the fallen officer is not consistent with a pathologist's report describing the downward trajectory of his chest wound. A different scenario, which is consistent, is suggested by Mr. Jamal's own account—that he was shot first by the officer as he approached. Furthermore, the third prosecution eyewitness portrayed the two men as facing each other.

Why did the police never pursue obvious leads and investigate the possibility of another gunman? Mr. Jamal had long been a controversial figure. As a teenager he helped found a chapter of the Black Panther Party. Later he became a journalist and radio commentator known for his support of the activist black MOVE community and for his condemnation of the city's police force as habitually brutal to blacks. To uniformed men in mourning for one of their own, he was an enemy delivered to their mercies.

During Mr. Jamal's years on death row, he has written cogently of prison life and has attracted many supporters. Groups across a broad spectrum have collected money for his defense. Amnesty International, the PEN American Center and Human Rights Watch have all questioned the fairness of the trial. All this has only strengthened the law-enforcement community's determination to see the "cop killer" executed. And Mr. Jamal's recently published book, *Live from Death Row*, has gotten him disciplinary isolation for his trouble, so that what the Fraternal Order of Police hopes are the last 40 days of his life may pass as wretchedly as possible.

If the death penalty must exist in this country, it is the burden of the public servants charged with applying it to do so only from the most unanswerable and awesome judicial imperatives—or state-administered death becomes morally indistinguishable from any other murder. Without a stay of execution and the most scrupulously objective retrial, how can Governor Ridge look at the facts of this case and say that they meet this test? Will the pain of Officer Faulkner's widow, who supports Mr. Jamal's execution, be resolved if it turns out that the wrong man has been executed and her husband's killer still walks the streets?

•••

MANNING MARABLE
Justice for Mumia Abu-Jamal

The American criminal justice system is, in part, an institution that perpetuates black oppression. It is no accident that, for example, nearly one-third of all young black men between the ages of 18 and 29 years old in the U.S. are either in prison, on probation or parole, or awaiting trial. None should be surprised that African Americans and Latinos convicted of crimes routinely receive much longer prison sentences than whites who commit the same crimes.

The outstanding element of coercion within the system of legal punishment remains the death penalty. As criminal justice scholar David Baldus observed, several years ago, any black person is 4.3 times more likely to be given the death penalty than any white person under the same circumstances. Since 1900, thousands of African Americans have been either executed by prison officials or police, or lynched by white mobs—all for the defense of white supremacy. In the past century, the total number of white Americans executed for either the murder of a black person, or the rape of black women, is fewer than five.

It is in this repressive context that we must consider the case of Mumia Abu-Jamal. An outstanding African-American radio journalist and political commentator, Abu-Jamal established a strong following in Philadelphia in the early 1980s. Abu-Jamal's reports documenting widespread police brutality and political repression in that city were broadcast nationally on National Public Radio and on other networks as well. In 1981, Abu-Jamal was arrested and charged with the killing of a police officer, Daniel Faulkner. Abu-Jamal had been shot by the police at the scene and then was beaten into critical condition.

In his years on death row in Pennsylvania, Mumia Abu-Jamal has refused to be silenced. His political analysis and commentaries have been published in a book, *Live from Death Row*. But on June 2, 1995, the Governor of Pennsylvania signed Abu-Jamal's death warrant. If nothing had been done to halt this legal process, Abu-Jamal would have been executed on August 17, 1995.

Intellectuals, public officials, journalists, and hundreds of prominent public leaders—nationally and internationally—have rallied in support of Mumia Abu-Jamal. In the struggle to stop the execution, we are doing more than just saving the life of an innocent man. We strike a blow to freedom against a criminal justice system pervasive with racism. We take a stand for justice against a legal system that punishes thousands of black and Latino young men for crimes while white men are permitted to go free. By fighting to save the life of Mumia Abu-Jamal, we struggle for a truly just and democratic society.

•••
MARVIN X
Free Mumia Abu-Jamal

Creator got things fixed. If you don't do the right thing, you can't go forward and you can't go backward.
—**Sun Ra**

MUMIA.
Guilty? Innocent? Shaky facts. Shaky trial. Evidence tampered.
questionable witnesses: a lying whore
arresting officer don't testify
sent on vacation
possible murder man flees scene. never found.
Governor say kill Mumia. Lawyers appeal. judge stalls. won't recuse. won't take off
black robe for true color white robe. Drinks nightly with KKK
Judge wants clock ticking to death date.
play on people's heartbeat. maybe his heartless heart will fail.
LIVE. FROM DEATH ROW.
"Hey, Grandpa."
FREE MUMIA.
"WHEN YOU COMIN HOME, GRANDPA?"
FREE MUMIA.
Black nigguh journalists say, "We can't help him. he taxi driver,
not journalist."

yeah
and you nigguhs
not journalists
white man parrots
boot licking, ass licking
pharaonic scribes, magicians
Free Mumia

he had a .38
pig killed with .44
what's really goin on?
free Mumia.
Rev. Bevels say, "White man wanna kill a nigguh so they can get a nut."
ole time lynching
bar-b-que a nigguh
bring yo kids
burn a nigguh
get a nut
you burned one too many, Bud.
not this one.
"Every nigguh ain't gonna bend over and let you fuck him in the ass," said Rev.
   Bevels.
Praise the Lord.
MUMIA special. ain't dumb. can write. talk.
LIVE FROM DEATH ROW.
burn him on Marcus Garvey's birthday
white arrogance
pigs invade wedding in Lord's House
contempt for God
contempt for African people.
FREE MUMIA.
YOUR SCHEMES. DEATH DATE. INTIMIDATIONS. Forced ZANZIBAR to cancel
benefit.
worthless acts of faithlessness. cowardice.
unmanliness, punkism.
FREE MUMIA.
BY THE POWER OF A UNITED PEOPLE
FREE MUMIA
AND ALL POLITICAL PRISONERS.

•••

STANDING DEER
If They Were Going to Kill My Brother

If they were going to kill my brother I would raise him... rescue him
steal him away from the murderous thugs of the state.
They don't need his life nohow! They can sell it for twice what it's
worth 'cause there ain't that much money in the world.
So what for do they want it?!?
He don't mean nothin' no way 'cept to those who love him
and need him and can't do without him.
I always wonder why we let freedom fighters rot their lives away in
some jail or go down in a murder-for-hire plot rigged by the state.
Folks be marching and hollering and carrying signs carrying his name
demanding his freedom, but if signs and words could free him he
woulda been free a long time ago.
This is not about revolution and we don't need the masses to rise up
and wrest away the means of production from the criminal class.
This is about our brother's life. His life!!! and it only takes a few of us
who don't want him dead.
There is no magic in a uniform and badge even if the State, Nation and
World Rulers are behind those symbols so if somebody wants him free
there he is over there in that dungeon guarded by folks
that bleed when they're hurt just like you and me.
Jonathan, the child/man had the idea and the brains and the courage...
he just didn't have the understanding that the state will throw away
functionaries within their apparatus like they were dirty toilet tissue,
and never look back.
Frederick Douglass said: "Power concedes nothing without a Demand.
It never has and it never will."
Carlos said: "You do things with bullets because bullets are real."
It has to start somewhere and sometime
What better place than here?
What better time than now?
Free Mumia Abu-Jamal!!!

•••

KEELYN BRADLEY
a battle hymn

(on the eve of Mumia Abu-Jamal's scheduled execution
Philadelphia august 16, 1995)

we are more than just warriors
our cries shrill
in heavy breath
and our weapons bear heavy
on our souls
we are more than just warriors
our tears have left stains on our cheeks

there will be another day
there will be another day
we been told to wade in the water
for another day
but our hunger still goes unfed
and there will be no rivers
to bathe in tomorrow
we been told that there would be another day
but it's been a long time coming

there are trees in these walls
the woman said there are trees in these walls
and her message fell on deaf ears
and her words went unspoken
the woman said there are trees in these walls
and went about making room to see them

the child says my feet are tired
my feet are tired and my journey is far
but i've got to keep up
the child says my feet are tired
but i've got to keep up
and he runs until the pain bids him to sleep
and then he rests awhile

the years will find us
beating our fists in empty ritual
pleading legend

in unmarked graves
grieving our sacrifices
the years will find us
struggling to find
what we knew was
from the beginning
we are more than just warriors

we are a collection of our fears
we are the strength of our hate
we are the depth of our pain
our struggle is love
our struggle is love
we are more than just warriors
we fight as wounded kin
come to take our son home

•••

TONY MEDINA *

Notes on a Hanging Judge

Judge Sabo's
an accomplished liar,
Death's architect,
The Devil's physician,
Satan's pinch hitter,
shoe shiner of doom,
the maitre d' of nightmare,
torture's midwife,
hysteria's chauffeur,
a disease on the heel of famine,
the butler of bad news—
guilty of causing trouble,
a cheap nickel & dime
seamstress sewing eyelids
in morgues,
stealing the nickels
from dead peoples' eyes,
eternal member of the Fraternal
Order of Pigs, wallowing

in the mud of corruption,
sending 3 1/2 baseball line-ups
from the Negro Leagues
to death,
score keeper of misery
who validates parking
in the hereafter
who takes dictation
from the lips of evil,
horsewhipping hope
for an extra part-time salary,
gracious host to life-threatening diseases,
who throws house parties
in his small intestine
for maggots
so they could feel
at home,
who writes obituaries
for children not yet born,
whose judicial review reads
like the screen play to
The Faces of Death
(where you can't miss his name,
permanently graffitied and
juxtaposed as the credits roll),
a state-sanctioned serial killer
authorizing bloodlettings
as if they were holy communion,
bringing the church & state together
in a sick baptismal orgy
of Herodinus despair,
euphoric with flashing fangs
and drooling tongue
who's so patriotically perverse
and sickly demented
that before every judicial decision
pertaining to a person's life
Nixon appears to him
in an apparition saying:
Give 'em hell, Harry!
A devil-may-care rude, uncouth
impolitic barroom psychopath
crippled with ill emotions

and equally ill intent,
attributed with coining
the phrase: *Heads will roll!*
and inspiring the line:
It's enough to make you sick.
His mind is a one-judge town
and his mental capacity
gives him the audacity
to sleep and pass judgment
simultaneously while
passing gas through his mouth,
nodding off in his own slobber,
a pathetic sociopath
who polishes the D.A.'s nut sack hairs
with his tongue and forefinger
who gives out merit badges
for outstanding achievement
in police brutality
who uses his false teeth
for a gavel, marking his bench
with warrants and dates with death
as if they were notches on his belt,
a devil in a black robe and
blood-soaked wing-tip shoes,
no mystery to anyone
familiar with the history
of U.S. jurisprudence
who refuses to recuse
or retire himself from the bench
for fear he might miss out
on a prisoner's forced expiration date
as if it were the winning number
on a lottery ticket
whose eating habits were made into
a major motion picture
starring Anthony Hopkins
entitled *Silence of the Lambs*
whose favorite song
is the theme song
to *The Exorcist*
whose sexual hang-ups
do not include
sodomizing barnyard animals,

groping little boys in confessionals,
and masturbating to the background
music of *Night of the Living Dead*
whose picture appears
beside the word necrophiliac
in any foreign or domestic dictionary
who decreed it illegal
to be happy
whose cheap Woolworth's
driver's license photo
is standard advertisement
for the year book photos
at Mass Murder State College
whose high school senior class
voted him most likely to hate
who only mourns
when someone dies
with a smile on their face
who's so cunning
he can invade the psyche,
spirit, and mental energy
of disgruntled postal employees
through hypnotism
and mental telepathy
whose vision
(like his memory)
is failing but is still
easily bothered
by people he perceives
to be in the vertical position
(unless their legs are dangling
in midair, defying perpendicularity),
volunteer salesman of coffins,
elevator operator to morgues,
low-paid museum guard of mortuaries,
the Uncle Sam recruitment officer
for maggot world supremacy,
the skull and cross bones
poster boy for poison
who was escorted to his
high school senior prom
by the Grim Reaper
whose mother was a mummy

JOHN ABNER

raped through the ace bandages
and strips of gauze by Dracula
King Kong and the Werewolf,
and whose combined sperm
made it through
to form him,
Judge Sabo,
timekeeper at the gates of hell,
umpire and referee of
sadomasochistic suicidal ritual,
judge, jury, and executioner
of living dreams
who cannot sleep

while someone else
is breathing
who's so vile
and senile
he thinks he's his own father,
a no-name, low-life
gas chamber cleaning attendant
at Auschwitz, laughing
in the blood red snow
of other people's ashes

•••••

11. All the facts are lies

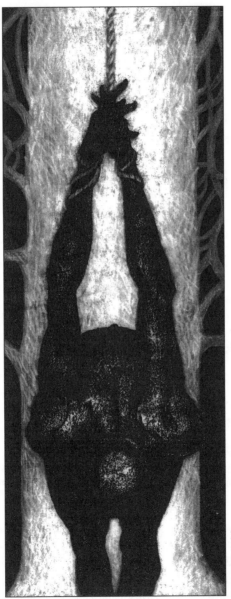

TOM FEELINGS

(the national scene 2)

WILLIE PERDOMO *

Dreaming, I Was Only Dreaming

My history professor
has a bad habit
of looking at me when
discussing slavery

I can't relate
to fields of slaves
making America

I can hear the cries

beautiful and strong

All the facts are lies

Right or wrong
I raise my hand
to ask a question:

Professor
Why do you
always look at me
when you
discuss slavery?
Last I heard
I was free...

I was free. The sheriff untied the noose around my neck and I ran to grab the sun that was sitting on top of the mountain. I slipped off a cliff and before I could close my eyes I landed in front of a white mansion. An old lady sat on a rocking chair and she was trying to make me dance with her rifle, swigging on some whiskey after every shot. She laughed like a drunken hyena while the whole world sat in a movie theater,
watching.

I snatched the rifle from her wrinkled hands and ran toward the crossroads. Before I could blink I was running through a jungle, trying to avoid the skeletons that were dangling off the trees and laughing like the old lady. Even the insects that were feeding onleftovers were giggling. By accident, I stepped on a baby's skull and I swore to God that I would give him my life if he let me out the jungle.

I escaped from a box that had no light and found a black and white photograph sailing in the wind. It was my grandmother. She was crying as my battalion marched past the New York Public Library on 42nd Street and Fifth Avenue. The stone lions started laughing like the old lady when we stopped to salute the flag. The soldiers stood at attention when I walked through the front entrance of Charlie's Bar & Restaurant. I asked for a menu and the waitress threw a pot of boiling coffee on my face. The crowd cheered and continued flinging their confetti. America was blessed.

A gunshot made the crowd scatter. Everyone ran to the train station to see the policeman who was drowning in a stream of blood that kept oozing out of the hole in his forehead. The chief of police held a news conference on the steps of City Hall. He held my hand up like a boxer who just won a championship. He told the crowd that I was the one who shot the policeman. (Or someone who "looked like me."He really couldn't tell because they were all wearing black berets, sunglasses and carrying automatic rifles. "Even the bullets were black!" He screamed as they escorted him to Bellevue Psychiatric Clinic.)

I held out my fist between the cage bars, raising my arm high like I wanted to ask a question. Blood dripped down my cheeks from a cut on my forehead. The policeman swam out of the stream of blood and he called my name. He wiped his red neck and smiled with his yellow teeth. Then he said, "Get up, boy. This ain't no dream. It's time to see the judge."

•••

TONI MORRISON
Racism and Fascism

Let us be reminded that before there is a final solution, there must be a first solution, a second one, even a third. The move toward a final solution is not a jump. It takes one step, then another, then another. Something, perhaps, like this:

1. Construct an internal enemy, as both focus and diversion.

2. Isolate and demonize that enemy by unleashing and protecting the utterance of overt and coded name-calling and verbal abuse. Employ ad hominem attacks as legitimate charges against that enemy.

3. Enlist and create sources and distributors of information who are willing to reinforce the demonizing process because it is profitable, because it grants power and because it works.

4. Palisade all art forms; monitor, discredit or expel those that challenge or destabilize processes of demonization and deification.

5. Subvert and malign all representatives of and sympathizers with this constructed enemy.

6. Solicit, from among the enemy, collaborators who agree with and can sanitize the dispossession process.

7. Pathologize the enemy in scholarly and popular mediums; recycle, for example, scientific racism and the myths of racial superiority in order to naturalize the pathology.

8. Criminalize the enemy. Then prepare, budget for and rationalize the building of holding arenas for the enemy—especially its males and absolutely its children.

9. Reward mindlessness and apathy with monumentalized entertainments and with little pleasures, tiny seductions: a few minutes on television, a few lines in the press; a little pseudo-success; the illusion of power and influence; a little fun, a little style, a little consequence.

10. Maintain, at all costs, silence.

In 1995, racism may wear a new dress, buy a new pair of boots, but neither it nor its succubus twin fascism is new or can make anything new. It can only reproduce the environment that supports its own health: fear, denial and an atmosphere in which its victims have lost the will to fight.

The forces interested in fascist solutions to national problems are not to be found in one political party or another, or in one or another wing of any single political party. Democrats have no unsullied history of egalitarianism. Nor are liberals free of domination agendas. Republicans have housed abolitionists and white supremacists. Conservative, moderate, liberal; right, left, hard left, far right; religious, secular, socialist—we must not be blindsided by these Pepsi-Cola, Coca-Cola labels because the genius of fascism is that any political structure can host the virus and virtually any developed country can become a suitable home. Fascism talks ideology, but it is really just marketing—marketing for power.

It is recognizable by its need to purge, by the strategies it uses to purge and by its terror of truly democratic agendas. It is recognizable by its determination to convert all public services to private entrepreneurship; all nonprofit organizations to profit-making ones—so that the narrow but protective chasm between governance and business disappears. It changes citizens into taxpayers—so individuals become angry at even the notion of the public good. It changes neighbors into consumers—so the measure of our value as humans is not our humanity or our compassion or our generosity but what we own. It changes parenting into panicking—so that we vote against the interests of our own children; against *their* health care, *their* education, *their* safety from weapons. And in effecting these changes it produces the perfect capitalist, one who is willing to kill a human being for a product—a pair of sneakers, a jacket, a car—or kill generations for control of products—oil, drugs, fruit, gold.

When our fears have all been serialized, our creativity censored, our ideas "marketplaced," our rights sold, our intelligence sloganized, our strength downsized, our privacy auctioned; when the theatricality, the entertainment value, the marketing of life is complete, we will find ourselves living not in a nation but in a consortium of industries, and wholly unintelligible to ourselves except for what we see as through a screen darkly.

•••

KECIA ÉLAN COLE
Day-Glo Armageddon

Napalm juice boxes
are selling deadly on the lunch line
bubbling over w/ the funk of
freeze dried government cheese pizzas

& two-year-old catsup packets
posing as vegetables
the fluorescent little bombs
pass thru 7th grade hands
voracious under tables
caked w/ food subsidies &
lack of learning
tossed sporadically around the junior high school
like disillusioned strokes of america
painting day-glo armageddon
across her stolen frontiers
we used to pray on
we used to pray to
before you
white rage revolution mouths
parched by the thought of payback
speak angry sweet rantings
of collection time
& past due debts
as though they had
400 years worth of cotton
trapped in the memory
of their fingernails
as though their grandparents
were snatched in midraindance
from a nyabingi wind
as they planted life inside
mother's soft brown hips
& now my feet don't know
the ecstasy of an earth kiss
or freedom
spent lifetimes
trying not to fear dying
& the death toll is now at 196
steady rising
john doe no. 2 is at large
arabs taking the Polaroids down
from their corner store Plexiglas
urged by customers to
keep the change
in the benevolence of guilt
convicted before the crime was committed
rednecks make brothers more patriotic
when they see newborns

strewn in the street
like chunks of federal building
& fear
tempered w/
the comfort of expectation
bulletproof babies
tuck themselves in at night
under blankets of demons
& past lives
surprised only by
everyone else's surprise
how aborigines
could be soothed by the illusions
blasting sitcoms in stereo sound
thru their living rooms
while wars transform into fiction
& death row's glutted stomach
steady rumbles
the rest of us felt our earth
cave into herself galaxies ago
feeling the weight of retribution
in Sharpesville, South Philly & Soweto
like it was today
because it is
& john doe no. 2 is
still at large
hiding beneath mid american black hills
displaced rampage feeds his famine
overcome by the howling
hunger of revenge
collection time has come
the debt is past due.

•••

XOCHIPIELLI

L.A. law (and order)

L.A. law is not a television
show, but an all-white jury
in Johannesburg—I mean Simi
Valley—that cannot see
the brutality of police
beating a black man
senseless for kicks

L.A. law is suburban law
and order reigning over
the inner city like 56
blows from a baton
—count them all—

L.A. law is not make
believe, but real hysteria
and alarm, jailing Chicano
zoot suiters in the 1940s
and letting the U.S. military
loose on them en El Pueblo
de Los, exercising their
right to terrorize people
of color—both foreign
and domestic—beating them
and stripping them naked
of those funny clothes
sus hermanos left before
shipping overseas—those
too big pants and jackets,
wide brim and long chain,
shoes shined so bright it's
almos' a shame to kick you
in your ass with them—no
real American would wear
such clothes both
yesterday and today

Sometimes L.A. law is
just a hunch those
niggers on the corner
are up to something

Too often L.A. law means
unarmed 14 year olds
shot dead by other 14
year olds or the police
—a dozen eyewitness reports
contradict the lone officer's
account, but those 12 are
not trained professionals

L.A. law stole El Pueblo
from Mejico, but not the
gente who still live there

L.A. law is a smoke screen,
a diversion

L.A. law is a frame-up:
manufactured evidence
and coerced confessions
—where were you on the
night in question?

L.A. law is a Hollywood
D.A. looking for a movie
contract (and the governor's
mansion)—did you see that
last performance on television?

L.A. law is a daily rail-
road that runs on time,
and it's coming to
a city near you

•••

SAUL WILLIAMS
Sha Clack Clack

I know you are but what am I?
I know you are but what am I?
I know you are but what am I?
Infinity

If I could find the spot where truth echoes
I would stand there and whisper memories of my children's future.
I would let their future dwell in my past so that I might live
brighter NOW.
Now is the essence of my domain and it contains
all that was and will be
and I am as I was and will be
because I am and always will be that nigga.

I am that nigga.

I am that timeless nigga that swings on pendulums like vines
through mines of booby-trapped minds that are enslaved by time.
I am the life that supersedes life-times.
I am.

It was me with serpentine hair and timeless stare
that with a glare turned mortal fear into stone time-capsules,
They still exist as the walking-dead.
As I do. the original suffer-head,
symbol of life and matriarchy's severed head,
MEDUSA, I am.

It was me, the ecclesiastical one,
that pointed out that nothing was new under the sun
and through times of laughter and times of tears
saw that no time was real time 'cause all times were fear.
The wise seer, SOLOMON, I am.

It was me with tattered clothes that made you scatter
as you shuffled past me on the street.
You shuffled past me on the street
as I stood there conversing with wind-blown spirits.
And I fear it's your loss that you didn't stop and talk to me.
I could have told you your future as I explained your present,
but instead I'm the homeless schizophrenic that you resent
for being aimless.
the in-tuned NAMELESS, I am.

I am that nigga.
I am that nigga.
I am a negro.
Yes, negro
Negro from necro, meaning death,
I overcame it so they named me after it.
And I be spittin' at death from behind
and puttin' "kick me" signs on its back,
Because I am not the son of
sha clack clack
I am before that, I am before.
I am before before.
Before death is eternity
After death is eternity

There is no death there's only eternity.
And I be ridin' on the wings of eternity
like yha, yha, yha
sha clack clack

I exist like spit-fire which you call the sun
and try to map out your future with sun-dials.
But tick tock technology cannot tick tock me.
I exist somewhere between tick tock,
dodgin' it like double-dutch, got me livin' double-time,
but I was here before your time. Before time.
My heart is made of the quartz crystals
that you be makin' clocks out of
and I be resurrectin' every third, like, tick tick tick
sha clack clack
No! I won't work a nine to five.
I am setting suns and orange moons
and my existence is this:
(still, yet, ever moving)
And I'm moving beyond time
because it binds me it can set me free
and I'll fly when the clock strikes me
like, yha, yha, yha
sha clack clack
But my flight doesn't go undisturbed
because time makes dreams defer
and all of my time fears are turning my days into daymares.
I live daymares, reliving nightmares that once haunted my past.
sha clack clack
Time is beatin' my ass.
And I be havin' dreams of chocolate-covered watermelons
filled with fried chicken, like piñatas,
with little pickaninny sons and daughters
standing up under it with big sticks and aluminum foil,
hittin' it, trying to catch pieces of falling fried chicken wings
and Aunt Jemima and Uncle Ben are standing in the corners
with rifles pointed at the heads of all of the little children.
"Don't shoot the children," I shout.
But they say it's too late, they've already been infected by time
But I need more time. I need less time. I need more time.
It's too late. They start shootin' at the children,
their existence smeared with chocolate, chicken, and watermelon,
and the children are dying 1 by 1, 2 by 2, 3 by 3,
4 by 4, 5 by 5, 6 by 6,

But my spirit is growing 7 by 7
faster than the speed of light
because light only penetrates the darkness that's already there
and I'm already there, at the end of the road,
which is the beginning of the road beyond time.
But where my niggas at?
Don't tell me my niggas got lost in time!
My niggas are dyin' before their time!
My niggas are dyin' because of time.

•••

DANNY SHOT
My Money

It's my money
not yours
It's my money
I need more
my money
It's not enough
my money
I keep it close
my money
nobody's going to take it away
give it away
to loud crude people
with funny names
and bad habits.

It's my money
I've watched it grow
into big money
piled majestically high
to the feet of God
who has a taste
for the sweets of gelt.
It's all my money
glittering sensually
in midnight dreams
of forbidden favors
bought and sold.
It's my money

the New Deal is done gone
no more government handouts
welfare cheats beware
socialized medicine...
I think not.
I buy paintings
to support the arts
Ha Ha Ha (suckers!)

It's my money
fuck the poor
and their many children
let them get a job
let them pay for school
let them eat welfare cheese
make them go away
beat them down
into the ground.
It's my money and
I want it back.

It's my money
gonna buy me
favors and friendships
of painters and
poets and
models and
cardinals and
maybe even
you.

It's my money
my reason for being
my money
my business
my life
life is a business
everything for sale.
America: I love
this decorated hell
that feeds me opportunities
and hears my voice
above all others.
My money

don't give it away
to those who claim to be in need.
Nobody needs it
more than me
I need my money.
I need:

> a new BMW
> a vacation house
> liposuction
> hair replacement
> season tickets
> tax deductions
> fur for my mistress
> Newt's ear
> an ambassadorship
> a magazine with my name
> on the cover
> Aspen, Colorado

My money
I spend it
as I wish.
My workers are grateful
that this is my money.
They show their appreciation
by washing my car
taking my suits to the cleaner
doing magic tricks for my children.
My employees,
they love me
because I'm tough but fair
fiscally responsible.

My money
not your money
don't touch it
mom and dad
worked hard for it.
My money
cultivated like an ancient orchard
bearing fruit for me and mine.
My money
don't stare at it
get to work

make me more
take your hungry eyes
out of my sight.
It's my money
I want more.

•••

LAMONT B. STEPTOE
Begging for a Nightstick

Every Blackman
in America
is a mug shot
a set of fingerprints
a second story man
a Mike Tyson
a King Kong
an O.J. Simpson
with gorilla hands
and a gorilla cock
in search of a screaming
blonde virgin

Every Blackman
in America wears a bull's eye
on his back
with nails protruding
from his head
begging for a nightstick
or hammer
to pound them into
the underground railroad
tracks that no longer
lead to safety
'cause the spy in the sky
knows where you live
how much you weigh
the formula of your DNA

Every Blackman
in America is a tin duck
in the cheap carnival
just outside town
waiting for a mob
of good ole boys
in high spirits
to make him dance
or swing

•••

LENARD D. MOORE

Rodney King

In the night. Lying there
like a melon beneath the stars.
He turns from aching billyclubs.
His pleas
rising in his eyes.
Pleas done gone ignored.

A camcorder
testifies a bruised dream.

O remembrances of
whips cracking
from centuries
not talked about.
His name echoes in blues,
in the hostile wind.
Los Angeles.
Los Angeles.
He
is lying there.
At the crossroads.
He turns: moaning.
Just a moaning
his weariness.
Blues screaming
beneath the stars.
Blues screaming
beneath the stars.

•••

MICHAEL C. LADD *

The Bottom of the Storm

I

We have witnessed the cacophony of consecutive explosions
yet not
precisely dropped
to blow away these hills
knocking on Beverly Hillbillies' front doors
like a cartoon bomb, gloved mechanical arm tap-tapping
politely waiting for the door to open
before it explodes
I am waiting on the same scenario
over and over again
until the repetition
creates a new reality of fire
burning like the eyes of a cockroach
still laughing in the Mojave desert
home to nothing but over-worked gamma rays
I am this cockroach smoking dust from poo poo nuts
until my brain is barbecue ribs
with crickle sauce like Curtis slams down
at the Ninth Wonder of the World
complete with corn and cool breeze

Yeah I want them to die in Crystal City
while I lick my six legs
thick with the taste of irrational redemption
ca-ca cash man blood baths
going out wading in guts
Ignoring consequences like Muslims in Chechneya
reckless, ruthless, but still alive
heavy with hell and very, very high
I want my own aircraft carrier
with Bed-Stuy for a crew
diligent and awake
with precision
this is my AM vision

Reprise:

At the bottom of the storm where the electricity of rhetoric sleeps
is the POW caressing nightmares looking through dreams
holding consciousness like a crystal ball
all snowy inside with an electric chair

II

The battleships are launched
it's muthafuckin over
sober up quick
we gonna leave with or without you
on this ark of fire and rage
taunting the noose
banging like sledgehammers
unruly muthafuckas out of control children
bringing on reality like violent diarrhea
full of hot peppers
yellow thin from dehydration
stinging burning the mayor's face
It's on, America
complacency will get the gag order
it's been begging for
the gag drenched in gasoline
and we with the Bic
lighter igniting the firefighters
too dumb to hose down corrupt unions
nesting in the governor's ass hair
it's beyond them
it's beyond the governor's ass
it is eating at his stomach
dancing in the acids
en route to his heart
we will throw that stone
into the hell sea that never gives back

It's on, America
catch up with yourself
we stick sticks of dynamite
in the eye sockets of
blow job casualty

newscasters
fighting truth with candy canes and winning
poop feeding press dogs
laxative junkies
killing peasants
blaming it on journalists
chasing their tails
sacrificing lives for their jobs
they will shoot themselves in the groin

we are shrapnel in popcorn kernels
in a pan hotter than scorched earth
die, nouveau nappers
there are no sappers to snuff us out
we new Viet Cong
more ruthless than Pol Pot with a heart
misguided missiles still blow baby
we are Bouncing Bettys
we have punji stakes jutting from our guts
we must catch a fire love the fire
burn the fire be the fire
let it burn again
let it burn

It's 1967 again renaissance time
America regenerate gyrate on understanding
The mayors want us babbling
The governors want us rioting
they want us unruly
they want us on stretcher cots not in boycotts
They want riots not marches
we might get war
regular standard fare guerrilla war
large amounts of friends and family in small pieces
lined up for identification
so they can crucify the identifiers
The mayor wants an excuse to recline on us in his curfew couch
he wants on site shootings
and Yankee Stadium full of buried mommies
a city full of black Oldsmobiles with red sirens
sucking in citizens like bad vacuums

I could go on
We could all be Mumia

but we will see our sneaker marks in blood prints

We should be Mumia

how do we stop the bleeding

We are Mumia

we need on-time tourniquets
we need student and union fusion
we need information infiltration
we need each other
as Americans
we need the silent creeping of understanding
and action upon action
until we are as over-worked as corporate executive jaws and cocks
with one difference we still working
like Palestinian stone throwers
El Salvadorean mortar men
Zimbabwean mothers caressing cheeks
Winnie Mandela bear hugs
change may be a violent wretched thing
but that's the trauma true love always brings
and it may just be how freedom rings

Reprise:

At the bottom of the storm where the electricity of rhetoric sleeps
is the POW caressing nightmares looking through dreams
holding consciousness like a crystal ball
all snowy inside with an electric chair

•••

CORNELIUS EADY
Rodney King Blues

I love the world,
But my heart's
Been cheated.

What's in my hands?
Pain, a low
Moan. That's
What it feels like.
Now every street
Shadows my steps.
A sin
And a shame.

What do I carry?
There's
Mr. Death

In his severe
Blue uniform,
Mr. Misfortune
And his legal fists.
A low-
-down funk.

What's on my heart?
'buke
And scorn,
Mr. Hard Luck's
Satisfaction.

Blue musk
Sorrowful shoes.
Rodney King Blues.

•••

MARIA MAZZIOTTI GILLAN

Coming of Age; Paterson

Blind as Oedipus, we grope our way
through a century gone dark,
where history has lost its power
and even war and death
televised on the 6 o'clock news

cannot shock us.
When children in Paterson
are beaten to death,
they do not even earn
one line in *The Herald News*.

I mourn the children in Micronesia
who are born without bones
as a result of nuclear testing.
I mourn the young men on street corners,
blown like refuse against Black Bear Liquors,
the young men whose shoulders speak
of 11 A.M. and no job and nowhere to go,
and the refrain in their heads: "what you gonna do?
what you gonna do?"

I mourn the wasted lives in Soweto and
South Africa, Nicaragua and Cuba;
then I walk these Paterson streets, knowing
we do not have to travel far to find
the worm in the heart of America:
the streets of broken bottles and crack vials,
the county jail with its guard dogs,
and the wives and children of prisoners,
line up from 5 P.M. to Midnight, patient as plaster
saints, waiting to be allowed inside.
The shoulders of the poor are an elegy.
They cry out for the lost
and forgotten,
wandering grimy streets
in search of a quick fix.

Let us join our voices, keening
for the man asleep in the doorway,
the liquor bottle in the gutter,
the child who toughs it out
in the Alexander Hamilton welfare hotel.

I mourn the black women in the dirty shelter
waiting for the Broadway bus; the Puerto Rican boys
in their thick gold chains and their wise guy smiles,
the child who trails behind, crying,
and the young woman lumbering down Main Street,
her heavy legs covered with angry

red sores, her body swaying
from side to side
and the embarrassed, downturned gazes
of the people who pass her by.

I mourn the young boy in the purple shirt
with the huge radio on his shoulder
blasting music into the street
and the cleaning woman
who says "I ain't black. See. It's them kind
make it bad for the rest of us."
When she should be working,
she climbs on the commode
in the handicapped stall in the bathroom
and smokes for hours, an out of order
sign pasted on the door
and her trash can wheeled in there with her.

In the streets of our cities
the poor rise again like dough,
no matter how we push them down.

•••

TRINIDAD SANCHEZ, JR.

America Is a Prison

The loss of a woman
separated from my son
is my real prison...a struggle
outside and within myself.
This paranoia full of suicides, murders,
drug overdoses is a grand central station
where only the strong survive.
It is a terrible, dangerous place
for keeping people filled with hate,
unrest, without a job or a trade,
where you learn to hate
being treated like animals
and loneliness is your only friend.
this is where a man is judged

by the number of cigarettes he has
not whether he is guilty or innocent.
This is no place to be,
this loser's home, losing situation
and pretty petty place
where time takes its toll
on the mind, body and soul—
should be condemned.

America is a prison,
a man made hell
full of persons buried alive
their madness breeding in the walls.
This overcrowded hate factory
is a toxic waste problem
yet not one person is here
for being convicted of polluting.
This classical paradox of doing time
is a facade, a $25,000 a year warehouse
$8,000 a year more than full costs
at Stanford University.
It is a big business, a corporate
multi-million dollar... TIMEBOMB!

These statements make no sense
just like prisons!

•••

ALLEN GINSBERG

A Ballad of the Skeletons

Said the Presidential Skeleton
I won't sign the bill
Said the Speaker skeleton
Yes you will

Said the Representative Skeleton
I object
Said the Supreme Court skeleton
Whaddya expect

Said the Military skeleton
Buy Star Bombs
Said the Upperclass Skeleton
Starve unmarried moms

Said the Yahoo Skeleton
Stop dirty art
Said the Right Wing skeleton
Forget about yr heart

Said the Gnostic Skeleton
The Human Form's divine
Said the Moral Majority skeleton
No it's not it's mine

Said the Buddha Skeleton
Compassion is wealth
Said the Corporate skeleton
It's bad for your health

Said the Old Christ skeleton
Care for the Poor
Said the Son of God skeleton
AIDS needs cure

Said the Homophobe skeleton
Gay folk suck
Said the Heritage Policy skeleton
Blacks're outa luck

Said the Macho skeleton
Women in their place
Said the Fundamentalist skeleton
Increase human race

Said the Right-to-Life skeleton
Foetus has a soul
Said Pro Choice skeleton
Shove it up your hole

Said the Downsized skeleton
Robots got my job
Said the Tough-on-Crime skeleton
Tear gas the mob

Said the Governor skeleton
Cut school lunch
Said the Mayor skeleton
Eat the budget crunch

Said the Neo-Conservative skeleton
Homeless off the street!
Said the Free Market skeleton
Use 'em up for meat

Said the Think Tank skeleton
Free Market's the way
Said the S & L skeleton
Make the State pay

Said the Chrysler skeleton
Pay for you & me
Said the Nuke Power skeleton
& me & me & me

Said the Ecologic skeleton
Keep Skies blue
Said the Multinational skeleton
What's it worth to you?

Said the NAFTA skeleton
Get rich, Free Trade,
Said the Maquiladora skeleton
Sweat shops, low paid

Said the rich GATT skeleton
One world, high tech
Said the Underclass skeleton
Get it in the neck

Said the World Bank skeleton
Cut down your trees
Said the I.M.F. skeleton
Buy American cheese

Said the Underdeveloped skeleton
Send me rice
Said Developed Nations' skeleton
Sell your bones for dice

Said the Ayatollah skeleton
Die writer die
Said Joe Stalin's skeleton
That's no lie

Said the Petrochemical skeleton
Roar Bombers roar!
Said the Psychedelic skeleton
Smoke a dinosaur

Said Nancy's skeleton
Just say No
Said the Rasta skeleton
Blow Nancy Blow

Said Demagogue skeleton
Don't smoke Pot
Said Alcoholic skeleton
Let your liver rot

Said the Junkie skeleton
Can't we get a fix?
Said the Big Brother skeleton
Jail the dirty pricks

Said the Mirror skeleton
Hey good looking
Said the Electric Chair skeleton
Hey what's cooking?

Said the Talkshow skeleton
Fuck you in the face
Said the Family Values skeleton
My family values mace

Said the NY Times skeleton
That's not fit to print
Said the CIA skeleton
Cantcha take a hint?

Said the Network skeleton
Believe my lies
Said the Advertising skeleton
Don't get wise!

Said the Media skeleton
Believe you me
Said the Couch-potato skeleton
What me worry?

Said the TV skeleton
Eat sound bites
Said the Newscast skeleton
That's all Goodnight

•••

ROBERT FARR
how's that?

amerika? where your chlorofluoro-carbon kings sit erect behind mahogany desks, demolishing secretaries. who can forget the ominous sound of CFCs, as harsh as a timpani played somewhat off key. we know there's cacophony in the boardroom. it's the hushed sound of a whistle being played backwards, from the in/side. it's the quick foot up the short ass of that eager, young kid, who sat next door. his office grown vaguely quiet. amerika, like all your other debates, this one has spilled over into Congress. Congress, who can't even tie its own shoes. who takes vacations—one week out of every four—as remedy to feeling accomplished. how can this be Congress? what coming together? what COMING together? meanwhile, corporate fat cats count up the tally, septuagenarian white boys like roger smith, whose "progressive" business policies bankrupted flint. chrysler's lee iacocca, whose slightly tarnished good guy image turns even browner with new factory layoffs. and how about the boys at perrier? pumping benzene for years into all that "natural" water. or jack welsh, at g.e., who turned schenectady into a glimmering graveyard, nothing but empty parking lots where buildings used to be. so much for the house that thomas built. over 14,000 layoffs, most of them in manufacturing, since 1980. more than 1/50th of the local workforce. think of all those faces. just think: but, you bet your ass the balance sheets looked good. you bet ol' jumpin' jack never went hungry, or homeless. you bet g.e.'s stockholders, most of them men, lined the pockets of success with some soiled green. all those blue suits. all those yellow ties. think of the wasted lives, as g.e. moved from fortune 6 to fortune 5. how's that for progress? how's that? as petrochemical companies flood us with tetrachlor, diazinon, malathion, ddt, agent orange, and carcinogenic briquettes soaked in something like kerosene, then burned underneath red meat stuffed with irradiated grain, and pumped full of antibiotics. how's that? and what about the CFCs, opening a hole as big as the ocean over antarctica, over california, over japan. yessir, it's just like Ronald Reagan, all over again. it's just like Ronald Reagan never left. or, maybe Ronald Reagan has always been here, we just thought he was john wayne. someone is always masquerading as john wayne. we know they're seriously homophobic, as they burst in to bust up grenada, nicaragua, el salvador, in some big, macho scene grabbing their penises. by the year 2,000, 18% of the ozone will be gone. (this is from the National Academy of Sciences.) after that, we burn our asses.

•••

PAUL BEATTY

Old Yeller Dreams of Days When They Wasn't Just Whistlin' Dixie

coon dog
raccoon
black coon
coonta kinte
back to africa coon
inner city riot burn n' loot coon
them niggers ought to be shamed of themselves...how much you selling that tv for coon
middle management coons
moody coons
put the ball in the hoop coons
athletic lip-sync the words to the national anthem coons
people who cry when they win coons
malibu beach barbie tan but not too dark coon
heckle n' jeckle looney tune cartoon coons
film school coons who wanna produce write and direct the same ol' soon to be a major motion picture
  young ghetto coons in turmoil fifty million fucking times over coons
free white an 21 coons
first coon on the moon coon
coon by yah my lord, coon by yah, oooh lord coon by yah
shut the fuck up censorship coons
ACLU freedom of speech at any cost, americans have a constitutional right to call you nigger bitch wop
  wasp honky faggot kike coons
folks who secretly like to be called nigger bitch wasp honky faggot kike coons
big city mayor up for re-election wearing a yarmulke one day a sombrero the next, "shalom, vota para mi" coons
hymietown coon
police chief coon
secretary of defense coon

prime time stuttering eye buggin n' shufflin baboons who think they different than Rochester, Stepin
Fechit, Beulah, 'whazzzaaapp?', 'whuchutalkinbout willis', 'get it girfriend' who don't remember hattie
mac once said, "The only choice for us is to be servants for $7.00 a week or portray them for $700
a week." coons
ebony magazine's annual most eligible bachelors and bachelorettes and the niggers who actually read
the goddamn article talking about "that banker is cute and i'd go out with the one in the navy" coons
ebony magazine's most powerful 100 African-americans who ain't changed shit coons
big buffed stand in front of the door and don't let any coons into the white clubs coons
i think the white folks are right as usual coons
white people who want to be down coons
white people who think they down cause they date black coons
niggers who play up to white wannabe black 'yeah you a soul brother let me have five dollars' coons
this is my white lover and i don't have to prove anything to you coons
this is my white lover and i don't have to prove anything to you coons who put their business in the streets
of the world by going on these syndicated afternoon talkshows and fucking up the rest of my day
coons
khengis coon
poets who call readings 'performances' coons
spoken word no images make a painful face take pity on me i'm from the projects
wanna be on tv look ma i'm a professional poet coons
art world power brokers who show off their stables of marginalized trivialized artists of color and other
coons
and now for the gay coon
the feminist coon
the rap poet coon
the latina coon
et tu, coon?
friends, romans, countrymen lend me your coons
a coon! a coon! my kingdom for a coon!
jesus h. coon
god coon
lucifer coon
hypocrite coon
contradiction free coons
blue coon
crip coon
blood coon
republican coon
republican democrat coon
webelo coons
post-modern coon
deconstructionist coon
the world owes me something coon

full coon
new coon
lunar eclipse coon
harmless coons
dangerous coons
suicidal coons
depressed coons
dehumanized coon
nevermind me i'm just a coon's coon

•••

PEDRO PIETRI

DO NOT WALK ON THE GRASS UNTIL AFTER SMOKING IT

TRUE TUNNEL VISIONARIES OF THE WILD WEST YES
I BELIEVE FOR EVERY DROP OF BLOOD THAT FALLS
FROM THE DREAMS OF TRUE BELIEVERS OF DEMOCRACY
ELECTED OFFICIALS GET THEIR POLITICAL ROCKS OFF
ON SOLID GOLD TOILET SEATS OF FALSE SELF-ESTEEM

I BELIEVE YOU BELIEVE WHOEVER DOESN'T BELIEVE
THAT THIS IS THE GREATEST COUNTRY IN THE WORLD
DOESN'T DESERVE TO BE SERVED BREAKFAST IN BED
AND IS BETTER OFF DEAD THAN TO BE ON WELFARE
(OH YEAH GOD ISN'T AS DUMB AS THE WORLD THINKS)

POOR PEOPLE ARE NECESSARY FOR DIGNITARIES LIKE
YOURSELF TO BE GATHERED HERE TODAY TO TALK SHIT
AS YOU RECONVENE FOR THE 2001 100TH 4TH CONGRESS
LIKE TRUE FELLOW UNMELLOW AMERICAN BUSINESSMEN
DISGUISED AS VERY HIGH OFFICIAL CIVIL SERVANTS
SERVING THE INTEREST OF THE RICH AND NOT THOSE
WHO WISH UPON THE STARS & STRIPES FOR PROSPERITY

BECAUSE THEY ARE SO BROKE THEY CAN'T EVEN PAY
THE INTEREST ON THEIR LIMITED ATTENTION SPAN
AND ARE NOT AMERI-CANS BUT AMERI'S WHO CANNOT
GET THEIR ACT TOGETHER TO OVERTHROW THE SYSTEM
OF DECEPTION ALIVE AND WELL THROUGH ELECTIONS
AND YOU DON'T HAVE THE RIGHT TO REMAIN SILENT

YOU HAVE TO VOTE REPUBLICAN OR DEMOCRAT (EVEN)
IF THE CANDIDATES RUNNING ARE BOTH FULL OF CRAP
ON BEHALF OF THE NATIONAL KEEP OFF THE GRASS
CAMPAIGN TO CONTROL THE WAY THE RAIN FALLS
ON DEMOCRATIC NONE OF THE ABOVE LISTED VALUES
MISSING FROM CONVOLUTED CONSTITUTION IMPOSED
BY THE DEFUNCT FOUNDING FATHERS WHO WERE
TOO DRUNK TO READ WHAT THEY HAD WRITTEN SOBER!

THE GOOD THE BAD & THE UGLY ARE IDENTICAL
GOOD FOR NOTHING HONEST PATHOLOGICAL LIARS
WHO WILL FAN THE FLAMES OF THE FIRE NEXT TIME
IN THE FOREST OF RECENT IMMIGRANTS AS RECENT

AS A FEW HUNDRED YEARS AGO WHEN THE VERY FIRST
PARKING METERS INVADED A POLLUTION FREE AMERICA
TO PROCLAIM IT THE LAND OF THEIR NATURAL BIRTH
AND BECOME A SUPER POWER THAT WILL EVENTUALLY
LOSE THE VIET NAM WAR AFTER SO MANY GLORIOUS
VICTORIES ON THE BATTLEFIELD DEFENDING FREEDOM
OF MOVEMENT EXPRESSION RECESSION & DEPRESSION

AS THE TRAFFIC CONGESTION GETS OUT OF HAND
AND EVEN IF YOUR LAST NAME IS RODRIGUES BUT
YOUR COMPLEXION ISN'T CAUCASIAN YOU TOO WILL
BE DENIED A BEER IN A BAR IN NEW ORLEANS G.I.

AY AY AY AY TO BE FREE TO BE HOMELESS IS A SIN

AGAINST HUMANITY & GOD AGREES BUT WON'T SAY SO
FOR FEAR OF REPRISAL FROM THE NEW WORLD ORDER
OF THE NATIONAL ENDOWMENT FOR THE ARTLESS ARTS!

FEEL FREE TO FART IN THE HOUSE OF CONGRESS SIR
AS YOU PONDER THAT OVERWHELMING QUESTION: HOW
THE HELL DID THAT SPIC BREACH SECURITY AGAIN?
THIS TIME I AM UNARMED AND EXTREMELY DANGEROUS
WITH THE FIRST AMENDMENT RIGHT TO FREE VERSE
THAT STATES A POET IS A POET AND A POLITICIAN
IS THE BEST FRIEND OF ALL AMERICAN MORTICIANS

AS I WAS SAYING BEFORE YOU ALL STARTED PAYING
ATTENTION TO SOMETHING ELSE THAT HAS NOTHING TO DO
WITH
WHAT THE MAJORITY IS SAYING TO YOU:
AND THAT IS TO GIVE TRUE EQUALITY A CHANCE MAN
FREE BAMBU PAPER FOR YOUR NON NICOTENE VOTERS!

HATS OFF (EXCEPT MINE) FOR POLITICIANS WHO
ARE NOT PRESENT HERE TODAY BECAUSE THEY LOST
THE ELECTIONS FOR BEING ANGRY NOT JUST FOR
CHUMP CHANGE BUT FOR REAL CHANGES IN AMERICA
THE BEAUTIFUL LAND OF MULTI-MILLIONAIRE BASEBALL
PLAYERS ON STRIKE CAUSE THEY WANT MORE MONEY
TO SWING AND HIT THE BALL AND MISS THE POINT
DURING COLLECTIVE GRACE CHANT FOR TV DINNERS:

LORD THANK YOU FOR THIS FOOD AND FOR KEEPING
THE HOMELESS OUT OF OUR NEIGHBORHOOD A-MEN!
WHICH WILL BE REPEATED FIFTY-ONE TIMES WHEN
EL CONSPIRACY AGAINST PUERTO RICAN INDEPENDENCE
IS COMPLETED & ACCENTS BECOME OFFICIALLY ILLEGAL
AND WHOSOEVER IS HEARD MAKING SENSE IN SPANGLISH
WILL BE CONSIDERED A THREAT TO NATIONAL SECURITY,

AND YES I AM HERE TODAY BECAUSE YOU CAN ONLY
SUCCEED IN GETTING RID OF YOURSELF AND NOT ME
OR ANYONE ELSE WHO CAME HERE THE SAME WAY YOU
AND YOUR PARENTS DID ON THE TIMES SQUARE SHUTTLE
TO BETTER YOUR STANDARDS OF DAYDREAMING OF
EVENTUALLY HITTING THE LOTTERY AND HIRING AN
ILLEGAL IMMIGRANT LIKE YOURSELF TO DO YOUR
DIRTY LAUNDRY AND BREAST FEED YOUR BASTARDS,

THE MOST RECENT ILLEGAL IMMIGRANTS (BECAUSE
THE BOTTOM LINE ALL THE TIME IS STILL A CRIME)
LOS UNICO NON IMMIGRANTS ARE IN RESERVATIONS
AND NOT IN THE HOUSE OF CONGRESS JERKING OFF

AND YES I AGREE WITH MY COUSIN ERNIE WHO SAYS
REALITY ONLY APPLIES TO THE CRUST OF APPLE PIE
IN THE U.S.A. HIP HIP HOORAY THEY ONLY VOTED
FOR YOU BECAUSE YOU ARE OF THE SAME RELIGION

AND THE CARDINALS & BISHOPS & POTENTIAL POPES
WILL CALL YOU A DOPE IF YOU CROSS PARTY LINES
AND YES I AGREE WITH MY BROTHER JOE WHO STATES
IT ISN'T SO, AT OTB THE WINNERS ARE ALL LOSERS
AND YES I AGREE WITH THE DISILLUSIONED MAJORITY
WHO WERE NEVER PROMISED A CHEESEBURGER DELUX,

WHEN THEY WAKE UP IN THE MORNING AND SHOUT
WHO THE FUCK DO THEY THINK THEY ARE FOOLING?
FREEDOM IS A STATE OF MIND OF BLANK THOUGHTS!
AND YES I AGREE WITH JOHN FISK THAT THIS POEM
FOR THIS HIGHLY PUBLICIZED SPECIAL OCCASION
SHOULD BEGIN WITH OUTBURSTS OF THE WORD "HELP"
FROM BEGINNING TO END AND BEYOND THE LAST LINE

BECAUSE THIS LAND IS NOT MY LAND OR YOUR LAND
UNLESS WE ARE WILLING TO SHARE WITH EVERYONE
EVERYTHING THERE IS TO SHARE EVERYWHERE YOU LOOK
AND YES I AGREE WITH MY FRIEND ALEX WHO THINKS
YOU SHOULD ALL GET LOST TIL YOU FIND YOURSELF
PANHANDLING DURING THE RUSH HOURS OF AMNESIA
WHEN VOTERS REMEMBER WHAT YOU LOOK LIKE & PUKE
ON THE TWO PIECE SUITS OF YOUR BROKEN PROMISES!

•••

JUNE JORDAN

Manifesto of the Rubber Gloves

So I'm wearing brand new loud blue
Rubber gloves
because
I'm serious about I don't wanna die
from
mainstream contamination
mainstream
poison waters poisonous
like
statistical majorities
that represent
the mainstream
poison waters poisonous

like
neo-Nazi perspectives
that reflect
the mainstream
poison waters poisonous
like
scapegoat policies
that distill
the mainstream
poison waters poisonous
like
the Congress and the Governor and
    the President
and the Supremely Clarence Retrograde
Thomas
Court
of Separated and Unequal
and Proud about That
Last Resort

I'm wearing brand new loud blue
Rubber gloves
because
I'm serious about I don't wanna die
from
mainstream contamination
mainstream
poison waters poisonous
like
the FBI and ATF
and the INS and Secret Service
Security Guards
with or without a cut on anybody's finger
and a pointless
overblown Armed Forces
afraid to fight
unless
it gets a not-a-single-cut-on-a-single-one-
of-your-fingers guarantee
backed by
a would-be
hero's welcome
first for hiding the hell

out of trouble
when the point
might very well
be
"The trouble"
The 6000,000 human beings dead
already
anyway

I'm wearing brand new loud blue
Rubber gloves
because I'm serious about I don't wanna
die
from
mainstream contamination
mainstream
poison waters poisonous
like
a serial killer
start anyplace
(next door!)
and slash and dismember
and move on

and on and kill more and more
a serial killer
absolutely
mainstream
tall and good
(looking)
nicely dressed
a dedicated
fast-travelling
serial killer
straight from the heartland oozing
mainstream
poison waters
a republican
a soft-spoken young man
a believer in Christ Jesus
a serial killer
like
The Pilgrims
like
the early
serial killer
settler
pioneers
beginning with the Indians
and then xyz
and then abc
and always
hunting down
the poor
and
the niggers
and
the kikes
and
the wetbacks
and
the chinks
and
the faggots
and
the dykes
and

the heathen who
unlike the serial killer
do
not
believe in Christ Jesus

I'm serious about I don't wanna die
from
mainstream contamination
mainstream
poison waters poisonous
at flood-tide heights
and depths
of programmatic and legislative and
     scatter-
shot self-righteous
consecration
to my death!

I'm wearing brand new loud blue
Rubber gloves
because
I'm serious about I don't wanna die
from
mainstream contamination
mainstream
poison waters poisonous
and swollen
all around me
and
as far as I can see

I'm serious
because
I don't wanna die
I don't wanna die
I don't wanna die

•••

NAOMI LONG MADGETT
Images

1.
One student (white),
leading a class discussion
of *Native Son*
and running out of things to say,
asked, "How would you feel
if you encountered Bigger Thomas
on a dark street
late at night?"

Another student (black, astute)
countered: "How
would you know it was
Bigger Thomas?"

2.
I pictured him as muscular,
dull-eyed and dense, his sullen scowl,
skin color, maze of hair
and criminal demeanor defining
my most horrendous nightmare.

How can I reconcile
that image
with this tender yellow
boy who could have been
my son?

•••

STACI RODRIGUEZ
where images are not sacred

give me a place where
images are sacred and
my politics safe
sweet land of liberty

where images are not sacred
and politics are not safe

where the president can one day O.K.
the killing of over 100,000 innocent children
and on the next call the Oklahoma Bombing
an evil crime!

where people sit in jail waiting
for their day in the Big Chair
while the real killers run the world
from their bedrooms
where the police protect private property
and destroy young lives

who said this was the land of the free
when the working class works the longest hours
for less and less money and live in projects
that look like penal colonies
with WW III helicopters
flying over them
where children dodge stray bullets
without the benefit of
bulletproof welfare cheese
searching for freedom
in the trash cans
of a country
where images
are not sacred
and no one
is safe

•••

JULIA LOPEZ

Colonialism on the Brain

No matter how hard I try I cannot run away from the
colonization of my brain.

I am haunted by the memories of myself,
8 years old,
in the South Bronx,

standing in the auditorium of P.S. 65,
hand over my heart,
wearing a navy blue polyester skirt,
(uncomfortably short),
bearing my chubby pale thighs,
a starched white shirt,
and a red bow tie,
singing:
"La tierra de Borinquen
donde he nacido yo..."
in a really bad Spanish accent,
and never having been to Puerto Rico.

Haunted by
the nights
Mami and Papi
duked it out
while my sister and I
6 and 4
hid ourselves in a corner
watching and crying
uncontrollably.

Hot Summer Nights...
Throwing ourselves,
without permission,
in and out
of the pump,
the rush of the water,
pushing us to
the other side of
the street
not going up the block
'cause thats where
the Gang
hung out.

Haunted by
the mornings...
On the roof
of Vilma's
renovated projects apartment
smoking a joint
laced with angel dust
(we didn't know it then)

getting ready for our
eigth grade senior
trip
to the Bronx Zoo.

Haunted by
Cano
dying of a heroin overdose,
and me
trying to play it off
when Cheo
offered me some acid
and I said no
I just wanted to
smoke pot
and relax.

Haunted by
my ex-boyfriend
Ray
twice my age
(he had a bald head)
and the night
the night I didn't want to do it.
He didn't care
he screwed me anyway
while I lay
on the bed
limp, motionless,
inhuman,
15 and feeling bad
knowing that
that was the way it was.

Memories of myself
just knowing I was black.

Not differentiating
between the shades of brown
within my family,
amongst my friends.

Until I was called a
spic
for the first time

by some rich white
ninth grader in Brooklyn Heights
who read Shakespeare
in grammar school
while I was still trying to
figure out the difference
between nouns and verbs.
But I was proud
so proud
of something I knew nothing about.
Except
that because of
Where I lived
and because
my mom spoke Spanish
and my father drank too much
and my sister danced salsa
and had a boyfriend whose
family business was
stealing cars
and my best friend
lost her virginity
at 12 years old
and I
ate rice and beans,
that because of this
it was OK
for the cops
to shoot us
in the back.

So proud...
because
the spirits of my ancestors
were secretly
telling me
that that's not the way
it was supposed to be.

The haunting memories
are the seeds of the weeds of
my colonization.
The roots infect every
aspect of my brain

overpopulated
with thoughts of violence, guns,
animals passing for human beings,
make believe gold, hate disguised
as love.

•••

JAYNE CORTEZ
What's Happening

What's happening
You'll know what's happening
when you see Pedro the poet
selling condoms and poetry books
and hear the man of god
choking on his sexual contradictions
you'll know what's happening
when you see computers going to sleep on
shoulders of their secretaries and
hear workers dismantling governments
you'll know what's happening

What's happening
An intellectual is marching around like
a great humanitarian but won't pay his
child support that's what's happening
And on the lower eastside of New York City
a Doris Day look alike is imitating the voice of
Louis Satchmo Armstrong while
the minister of unnecessary information
gets his hair curled
That's what's happening
The musicians are making facial expressions acting
like they're really playing something complex
                         and are not
That's what's happening
& me? Me?
I have already dropped a half inch of
slobber on a certain line
I have already placed parachutes on
two mountains of paper
OK It's only one word in three hours

but look at you
look at you
Your job is to be a singing raisin
He's a dancing cornflake
You're a smiling commode
She's a walking roll of toilet tissue
He falls on the beach like
a sack of empty bullet shells
She's forced to sit like a ground based
missile interceptor in the tourist area while
commander in chief invades Panama and
shoots Panamanians democratically to
enforce human rights and burn up another flag
That's what's happening
And there are other drug dealers butting
                          heads in the dark
other equal opportunity killers on
                          the horizon
other fraudulent financiers manipulating money
                          and doing the hand jive
other corrupt hotel chain owners with
nice clothes and dirty drawers
That's what's happening
Meanwhile
the meter "maids" are still giving parking tickets
and the gospel singers are still taking clichés
                          and beating them to death
and the xmas tree crews are out discovering the
deepest hole of their consciousness in the donut shop
and little ladies in long coats are walking in
competition with big ladies in tight pants
and here we are between the emergency exit of
                          a closing bank
and the ambulance entrance of an aging nuclear reactor
waiting for the economic recovery of our dreams
and that's what's happening
that's what happening

●●●●●

III. Bringing the temple down

MAC MCGILL

(MOVE)

LUCILLE CLIFTON

move

On May 13, 1985 Wilson Goode, Philadelphia's first Black mayor, authorized the bombing of 6221 Osage Avenue after the complaints of neighbors, also Black, about the Afrocentric back-to-nature group headquartered there and calling itself Move. All the members of the group wore dreadlocks and had taken the surname Africa. In the bombing eleven people, including children, were killed and sixty-one homes in the neighborhood were destroyed.

they had begun to whisper
among themselves hesitant
to be branded neighbor to the wild
haired women the naked children
reclaiming a continent
away

move

he hesitated
then turned his smoky finger
toward africa toward the house
he might have lived in might have
owned or saved had he not turned
away

move

the helicopter rose at the command
higher at first then hesitating
then turning toward the center
of its own town only a neighborhood
away

move

she cried as the child stood
hesitant in the last clear sky
he would ever see the last
before the whirling blades the whirling smoke
and sharp debris carried all clarity
away

move

if you live in a mind
that would destroy itself
to comfort itself
if you would stand fire
rather than difference
do not hestitate
move
away

•••

samson predicts from gaza
the philadelphia fire
for ramona africa, survivor

it will be your hair
ramona africa
they will come for you
they will bring fire
they will empty your eyes
of everything you love
your hair will writhe
and hiss on your shoulder
they will order you
to give it up   if you do
you will bring the temple down
if you do not   they will

•••

MOVE

Why the MOVE Organization Supports
Mumia Abu-Jamal

Long after the taking of... life, it is not only a loss to the executed, but the family bears the pain the deceased suffered while waiting to be executed. When you kill the sense of contentment in anybody, you have committed the crime of murder to everybody.
—John Africa

As a community-based journalist during the 1970s, Mumia Abu-Jamal was exposed to the teachings of John Africa. Unlike the vast majority of Philadelphia journalists who had (and still have) chosen to ignore the truth and were biased against MOVE, Mumia chose to be honest with himself and to admit that John Africa did have the truth. Therefore, Mumia was compelled to write and talk about MOVE truthfully.

In 1981, for example, when nine MOVE members were being tried for the murder of a Philadelphia cop, Mumia was broadcasting and telecasting events of the trial that other journalists dared not report, which caused enormous controversy with his supervisors and eventually landed Mumia Abu-Jamal on death row. Mumia's supervisors didn't want him to report the truth, because the truth would benefit MOVE rather than the politicians and officials who want to keep all of MOVE imprisoned. So it followed that Mumia's supervisors would finally accuse him of slanting the courtroom events in MOVE's favor. But Mumia never backed down. He consistently reported the contradictions in the testimonies of the cops and of D.A. Wilhelm Knaur, who was caught changing the victim's autopsy report to fit the state's case. Mumia also revealed that the judge had allowed the D.A. to get away with such slimy tactics.

Mumia's determination to do what is right enhanced his efforts in support of MOVE. And this is why we of MOVE support Mumia to this very day. In December 1981, months after consistently exposing the truth about the criminals running the Philadelphia justice system, four months after MOVE people were convicted of third degree murder and sentenced to 900 years in prison just for being a united family, Mumia was shot, brutally beaten several times by the police, arrested, and then beaten again.

During the early part of his trial Mumia had asked that John Africa represent him, because Mumia knew that John Africa could, without a doubt, effectively represent him and win his case. However, Judge Albert Sabo denied Mumia his right to have John Africa as his counsel, all too aware that John Africa had won his own case earlier that year.

MOVE believes that Mumia was framed for the murder of a cop to justify sentencing him to die in a vendetta to silence him forever for publicly demonstrating his support for MOVE, and for refusing to back away from the system's intimidation.

John Africa's MOVE Organization is fighting to eliminate exactly this kind of prejudice germ, which infects all of the world's life.

Long Live John Africa Forever!

•••

WHAT KIND OF SYSTEM CAGES the VICTIM AND AWARDS HER ATTACKERS?

DAVID HENDERSON
NOMAD ISLAND

leaning against the downtown sky line

twilight blues

       a thousand and one sirens

cigarette smoke is destroying the ozone layer

Leadbelly standing on 9th Street and Avenue B

looking at the sun descend thru the trees of the park

glistening his twelve strings

a city sinking below the ocean tide

a sea of white women

glassy windows under surf

to swim, like "Shine," for life.

the one cell theory of revolutionary cadres

nomad on an island

marsupial shoes

high end pop

posthumous slavery

scapegoats from the "third world"

pop zombis

the "Shine" syndrome,

Africa Anonymous

•••

RAS BARAKA *

Why Mumia Must Live and Go Free

Sunlight fire
Tomorrows not
promised yet
You know
Most people (in their right mind)
don't wanna be the
King
Most people don't wanna be the King
or the queen for that matter
people want freedom
people
pepepe pe pe pe people in their right mind want freedom
want freedom
people want freedom
people want freedom
like Sojourner bare chested on
Congressional floors yelling
Ain't I Women, Ain't I Women
freedom like
Ten Thousand black faces in blue suits
sweeping across southern plantations
or freedom like Assata
busting down prison walls

Most people don't want to be the King
Most people don't want to be the King or the Queen for that
matter
Most people don't want to be on their knees
or beg
or accept hand outs
or steal
Most people want freedom
Most people want freedom
in a very real way
Something that's just better than
what they have
or

don't have
A scratch, a pull, a push
a fight
proof that everything and everyone's not dead
Most people just don't want
poverty or dead children on
dirty sidewalks
or diseases and plagues
and high insurance and no health card
They don't want work for little or no pay
They just want their jobs back
and a decent education for their children
and a playground to play in,
and can't understand
factories that lay off millions
that throw away extra food
and burn surplus while families
live in boxes on cold streets
or shacks in South Carolina,
While some have acres of unused land,
abandoned buildings, yachts, diamonds and
riches
While most of the world is starving
and on their knees praying to a God
who has turned a deaf ear
Yes there are places where
the rats are millionaires
and people scrape through the ruffage
of back alley chinese joints
there are people who
don't want to be King
Most people don't want to be King or Queen for that matter
"Dirty laundry in the country can't hurt Uncle Sam"
there are people who
actually want war
And jails

And death
penalties

There are
people who would
dance around Mumia's electrocuted corpse
who would love to turn our mother's into breeders

and take babies from their families
from 1795 to 1895 to 1995
for money,
for profit, for capital
There are refugees all over the world
in concentration camps
stinking with death and unborn babies
behind barbed wire
closed in boxes eating wheat and water
with bloated bellies
in every place you can think of
every continent
in every language you can utter
a thousand colors of suffering and starvation
staring in the dead face of Imperialism
I mean there are some people who don't want to be King
or Queen for that matter
There are prisoners and exiles
in every corner of the Earth
Hunted and chased away by Inhumanity
ran out of their homes away from
their families
Attacked in front of Unamerican Committees
Cause they didn't believe
the earth was flat
or people and repressed
because they wanted workers
to enjoy their lives
or receive greater pay
and thought the people should run the world
and benefit from their own labor
They actually believed in democracy
that's why Sacco and Vanzetti are dead
That's why the Rosenbergs are dead
that's why Chris Hani is dead
Why the wailers are dead
Why Cinque is dead
Malcolm dead
Patrice Lumumba Dead
Nat Turner Dead
and why Mumia Must live
why we all must live
because we have been plagued

to keep our mouth shut
and our stories to ourselves
and hate one another for being
Who we are
because Capitalism has spent
billions
to wash the people's memories
away and divide us
to kill hope and love
from our hearts
That's why Mumia must live
that's why we all must livethat's why
Revolution must live
Revolution
Not just speeches, and marches,
or protest, jail, and guns,
It's not just about meeting and flyers
It's about ordinary peoples' will and
their push to live better lives
more fruitful
and more importantly longer
It's about having the ability
to enjoy life
and not live in misery and despair
so people can get off of their knees
and stand up and move forward
It's something you just can't get in a class
You get it everyday making
History
Moving from one point to another
It's about crying when you must
shouting when necessary
Hugs always
Creating a sense of humanity
and building democracy
It's about the love of life
and of people
Not out of Academia or political correctness
but out of the very hearts of our souls
even science is on our side
It's about loving freedom

> more than anything else in the world
> that is why Mumia must live
> and go free
> that is why Mumia must live
> and go free
> that is why Mumia must live
> and go free
> that's why we all must live
> and be free!!

All power to the people
Free Mumia Abu-Jamal

•••

MOE SEAGER

We Want Everything

These predictable exchanges
we pass on thin winds
Are we talking
or fanning ourselves?
Where's the gust!

You don't know me–
cause itself:
Take my hand, grip
it is malleable.
I'll come. Always at the ready.
On the brink of becoming ...

You're a black man in Philadelphia
I an orphan shaping poems in Paris.
There we say: Ça va? Bien, et toi?,
leave it at that.
Like two dogs lifting hind legs
at the hydrant.

Here it sounds: How's it goin' man?
It goes like this:
       Each time our children's hands
       ripped to paper ribbons
       snag of the thornbush
       forbidding them fruits of desire
       I stop cold on the boulevard
       un-curl palms scarred and cannot heal.

I am a civilized man
thus told - to hold my tongue
How absurd. I prefer to hold yours
       like a shell pressed to my ear
       resonance of inner cosmos
       speak - listen
       we want everything.

We must stop lamenting the rain,
shrinking from heat, humid days.
Weather is so much tide
ocean of air from which we swim.
Direct me to the nearest galaxy.
Shall we summon a boat?

What's happening? Ask me, again.
No. Yes. Yes ask me!
       You are to me, alchemy
       Look: space between us
       charged with protons of love
       passion particles osmosing the boundaries
       of the vacuum
We are about love
when we choose to be.

Bullets, blades, booby traps
sprung by the masters
parasites embalmed in pale faces
bank vault visions, myopic chill light.
Hermetic madness.
       C'mon Orpheus
       play me your opus
       I will empty my head
       like a tulip in April.
       We shall build the cult of imagination.

You don't know me
but I hear your howls
from the death camps,
Columbus' crematorium.
Migrating birds pass the news.
I wrench requiems from my sleep
brood in the mirror of morning café
spittle drops on counter tops
unhinge doors to corridors
days in discord
Arrested in motion on a bridge deck
hammered stone, cold steel rivets
to the base of my skull.

You don't know me
I've been writing to you for years
and crystal clear moments
I sing your song in the darkness
the migrating bird my witness.
      How you be?
      Go on - tell me
      tell me more,
      So much more.

•••

RICK KEARNS

No Charges/Police Flashlight Ballet

Sparks jump connection
flying other synaptic pole
cocaine guaguanco dyspeptic rage
messages in head of my distant
messages in the unmarked police
car told him it was time to
chill until he sees the gathering
blue swarm these are the same
ones they are the same sparks
jumping the plate in his forehead
the message is they will kill me
they will kill me now for damn
sure my distant cousin I think

as I look at autopsy metallic
photo of gash in head he is
thinking he is thinking I have
to get the hell out of this
doors are locked he is strong
from breaks window and crawls
out before swarm of la hara the
same ones like the cop who shot
him point blank in forehead says
oops, accident, no charges against
cop brain surgery for Moises
brain surgery for Moises DeJesus
they are the same ones he is
they all look the same he is
running he is running into
wall of Philadelphia police car
barricade call had gone out man
with gun he is running he has
no gun runs into wall of police
cars struggles throws them
off as others pile on they are
throws them off as others pile
on they are swinging heavy
police issue flashlights they
are the same ones they are
swinging heavy police-issue
flashlights he is subdued into
he is brought down subdued into
coma is dead not long after
they knock him out again as he
tries to escape from ambulance
as they arrive to hospital these
are the same ones sparks jumping
flight and darkness he is knocked
cold knocked cold out he is dead
not long after he is dead not long
after APB to man with gun who has
no gun is another dead Puerto Rican
is another dead Puerto Rican en
el barrio de NORTH Philly he is
wearing a gash to his grave and
the DA says cops will not be
charged DA says witnesses mean
nada DA says another dead Puerto
Rican

DA says
sparks jump
autopsy photo
wailing mother
cousin I think
no charges
no charges.

•••

GASTON NEAL

Mrs. Eleanor Bumpers, Age 69

TWO SHOT GUN BLASTS!!
Ah chain of mistakes and circumstances (so the Mayor said)
TWO SHOT GUN BLASTS

> One tore her hand off
> One destroyed her chest

TWO SHOT GUN BLASTS
Ah chain of mistakes and circumstances (so the media said)

> One tore her arm off
> One destroyed her chest

Ten thousand New York police marched
and said the SHOT GUN BLASTS was RIGHT!!

> One tore her hand off
> One destroyed her chest

The police Chief said
The media said
The social worker said
The mayor said
Ah chain of mistakes and circumstances
Ah chain of mistakes and circumstances

> One tore her hand off
> One destroyed her chest

and TEN THOUSAND NEW YORK POLICE MARCH
AND SAID
the SHOT GUN BLASTS
WAS RIGHT

•••

MARILYN BUCK

One White Girl Ponders Strange Behavior

It is strange to me
that so many white folks
were upset and enraged
by the federal carnage
at the fundamentalist farmhouse
at Waco
After all these same "folks"
were not distraught or outraged
by the Philadelphia firestorm
where Black women children men
were massacred and
Black people's homes became ashes.

It is strange to me that the police and FBI
are not running around
kicking in white folks' doors
or stopping all blond or brown-haired men
wearing Levis or Brooks Brothers suits
or Stetsons or John Deere caps
You know:

      a search, brutalize, blow away mission
      like those in   South Central LA
               Washington DC
               Harlem or El Barrio.

After all, wasn't it
all-American white males
who blew up the Federal Building
in Oklahoma City?

•••

LAMONT B. STEPTOE

OSAGE

Osage
Indian name
Osage
Indian name/song

name/song
name/song
name/song gone bad
from the polluted waters
of the American night
Name/song
draped in Black
name/song
now one with Wounded
Knee
now one with My Lai
now one with Songmi
now one with Soweto &
Sharpeville
now one with Sabra &
Shattilla
name/song
fetid with the stench
of human sacrifice
Osage-Osage-Osage
the fire burns
the fire burns
the fire burns
the fire burns
the fire has never gone out
the fire has never gone out
the fire has never gone out
there is always a fire for us
there is always
a rope, a chain, hot tar
burning cross
a stake and flame
to abolish our name
there is always a fire
for us
involuntary cremation
has too often been our
sentence
the fire burns
the fire burns
the fire burns
we join Joan of Arc
in the flames
we join
all the nameless Black men

women and children
in the flames
stare into any fire
and you shall see our eyes
looking out at you
we live
in the fire now
we live in the fire now
the fire burns
the fire burns
the fire burns
we control the fire now
we are the genies of
the fire now
we are the genies of the fire
the fire burns
the fire burns
the fire burns
Wounded Knee
West Philadelphia
brought to you by
ABC, NBC, CBS, FBI, CIA
ABC, NBC, CBS, FBI, CIA
ABC, NBC, CBS, FBI, CIA
Wounded Knee
on Osage
on the 13th of May
a hell
of a day
the fire burns
the fire burns
the fire burns
O' Philadelphia
is this liberty?
Is this liberty?
in the shadow of Independence?
O' sky
O' wind
O' ground
O' waters
O' trees
I still hear
your sobbing
you have not forgotten
this act of war

this act of barbarity
this act of a beast
My tears
flow like the water
they used to drown your voices
gone-gone-gone-gone
is something in the air
gone-gone-gone-gone
and now this city lies
under heaven its aura
stained with blood
its people
shocked to silence
or secrecy of rejoicing
none
can look
each other in the eye
all
are guilty of something
the mark of Cain
is everywhere
the fire burns
the fire burns
the fire burns
America bombed
while the country's out shopping
it will go away
it will go away
it will go away
it won't
it won't
it won't
the fire burns
the fire burns
the fire burns
there's always a fire
for the descendants of Kings
Black as the bones
in the ashes of Osage

N.B. To date, no city officials have been indicted for the eleven Black lives that were lost in the Osage Avenue government bombing of MOVE.

•••

At 13th and Locust
a pair of boys talk basketball
in the shadow of the stars...

their mother stands watching
in the window she wonders
at how fast they've
grown...

a patrolcar
passing
slow...

sizes them up
as suspects rather
than children...

if they were decent folk
judges the cop
they wouldn't be outside at night...

their mother calls
the boys in quickly...
things happen...

...and she doesn't
want to lose
her family...

many years have passed...

but the spot is still

warm with conflict...

LANCE TOOKS

KEVIN POWELL

altar for four

I.

four little girls

        bombed for equal rights
a prayer yes yes say a prayer, brother
for the forgotten
           we
                  shall
                            overcome
our overcomes and our overcames

DEAD

four little black girls

bodies greased, pressed and folded against the church
pews
their heads
like halos
glow beneath the lord's window
no, sister
that window is not there anymore
it exploded on four little girls
the way that water hose broke old mister young's back

oh people, can you hear me?
                what do we want?
        freedom!
                when do we want it?
        now!
thirty years and counting
been countin' for thirty years now
done run out of toes and fingers to count on

II.

john coltrane
where have you gone?
we can still feel your sax dragging its tongue
along the carpet they call alabama
sweet sweet alabama
land of the cotton
why are those four little black girls
still bleeding in your belly?

III.

brothas and sistas, hah!
i'm here ta tell ya, hah!
that the laaawd don't like ugly, no! lawd don't like no
ugliness
are y'all wid me?
i said are y'all wid me now?
these little girls ain't done nothin' to noooo-body
i said noooo-body
and for that they dead lawd
look at them sweet jeee-sus!
ain't got no toes left, hah!
ain't got no fingers left, hah!
can't count the time no more lawd, hah!
time done stop lawd, hah!
i said time done stop, hah!
what we gonna do lawd?
we gonna pick some flowers, hah!
and bury our future, hah!
and we gonna build a new house lawd
and we gonna paint it blue lawd
i said we gonna paint it blue, hah!
so we can feel that old-time spirit a-goin', hah!
feeel it! thank ya jesus!
feeel it! thank ya jesus!

IV.

at 16th and 6th they say it's
                        not a home anymore
they say all the homes have been torn down
                               that blackfolks don't live here anymore
just dusty flesh and charcoal bones
                        with steam-iron memories
of this march or that song
they say
               the railroad tracks have moved
that just because you can cross 'em now
don't mean you gotta new home
you still gotta pack a gun
still gotta poke it into the sky like this:
bang!
they say:
               we're not bitter
                        just hungry
                               need some nourishment
                               and some time
                               and some homes
                               and some freedom...

•••

MARI EVANS

Alabama Landscape
(In Memoriam)[1]

I

See the ancient underbrush
the disciplined entanglement
wild welt of trees and gullies
traps of mud and broken branch
the hairline brook, the secret water
see the stirring, see him coming
modulating thru the silence
leaping sinkholes, torn confusion
buckling knees then grace regained

he ducks and dodges
     Black man running
   claiming Freedom
thru the ageless sun and shadow
vanishes from sight he is at once both
Past and Present, history repeated
    history relearned

II

History relived

the Present savagely contrived, the
Past still swollen, still unhealed and
  All transition merely language.
What was tar, and rope, and flame, was
    rape and scourge
    is magnum now,
is unrelenting chokehole

  Sanctioned lynchings
    Still orgasmic

III

The time is surely near
when we reluctantly have learned
what lessons time intends to teach
And such intransigence as now
is veiled and hid we will release
When "for their thousand blows" return
    a thousand ten
However unannounced, the Truth is clear:
Until we stand, until we act
the murders, the oppression still
    the unabated war
   we seem unable to define
    goes on

Black man running
thru the ageless sun and shadow
  Vulnerable
     still unavenged

History repeated past all logic
Who is it bides the time and why?
   And for how long?
There will be no one left, for ovens

---

[1] For all the Black victims of "police action" lynchings throughout the United States, and especially for Michael Taylor, aged 17, who "committed suicide" by shooting himself in the temple while sitting in the back seat of an Indianapolis police car with his hands steel-cuffed behind him.

•••••

IV. Condemn death to death / This is no place to be

(prisons)

AMINA BARAKA *

Dirge for the Lynched
(for Ida B. Wells)
1862-1931

hanging from a tree

dead hair
dead scalp
dead eyes
dead nose
dead mouth
dead ears
dead neck
dead torso
dead shoulders
dead arms
dead hands
dead legs
dead feet
dead muscle
dead tissue
dead blood
dead skin

hanging from a tree
dead black bones
hanging from a tree

tarred & feathered
beaten & tortured

lynched Black People
hanging from a tree

when they come, the Bourgeoisie
blowing their bugle
to fight their wars
let's take their confederate flag
& burn it from a tree

when they say we are not Patriotic
let's remind them
of ALL the BLACK BODIES

hanging from AMERICA'S trees

•••

SAFIYA HENDERSON-HOLMES
death row ain't

when speaking of death
as penalty: eye raping eye,
murder loving murder
do not say row,

as in linear, as in a sequence
of time, place and conditions
of things. do not say row
as if to imply reason, logic,

a consistency with a parallel
somewhere in space.
when speaking of death
as penalty: eye raping eye,

murder loving to death
murder, say death schism,
death fang, death chaos,
death gone mad and malignant.

and when speaking of death
as penalty do not say man
or woman, as if this punishment
can be given to a humanbeing

and therefore evolved,
elevated above the non-
upright species and somehow
advanced and progressing.

when speaking of death
as penalty by lethal injection,
poisonous gas, electric chair,
a stoning, a hanging, say war is eminent,

the enemy everywhere, viral,
doubling within and without,
say to all those not yet born,
abort,

hit the dirt.

•••

DENNIS BRUTUS
In the Courthouse

The prisoner comes in
erect, subdued
surrounded by guards
greeted by his lawyers;
he has grace, is calm,
the shadow of death trails him
but one senses his strength

Mumia Abu-Jamal Case

9-5-95

•••

JOHN EDGAR WIDEMAN
Doing Time, Marking Race

I know far too much about prisons. More than I ever wished to know. From every category of male relative I can name—grandfather, father, son, brother, uncle, nephew, cousin, in-laws—at least one member of my family has been incarcerated. I've researched the genesis of prisons, visited prisons, taught in prisons, written about them, spent a night here and there as a prisoner. Finally, I am a descendant of a special class of immigrants—Africans—

for whom arrival in America was a life sentence in the prison of slavery. None of the above is cited because it makes me proud or happy, but I feel I should identify some of the baggage, whether bias or insight, I bring to a discussion of prisons.

The facile notion of incarceration (read apartheid) as a cure for social, economic and political problems has usurped the current national debate. *Which candidate is tougher on crime* was the dominant issue dramatized in TV ads during the last election campaign. And the beat goes on.

"Tougher" seems to mean which candidate behaves more like the bullies I encountered in junior high school, the guys whose fierce looks, macho words and posturing lorded it over the weakest kids, stealing their lunch money, terrorizing and tormenting them to gain a tough-dude image. Cowards at the core, bad actors mimicking the imagined thugs who keep them awake at night.

What bothered me most about the hysterical, bloodthirsty TV ads during the last election was the absolute certainty of the candidates that the prison cells they promised to construct, the draconian prison terms and prison conditions they would impose if elected, would never confine them or those who voted for them. Ignorance, racism, naïveté couldn't account for this arrogant, finger-pointing certainty. The only way they could be so sure was to know the deck was stacked, know that they enjoyed an immunity. The ones they were promising to lock up and punish, by design, would never be their people. Always somebody else. Somebody other. Not their kind. The fix was in. Without referring explicitly to race or class, the candidates and their audiences understood precisely who the bad guys were and who the bad guys would continue to be, once the candidates assumed power. I recall a sentencing hearing in a courtroom, the angry father (white) of a victim urging a judge (white) to impose upon a young man (black), who'd pleaded guilty, the most severe punishment because "they're not like us, Your Honor."

Honest fear, thoughtful perplexity, a leavening of doubt or hesitancy, the slightest hint, then or now, that what the candidates insinuated about the "other," about criminals and misfits, also implicated them, would be a welcome relief. Instead, the rhetoric continues, Manichean, divisive and absolute, the forces of light doing battle with the forces of darkness.

As an African American, as a human being, I haven't yet shaken the sense of being personally assaulted by the campaign appeals to the electorate's meanest instincts. Nor have I been able to forgive the success of the tactic.

Sure enough, our country's in deep trouble. Drastic measures are required. But who says we must always begin at the bottom, taking from those who have least? Why heap more punishment on the losers, the tiny majority of lawbreakers who are dumb enough or unlucky enough to get caught and convicted? Building more prisons doesn't decrease crime. Removing federal money from some citizens' hands (the poor) and placing it in others' (the rich) doesn't save the nation billions. Why are such patently false cures proclaimed and believed with such passionate conviction?

Why not start at the top? Limit maximum income. Reduce military spending. Wouldn't it be better to be swept from the earth while trying to construct a just society, rather than holding on, holding on in a fortress erected to preserve unfair privilege? What indefensible attitudes are we assuming toward the least fortunate in our society? Isn't shame the reason we are desperately intent on concealing from ourselves the simple injustice of our actions?

We're compiling a hit list. Retrogressing. Deciding once more it's in the nation's interest to treat some as more equal than others. Belief that America is burdened by incorrigibles—criminals, the poor and untrained, immigrants too different to ever fit in—is an invi-

SHAWN A. ALEXANDER

tation to political leaders who can assure us they have the stomach and clean hands to dispose of surplus people pulling the rest of us down. We're looking to cold-eyed, white-coated technocrats and bottom-line bureaucrats for efficient final solutions. If this sounds paranoid or cartoonish, you must be unaware of facilities such as Pelican Bay in California, already in operation: chilling, high-tech, super-max prisons driving their inmates to madness and worse.

The sad, defeatist work of building prisons, the notion that prison walls will protect us from crime and chaos, are symptomatic of our shortsightedness, our fear of engaging at the root, at the level that demands personal risk and transformation, the real problems caging us all.

In the guise of outrage at crime and criminals, hard-core racism (though it never left us) is making a strong, loud come-back. It's respectable to tar and feather criminals, to advocate locking them up and throwing away the key. It's not racist to be against crime, even though the archetypal criminal in the media and the public imagination almost always wears "Willie" Horton's face. Gradually, "urban" and "ghetto" have become code words for terrible places where only blacks reside. Prison is rapidly being re-lexified in the same segregated fashion.

For many, the disproportionate number of blacks in prison is not a worrisome issue; the statistics simply fulfill racist prophecy and embody a rational solution to the problem of crime. Powerful evidence, however, suggests racism may condition and thereby determine upon whom the war against crime is waged most vigorously. For instance, a recent study, summarized in *The New York Times* on October 5, [1995], indicates that although African Americans represent about 13 percent of the total population and 13 percent of those who are monthly drug users, they are 35 percent of those arrested for drug possession, 55 percent convicted for possession and 74 percent of the total serving sentences for possession.

We seem doomed to repeat our history. During the nineteenth century institutions such as prisons, orphanages, asylums and poorhouses developed as instruments of public policy to repair the gaping rents in America's social fabric caused by rapid industrialization and urbanization. Politicians driven by self-interest, hoping to woo businessmen and voters with a quick fix, avoided confrontation with the underlying causes of social instability. Uncontrollable brutish instincts, inferior intelligence, childlike dependence were attributed to the lower classes. Public policies, focusing on this incorrigible otherness, defined the state's role as custodial, separating and controlling suspect populations. State intervention into the lives of the poor neither diminished crime nor alleviated misery but did promote fear and loathing of the victims of chaotic social upheaval.

Today young black men are perceived as the primary agents of social pathology and instability. The cure of more prisons and longer prison terms will be applied first to them. They will be the ones confined, stigmatized, scapegoated. Already squeezed out of jobs, education, stable families and communities, they are increasingly at risk as more and more of the street culture they have created, under incredible stress to provide a means of survival, is being criminalized (and callously commercialized). To be a man of color of a certain economic class and milieu is equivalent in the public eye to being a criminal.

Prison itself, with its unacceptably large percentage of men and women of color, is being transformed by the street values and street needs of a younger generation of prisoners to mirror the conditions of urban war zones and accommodate a fluid population who know their lives will involve inevitable shuttling between prison and the street. Gang affiliation, drug dealing, the dictates of gang leaders, have replaced the traditional mechanisms that once socialized inmates. Respect for older, wiser heads, the humbling, sobering rites of initiation into a stable prison hierarchy, have lost their power to reinforce the scanty official impetus toward rehabilitation that prison offers. The prison is the street, the street is prison.

If we expand our notion of prison to include the total institution of poverty, enlarge it to embrace metaphorical fetters such as glass ceilings that limit upward mobility for executives of color, two facts become apparent: There is a persistence of racialized thinking that contradicts lip service to a free, democratic society; and for people of color, doing time is only one among many forms of imprisonment legitimized by the concept of race.

The horrors of the prison system, the horrors of racism, depend upon the public's willed ignorance. Both flourish in the darkness of denial. As long as the one-way street of racial integration and the corrosive notion of a melting pot confuse our thinking about national identity and destiny, we'll continue to grope in darkness. We need to be honest with ourselves. Who we are, what kind of country we wish to become, are at issue when we talk about prisons.

•••

PIRI THOMAS
A First Night in El Sing Sing

As I stand on the hill, on top of the rocks,
I stand and look and stare inside,
I remember the whole, the mass, the past—
I see the gray figures, walking alone,
I look and remember—I was there with you once—
I was with you...

I search into the building,
Many years ago break through the walls,
I see my cell block, my cell, my bunk, my wash bowl,
my ca-ca bowl,
I see my grim bars, around and around,
The long march upward to the dining room mess.

I do not see them playing, I hear only the marching,
The long line, upward climb, a gray—a sea gray,
A mass of thousands of identities, thousands of locks,
thousands of keys.
"Look," I cry, "the cells are open"—
Wake up—I can't, I'm not asleep, I'm dreaming, Piri.

Can you hear the clicks of thousands of keys being turned?
The soft pad-pad of the back, the man, and you turn your back
so he'll not see your face.

You grip wash bowl—the dizziness will pass.
Sit on your bowl—crap—move your bowels—
Defecate—oh, man, do something, don't just sit there.
Make them shadow bars go away.
Count the bolts on your cell, how big is it—
6 x 9 x 8—who cares.
It could be Grand Central Station, it's too small for me.

Smoke a smoke, read a book, plug your earphones—
Shut out, drown out, don't listen, don't hear, don't look, Don't let it go.
Forget the green dark pressure that pulls you in a short while back.

Forget the last hard-flung look before your back was trapped by a hard-flung
gate,
Forget your loss of clothes, identity, forget your bug-killing shaves,
And the spread-your-cheeks inspection, or "lift your feet, puleeze."
Forget the damp-filled cell in the box, no room in reception.

Forget the two matches left in the book,
And three tailor-made smokes.
Forget your splitting these in half
And now four matches and still three tailor-made smokes.

Forget laying on the dingy mattress—
Inhaling time with no space.
Forget the damned feelings, the hammering, damned feelings,
As it roars on you—
Hard—into your mind.
You drag on your burning cigarette.
Oh, God, here it comes.
Fifteen fucking years—of this.

        *

Hey—you're not a numba
You got a name—
They only got your body
not your brain.

•••

DAVID MILLS
All Things We Didn't Consider

Blacks had no rights the white man was bound to respect.
—**Dred Scott**

I

There is no moon and there is
Only a smidgen of light at 4 a.m. in a bony
Cold medallion cab. December
Has a bad attitude, sucking her buck teeth
Turning her back, taking it all
Out on me. This is the red light
District: steam and dice taste
The same in a hungry man's hand. I saw what looked
Like my brother's VW driving the wrong
Way down a one-way street.
Then this cop's flashlight swimming
in his skull, deep strokes
Chunky pieces of his dreams howling
As they flinch on the cold pavement. I drop
Off my fare and pull my .38
From the front seat. This is the city
Of brotherly love. But the blood
In these veins is bubbling and not
Always mine. I don't know why
My liver opened its blood shot
Eyes, as the cop's bullet carved
It's vicious initials on my spine: D.F.
I do know my .38 went off
Before I drank the last light
Of that bucktoothed night

II

In the interrogation room
They cuffed me to a chair bolted
To the floor, rammed me
Into a pole, pinched my testicles
With scissors, twisted, rained

On me: lead pipes, black
Jacks, brass knuckles, handcuffs. A telephone
Book above my head: hammered
A nail into it until the bones
In my neck buckled and sang

III

Airplanes stalk the sky
writing Addison-Wesley supports a cop
Killer. As I'm swept into this kangaroo
Court the police carry placards humming
For my blood. But I had a .38 and the fatal
Shot was a .44. Their only witness:
a 36B cup full of come ons and evaporated milk
She feeds her johns until they bleed
From the middle of their teeth. Her tongue
Shatters like glass every time
She tells her story because her feet
Know that night's deepest secret

IV

My daughter's arms ate all the air
In the visiting room the first time
She came to see me.
But then her laughter ran
Into the Plexiglas. I'm shackled
So I lullabied her bones. How could I
Tell her that they just brushed my teeth
Cleaned my ears and wiped my ass
With a billyjack. I kissed her
Through the mesh and prayed
That the love letter I dug into
My lips with metal might rub
Off on hers. Prayed that the silence I return
To is not final. Prayed that my
Ears will burn tonight, slowly

V

Clinching his belly, dashing to
The can, he thinks he's broken me
Down. He worships the thunder
And burp in his guts, as his anus bleeds
Claps and strains to squeeze my name
From his ass. And I feel the bowels
Of Death Row trying to move
Me. I know my name
is near. But I've got to finish this
Story I've got to peel the music
Off this news. I've got to
Find out how the blues tastes
In the back of the devil's mouth. QWERT
YUIOP ASDF? GHJKLZXCV/ BNM
Now it's my tongue scrubbing
The commode pleading with the bowels
Of death row not to move. The cement
Beneath my feet splits and a fountain
Of stars pushes through the floor
Bouncing me on their warm bellies:
FREEDOM! (is a full time occupation)
And there are seventy eight
Other men who spend twenty
Two hours a day in a 6 by 10
Cell: these conditions are supposed
To last two months I've lived
Like this for over ten
Years. Excuse me this isn't life
It's a pantomime of life
It's a sink a cot a toilet its knowing
Everyone of these men
Has a date but not everyone
Knows their name: Old Head longed
To curl up in Nina's belly button
One more time, longed to hear
Betty Carter's scat tickle Norfolk's
August sun, but stomach
Cancer's last dance found him
Without a partner. And we exist
In the shadow of the bowels
Of the death house and everyone

Has a date but not everyone
Knows their name: Harry who shrieks
From his cell out of an internal orgy of psychic
Pain NIGGER! the letters spinning
In his spit. Harry once wore the c.o.'s keys
Now he hears the tangy jangle
Of keys: NIGGER! 15 hours
Of this and his screams
Start to bleed from my sink
I can only wipe it up with music. There
Are no typewriters, no TV just a little
Headset I plug into the wall
See twenty hours of silence is not
Always quiet. WEST our one station
Plays stuff like: "I'm proud
To be an Okee from Muskogee."
So I try to eat my own breathing
Snatch the black hood the prison
Chaplain slid on my heart
When he tried to baptize me
With a swastika. Talk to myself
And rub the conversation
On my thighs since I can't read
Any books and only get one
Visit a month because I let my locks
Grow. They tried to cut 'em off
But I'm a hydra and they found two
Dreads itching and hissing in a c.o.'s
Throat. Babble on Babylon remember
Scottsboro Habeus Corpus Jim Crow
I'm almost done just let me tickle
This sentence, which I heard some years
Ago. I'm still not sure if it ends
With a period or a question mark. I know
There are more days behind me
Than there are ahead. But I got to
Make this paragraph crack
Up: picture that: a journalist's final deadline

•••

ABIODUN OYEWOLE of The Last Poets
POLITICAL PRISONERS

AND THE CROWD YELLED OUT
"FREE ALL POLITICAL PRISONERS"
THEN THE SKY TURNED DARK
BLOOD POURED FROM THE CLOUDS
THE OCEAN BEGAN TO ROAR
AND THE SHADOWS OF A BILLION
NAKED BLACK SOULS
WERE THROWN INTO A HUGE PIT
IN SPACE SPINNING
WITH NO REAL REFERENCE OF TIME
AND WE WERE FORBIDDEN TO SEE
EYES GOUGED OUT WITH HOT POKERS
IF WE SAW SOMETHING OTHER
THAN A SLAVE IN OUR HEARTS
IN OUR MINDS IN OUR EYES
AND THE CROWD YELLED OUT
"FREE ALL POLITICAL PRISONERS"
AND CHAINS RATTLED ON SHIPS
CAUSED SHIPS TO WRECK
BREAKING THE CAGE
FREEING THE BIRD
AND SOON ANOTHER TROPICAL ISLAND
WAS GRACED BY THE PARENTS
OF MOTHER EARTH
ONLY TO BE CAPTURED AGAIN
AND MADE INTO SUGAR CANE
AND CALLOUSED COTTON AND HOT MOLASSES
AND AFRICAN RHYTHMS BEATING INSIDE OUR HEARTS
AND STILL SOME CHERISHED THEIR SLAVERY
VOLUNTEERED FOR IT HELD IT CLOSE TO THEIR HEARTS
IN SPITE OF THEMSELVES
AND THE CROWD YELLED OUT!
"FREE ALL POLITICAL PRISONERS"
LIKE NAT TURNER, HARRIET TUBMAN, JACK JOHNSON,
LEADBELLY, PAUL ROBESON, STAGALEE, ANGELA DAVIS,

ASSATA SHAKUR, AFINA SHAKUR, THE PANTHER 21,
TUPAC SHAKUR, MARTIN, MALCOLM, MANDELA, MIKE TYSON,
COLIN FURGESON, JALIL H. RAP BROWN, WILLIAM B. WILLIAMS,
CLARENCE THOMAS, DELORES TUCKER, O.J. SIMPSON,
ANITA HILL, TAWANA BRAWLEY, KABILA, WINNIE, CUBA,
MUMIA ABU-JAMAL AND ALL THE BROTHERS AND SISTERS
WHO HAVE BEEN FIGHTING FOR AND AGAINST THEMSELVES
IN A WORLD DESIGNED ONLY
FOR A FRONT WITHOUT A BACK

•••

RASHIDAH ISHMAILI *
Missing Person–2

Prisoner X does not exist anymore.
His cell has been cleaned.
No trace of his is left.
Call a witness if you dare.
Dispute if you care, with his guards.
The jailors will tell you.
He is not here is he!

But I tell you, he was here!
Prisoner X was here.
His cough awakened us daily.
A dim glow of smuggled candle light
lulled us to sleep nights.
We knew another day had passed.
We had lived another day.
I tell you, he was here!

Guard P knows I do not lie.
He is the one who came each
evening with food for him.
We all saw him spit in his plate.
Guard P is not a tall man.
No distinguishing features,
ordinary. This greying hair.
A gold band on his finger.
Ask him! Ask him! I tell you
he *was* here!

The others are afraid.
They will not talk.
If you speak to them,
they will not talk.

Their time is near and
their bodies ache for
women left waiting in the past.
But I, there is no one
waiting for me. My house
was searched and burned.
No one waits for me.
I have vanished. No one
knows me here. Only him.
Prisoner X. He knew me.
Knew me!

I tell you he was here!
In the dead of night
when silence was broken by snores
of guards and guarded, he read to me.

I who learned to decipher A from B.
You see! Before I could not read.
We would not enter their schools.
I could not read.
I tell you, he was here!
Well, I will write about him.
I am unafraid and my time is
so long. No one waits at home for me.
Death is certain. Let me begin.
Guard P is a pervert.
He defecates on the Bible each night.
His calls to prayer are muffled belches.
He cannot spell. His reports are false.
His name appears as an appendix to
Prisoner X. It was he who made the
statements. Guard P cannot spell.
I tell you, he was here!

Well, anyway, the night of the blackout
Prisoner X did not write. His cell was dark.
The others said he had magic. He could fly.
On that night I did not see him.
The others said he could fly.
But when dawn came, his cough,
that familiar sound came as
our call to prayer. Guard P
walked with a limp. Sgt. J.S.,
the black one, was absent. Guard P said
he was sick. He knew. Prisoner X knew.
But, he was silent!

Sgt. J.S. could read and write but
could not carry a gun.
could not eat with other guards,
could not reprimand Prisoner A
But Sgt. J.S. was black and the
prisoner was white. Sgt. J.S. could not
go home nights because this is a
restricted zone and he is not from here.
Sgt. J.S. could only beat Prisoner X
because, he too is/was black.

But when the day of the explosion came
and rocks were dislodged,
and the tower fell,
and the current disrupted—
Chief Warden P.B. came to inspect.
And all, all were present. But
Prisoner X smiled. He was there.

Chief Warden P.B. walked up and down.
His eyes were piercing and gleamed
in the sun. They fixed themselves
on each man and accused. Each man
stared and stared at his feet. But he,
Prisoner X, he looked at him. Then
Chief Warden P.B. spoke but Guard P said
he was there when Sgt. J.S. struck him
across his face and Prisoner X had fallen
beneath the blow. Chief Warden P.B. asked
if he had spoken the names. The names of
the others. But Prisoner X smiled and we knew.

We knew he had not!
Guard P assured Chief Warden P.B.
that one more night of Sgt. J.S. and
the prisoner would speak. Chief Warden
P.B. looked at Sgt. J.S. and accused him
of sabotage and threatened imprisonment
if he did not get responses and quick!

That night, that night—we heard it.
We all heard though they, the men
will not talk. Will not speak.
Their time is short and their women
wait hungry and alone. But we,
we heard blow after blow. No cries.
No pleas. First, the sickening sounds
of bone-crush-blows. And then water.
Running water turning red. His blood.
His blood! You see! He did live.
Does death bleed?

Sgt. J.S. cursed and beat. And we,
we cursed and cursed him. Guard P
was home in bed. His wife will swear
to that. She was under his fat belly.
He had nothing to do with it. Guard P
is white and he can hit black and white.
He lives in a restricted zone and
cannot be fetched by night guards/
A note was sent but he cannot read.

Sgt. J.S. yelled and beat. His armpits
ran wet with water and exerted pressure
of blow after blow. He pleaded with Prisoner X
to tell, tell him all. He, Prisoner X
would be spared. Just speak. Give one name.
And then, I swear this is true, Prisoner X
vanished! And in his cell, Sgt. J.S. stood
bloodied. Locked in!

The morning came silently. We were awakened
by a cry of fear. He was not there! He was gone!
The man, Prisoner X vanished. Sgt. J.S.
lay on the floor. His face bloated
and spotted with blood which was not his.
Guard P came in to inspect. Sgt. J.S.
was in the cell. His eyes were gone!
His prisoner was gone!
We heard the blows.
We heard the cries.
We listened in disbelief.
"But, I tell you," said Sgt. J.S.
"He was here! He was here!"

The others have all gone back to their areas,
back to their women. I am here alone
in this cell. No one waits for me. And I tell you
he was here. The men said he had magic.

He could fly. He could fly!
Tomorrow I shall look for him.
In the morning I shall strain
to hear his cough call me to prayer.
I shall search the red sky for his face

among the faces that stare at the
scaffold and me. And when I go,
who will be able to say, "He was here!
He lived."

•••

RAUL SALINAS

News from San Quentin: August 21, 1971

A Tender Warrior
             fell today
victim
             of the JAIL MACHINE!!
And in Leavenworth Prison
             rank right-on-ers
of the chilly clenched fist set
             (complete with afro-do)
dig soul music, man...Soul Music!
             & dream of
                           one
                                    more
                                             Kadillac!
Those few
             who have been touched
                           by
                           MADNESS
in silent darkness pray
             to the spirit of Ho Chi Minh
and grow impatient/intolerant
             of the oppressed...
those who wish to stay that way.
             There's no turning back for us.

A Tender Warrior
             fell today
a flame that burned for
             revolutionary eons
was doused/
             slowly ebbed its glow.
We all grew a bit today,

             brother george.

Our struggle became more intense!

•••

JILL WITHERSPOON BOYER
George Jackson

The newsboy hands us
his death
and smiling leaves us wondering
what to do with it.
We shift from foot to foot
old discontents,
as the careful comfort in our lives
flicks off the bullet
that found the soft spot
in his back.
Still, some vague thing
about freedom
makes us nervous to know
where he went.

He falls hard into our memory
of others gone
for something or nothing,
Righteous rebel, he was tracked to the heights
of his road
that bent dangerously proud.
Though his spirit rose through deliberate fires,
he couldn't escape the ones
who sent the bullet.
But even those who knew their jobs
so well
only got his flesh,
because they couldn't strike
the awakened worth of him.

And we, reading his blood,
we jerk on tenterhooks
for fear a trail of broken chains
may lead to us.
Servants of safety, we live in our skins.
Our chorus is, "He can afford to be free
who has nothing to lose.

But those who have jewels
must stay in the grace of thieves."
And so we pull a cover
over our weapon of will
and yield to forgetfulness of him
with already drying tears.

•••

LARVESTER GAITHER

Conviction or a Fine?: Are There Political
Prisoners and POW's in the Good Ole U.S. of A.?

Public attention has been directed towards the issues of the death penalty and political imprisonment as a result of the media coverage of a Philadelphia journalist named Mumia Abu-Jamal. Abu-Jamal is recognized as a political prisoner by human rights activists through-out the world because of his uncompromising journalism, criticism of Philadelphia police brutality, past membership in the Black Panther Party, and affiliation with the separatist organization MOVE. In 1982, many believe Mumia Abu-Jamal was falsely accused of the murder of Philadelphia police officer Daniel Faulkner—a crime punishable by death. He was scheduled to be executed on August 17, 1995. There was a renewed sense of immediacy on the part of political activists and anti-death penalty advocates in response to the execution date. Appeals were made on Mumia's behalf throughout the world—from South Africa, Germany, France to Brazil. German Foreign Minister Klaus Kinkel made a special request to Pennsylvania Gov. Tom Ridge to halt the execution. Also, French President Jacques Chirac gave his support to overturn the death penalty against Mumia Abu-Jamal. Finally, on August 7, 1995, Mumia Abu-Jamal was granted a stay of execution to, according to the ruling Judge Albert Sabo, "give him more time to complete the appeals process before the execution date in his death penalty case."

Because of Mumia's case, the whole panorama of debate around the two issues has widened considerably. The questions remain: First of all, is the U.S. criminal justice system a political institution designed to criminalize black people? Second, is the death penalty a long-standing mechanism of social control? And, finally, are there political prisoners and Prisoners of War in the Good Ole U.S. of A.?

There is the question of definitions: A political prisoner is usually defined as a person incarcerated for actions carried out in support of legitimate struggles for self-determination or for opposing the illegal policies of the United States government and/or its political sub-divisions. The most obvious reason why the American public doesn't hear much about political prisoners is because the United States government doesn't recognize political prisoners within its borders. Furthermore, it has not and does not recognize any of its policies (i.e., slavery, genocide of indigenous people) as illegal. And then, most American political prisoners are charged with crimes—albeit crimes they did not commit. The criminal charges are used as subterfuge for discrediting their political activities and neutralizing or destroying their effectiveness. The media—which religiously corresponds with government lines of policy—frames the issue around their guilt or innocence as opposed to their politics; in most instances, the media does not cover their cases at all. Thus, unless the public is politically educated around the issues, they will view these cases as criminal rather than political. Or, in fact, they will not view the cases at all.

Usually, when the issue of political imprisonment or prisoners of war comes up, our attention is misdirected to another time and place. Our minds quickly escape to South Africa, for example, where we witnessed Nelson Mandela, after twenty-seven years of imprisonment for his political convictions, emerge as head of state. Or, in the case of prisoners of war, we think of Vietnam veterans who are missing in action (MIAs). We don't think of Leonard Peltier, Sekou Odinga, Geronimo Pratt, Herman Bell, Mohaman Geuka Koti, Robert Seth Hayes, to name a few. According to Dhoruba Bin Wahad, initiator of The Campaign to Free Black and New Afrikan Political Prisoners and P.O.W.s in the United States, since the political prisoner campaigns waged by the Black Panther Party to free Huey Newton and Angela Davis...there has not been a systematic national campaign for freedom of our political prisoners built from the grassroots to the highest level of political power in our community. Clearly, the lack of political education contributes to much of the public's complacency.

However, despite our apathy and unawareness around these two issues—death penalty and political imprisonment—both historically symbolize the principle relationships to power between African American people and the U.S. government apparatus. Michael Warren, who represents Dr. Mutulu Shakur, a political prisoner who was a long-standing member of the Black Liberation Movement and allegedly a part of the Black Liberation Army, argues that "there has been constant discussion on political prisoners and prisoners of war, and the need to link the two to the death penalty." But he agrees that the case of Mumia has contributed much to make more people see the connection.

In 1959, George Jackson was sentenced to prison as a common criminal. He was given a one-year-to-life sentence for a $70 robbery in California. However, as George Jackson became politicized, he devolped into an effective spokesperson against harsh and unfair prison conditions and was considered one of the great revolutionary thinkers of the twentieth century. By the time his book, *Soledad Brother: The Prison Letters of George Jackson* was published in 1969, he was one of the most recognized political prisoners in America. Less than a year after the book's publication, he was assassinated while still in prison.

Gary Graham was a seventeen-year-old misguided youth when he was accused of the murder of fifty-one-year-old Bobby Grant Lambert in 1981. Gary roughly matched the description of Mr. Lambert's assailant in that he was a young black male. Although Gary admits to being a common criminal at the period of his arrest, today he maintains his innocence, and legal work on his behalf shows that there is ample evidence to support his innocence. "The criminal justice system tends to focus more sharply on the young Black teenager, particularly males. It acts as a reflection of the larger society's racial prejudices and fears," says Gary Graham. Since Graham's imprinonment, he has emerged as a politicized anti-death penalty advocate. Because of local, national and international support, Graham has survived three stays of execution. Although Gary's imprisonment was initially a criminal case, the nature of his imprisonment today is clearly political. Chokwe Lumumba, who heads the Malcolm X Grassroots Movement, argues that Gary's plight against his execution has helped to mobilize a whole consciousness against the death penalty in the state of Texas. "Gary Graham is one of many brothers who might not have been well known as a political activist prior to going to jail. What happens in many instances is that people, when they get to jail, become politicized. And in doing so, often they inspire prisoners around them to do the same. And not only prisoners around them, but people on the outside of the jail," he said.

Criminalizing a Race

Mumia's case clearly symbolizes two diabolical currents in history. "By looking at how the government was able to criminalize Mumia's political work, we see an example of what this government was able to do during the period of slavery. The same methods of social control used during the period of slavery—from physical control (attempting to escape from slavery was a crime punishable by death) to the destruction and separation of families—we see in the case of Mumia Abu-Jamal," says anti-death penalty advocate Ashanti Chimurenga. Chimurenga, who currently heads the efforts to save Gary Graham, feels that we should view both political imprisonment and the death penalty from a human rights perspective. She says that they both represent two forms of repressive government practices. "There's a continuity between *Slave Codes* and the outgrowth of slavery on the part of the government to terrorize and criminalize an entire community of people. Because we know so little about the history and the current reality of these policies, we are not as terrorized as we should be," says Chimurenga.

In the book *Criminalizing a Race*, Charshee McIntyre puts forth the argument that once early attempts at colonization proved too expensive, prisons served as alternative places to removing "Free Blacks" from society:

> Since the 18th century, the prisons have been the logical holding
> place for African Americans. Through constantly reinforcing the
> idea that those of us not in them really represent prime candidates
> for prisons, these institutions keep us in this society's outsider posi
> tion. To Whites, Blacks not incarcerated simply have not been
> caught or the prisons lack room to accommodate our entire popula-
> tion. In other words, because Whites have proffered an idea of
> African American criminality, we have lived for two hundred years in
> an environment that constantly threatens our freedom. [pp. ix]

She writes further:

> The notion of Blacks' having social mobility escaped most
> Americans. States included all Blacks in their *Slave Codes* which
> reflected how most affluent Americans expected some kind of disor
> der from free African Americans. [pp. 185]

Today's conservative rhetoric is nothing new. Code Words and phrases such as "War on Crime" ("Crime" meaning Black Youth), and "The Crisis of Public Order" (the title of Adam Walinsky's cover story of the July issue of neo-liberal publication, *The Atlantic Monthly*), which warns:

> We Have Fled Our Cities. We Have Permitted The Spread
> Of Wastelands Ruled By Merciless Killers. We Have Abandoned
> Millions Of Our Fellow Citizens To Every Kind Of Danger And
> Degraded Assault. And Now A Demographic Surge Is About To
> Make Everything Worse.

"Stranger Murders" (murders no longer take place among family members, acquaintances, etc. but from violent teens). Of course, there's a whole entire lexicon for reinforcing these images which oftentimes reverse the realities.

Introducing COINTELPRO

Abu-Jamal's case is no precedent where the issues of political imprisonment and death penalty converge. And it is not an issue limited to African American communitites of resistance. In spite of a last moment stay of execution granted by Justice William O. Douglas, on June 19, 1953, Ethel and Julius Rosenberg were executed. They were tried for espionage even though the major evidence was furnished by individuals who admitted to being spies, were in prison or already under indictment. Their case had received unprecedented worldwide support. Scientist Albert Einstein and French philosopher Jean-Paul Sartre, among many other prominent figures, had made appeals for the husband and wife. However, Supreme Court Chief Justice Vinson dispatched jets to the various places around the country where the other justices were vacationing and, together, those justices canceled Douglas' stay. Years later, a subpoenaed FBI document showed that the Judge had already promised the Attorney General and other high-level officials that the Rosenbergs would be executed. This was an important case, because it set the tone for what would happen to those whom the government would deem "traitors" or "threats to internal security." The Rosenbergs typified the era of McCarthyism.

The sixties marked not only a new era for an awakening blackness, but an age of covert government repression, surveillance, and elimination. As the civil rights movement gave way to the Black Power and Black Liberation movements, the FBI, under the leadership of J. Edgar Hoover, declared war on organizations such as the Black Panthers, American Indian Movement, and hundreds of others—including writers, artists, musicians, etc. For black Americans, here is where the term "prisoners of war" in the U.S. becomes even more clear in today's context. Those who organized to defend the community's interest or spoke out against the repression were either killed in assassination plots, neutralized, or labeled criminal, convicted and imprisoned. The counterintelligence activities carried out by the Federal Bureau of Investigation was an act of war against radical, reformist, and even integrationist organziations and, at minimum, state-sanctioned terrorism against the general African American communtiy. While Congressional hearings concerning the Waco affair have gained national sentiment, Congressional hearings in regard to COINTELPRO have never been considered.

However, COINTELPRO has to be considered as a component of the overall policy towards African people or any individual or group who effectively opposes its policies. Beginning in 1973, several lawsuits forced the government to release documents highlighting its various campaigns to undermine and disrupt organizations and legal activities against the state's policies throughout the sixties and seventies. Although COINTELPRO contributed much to the underdevelopment of black leadership and consequently the black community, with historical caution, it has to be viewed as part of an overall policy towards the African community, with underpinnings dating back to, as McIntyre argues, the inception of the criminal justice system, and as Jonathan Jackson further puts it, evolving well into the twentieth century.

In the new introduction to *Soledad Brother*, Jonathan Jackson, Jr. makes the following observation:

> COINTELPRO...was really a symptomatic, expendable entity; a small
> police force within a larger one (FBI), within a branch of govern-
> ment (executive), within the government itself (liberal democracy),
> within the economic system (capitalism).

Jackson goes on to point out that "doing away with COINTELPRO or even the FBI would not alter the structure that produces the surveillance/elimination apparatus." This is an important observation because as the struggle around political prisoners, abolition of the death penalty, and prisoners of war builds steam, as well as other movements for social, political, and economic change, an incorrect analysis of what we're up against will prove more detrimental than ever; particularly given the new and more entrenched association between the social, political, and economic situation and today's new prison industry.

An unbalanced attention towards the draw blood policies of COINTELPRO focuses in on merely one aspect of political imprisonment and repression. Mumia Abu-Jamal, for example, is one of a small number, if not the only, widely recognized black "political prisoner" on death row today. There is a strong need to focus on the whole spectrum of political imprisonment and beyond that, the entire spectrum of this economic, social, and political system.

The New Political Prisoner

Draconian policies toward the African American community have always created conditions which give birth to various forms of resistance. The '90s are no different. The Crime Bill will fundamentally enhance the political, economic, and racial injustices carried out against poor white, Chicano, African American youth in the United States. "There is a real connection given the economic climate. The fact is that in a post-labor era, where people of color have not been trained for the type of technological positions in the current and emerging work force, there will be a surplus of people who are idle, and by virtue of being idle they will think about the conditions around them and will engage in activities to alleviate those conditions," says Attorney Michael Warren.

On one hand, the present generation of young people haven't demonstrated the kind of political-centeredness we saw in the sixties and seventies. Although today's youth embody the spirit of rebelliousness we witnessed with Fred Hampton, Assata Shakur (currently exiled in Cuba), H. Rap Brown, Stokley Carmichael (aka Kwame Touré, currently exiled in Guinea) and others, it is a rebelliousness that is rarely politicized. By the looks of things, there will be fewer youths going to prison for political activism. On the other hand, the criminal justice system is more sophisticated in its racial politics than it has ever been. With hundreds of new crime laws being enacted, the privatization of prisons, the sky-rocketing teen population and the marketing of the image of Black youth as criminal, there will be a new kind of political prisoner in the years ahead.

With the rise in crime rates, the death penalty is not likely to be overturned anytime soon. Just recently, New York became the thirty-eighth state to reinstate the death penalty. With the new Crime Bill, there are over sixty new death penalty provisions—new federal laws that will override some states that have no capital punishment. "The pace of executions this year is poised to break the modern record of 38 deaths set in 1993, partly due to strong public support for capital punishment and the eagerness of political leaders to claim credit for fighting crime." (AP Wire of 8/17/95)

Timothy Pratt, the brother of Black Panther political prisoner Geronimo Pratt, feels that in order to offset this, the government's crime (criminalization) policies should be closely scrutinized. "We should look at the drastic increase in Black male imprisonment beginning in 1969," says Pratt. He goes on to point out how "one study showed that longer lengths of sentencing did not deter crime, but increased crime. But the *Crime Bill* pushes for longer sentences. Drug offenders should be treated as patients in need of medical help. But the U.S. government treats them as common criminals. And thirdly, the juveniles should be treated as juveniles. However, we've seen where the legal age for a juvenile has been pushed down to age 14. So there is definitely a connection between the U.S. government policies and crime."

It is clear that there is a lot of work to do around the two issues of death penalty and political imprisonment. "Every state's got a lot of penitentiaries and every penitentiary's got a lot of brothers," said Gil Scott-Heron at a recent fundraiser held in Houston for Gary Graham. "We don't claim to know as much about particular individuals as the people working on these cases, but we claim to know about the circumstances that black people are put into all over the country."

If nothing is done to change this condition in some way, many more of the young people of today's generation may soon be faced with government-sanctioned executions. The laws have been enacted. What comes next is the execution of those laws. Viewing the present condition of this country against the backdrop of its history, Attorney Michael Warren says, "Mumia represents what will happen to black people in general, but specifically to those who offer their services in a vanguard capacity to the struggle to change the existing conditions African Americans face."

•••

RAYMOND R. PATTERSON
Words

Each night with words
to wall out prison walls

brick by word brick by word
from darkness lifting

into wordless space
words from syllables of rage

to rise through caged tiers
towards the clear speech of stars.

Can you see now in the dark
in the top of the makeshift scaffolding

the prisoner lifting
the final words into place

some jailer below
shaking his keys and shouting?

•••

SUSAN ROSENBERG
Shadow Life

Entombment like black smoke
will do damage deep in.

All the way in it twists
and coils into jagged
shards of eliminated time
creating a
shadow life that never sees light.
No sun rays here
to shake spirits free

What will it be
the upcoming state sponsored
execution?
Is it injectable?
Is it electrical?
Justice denied, yet again?

If the state murders
Mumia
all of us
will be diminished.
The deepest damage will
spread
and the particles that racism
breed
will extend the shadow of life.

Their message so clear
Do Not be Black
Do Not be radical
Do Not be a political prisoner

There is still time to
SHAKE IT LOOSE
to pry open this iron fist
to shake spirits free
into the light
To free Mumia Abu-Jamal

•••

LENINA MORALES NADAL
to the warrior with child

This poem was inspired by Puerto Rican political prisoner Carmen Valentín and her poem "To Our Revolutionary Children"("A Nuestra Hijos Revolucionarios"). It is for her, Mumia, and all other political prisoners. Let the spirit of their native children inspire them.

this is a poem for the revolutionary child
child who drew countries before flowers
hospitals before gardens
this child
who rode on the backs of pregnant warriors
before coddling plastic white dolls

this child
who licked her face with mud
before hiding her mouth
with kissy-face lipsticks

this child
who was a Bolshevik Latin Suburban MUJER
before birth
whose mother labored
holding notepads
to fight and write in a country called Iraq
before telling this child fairy tales

this child
was told to lift her adobe colored face and sing
to a flag w/ too many stars
was told to listen to loudspeakers and follow

No. Flow
flow to the drumbeats and trios at midnight
these were her loudspeakers

this child was love
the product of
a grandfather who smashed wine bottles against officers' necks
when they silenced his liberation song
a grandmother who grasped english words
in her fists to throw like stones
at public school dictators

this child felt love
from the sweet sweat smell of mothers who raised her
Mothers
preaching defiance in their slippers
praying to Gods disguised as men
and weeping *tristeza* songs
while nourishing life

this child is woman
wearing my flag on her chest
my country's in her feet
and these *colores* don't run US
these *colores*
defy
gray
stoned
women
holding torches.

•••

MUMIA ABU-JAMAL

Freedom of Religion = Bondage of the Flesh

MILLIONS OF EUROPEANS FLED TO AMERICA SEEKING "RELIGIOUS FREEDOM" BUT DENIED <u>ALL</u> FREEDOMS TO INDIANS and AFRICANS WHO WERE FORCED INTO PEONAGE AND SLAVERY — WHAT "FREEDOM" DID THEY HAVE?

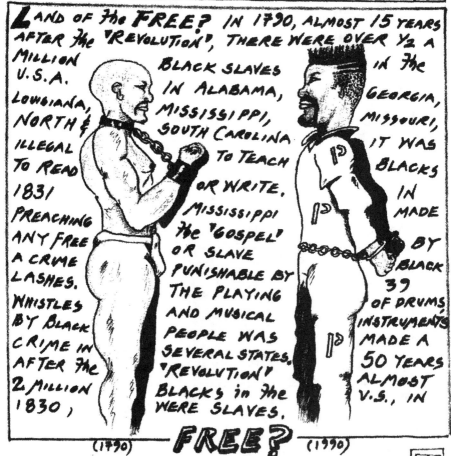

LAND OF THE **FREE?** IN 1790, ALMOST 15 YEARS AFTER THE "REVOLUTION", THERE WERE OVER ½ A MILLION BLACK SLAVES IN THE U.S.A. IN ALABAMA, GEORGIA, LOUISIANA, MISSISSIPPI, MISSOURI, NORTH & SOUTH CAROLINA IT WAS ILLEGAL TO TEACH BLACKS TO READ OR WRITE. IN 1831 MISSISSIPPI MADE PREACHING THE "GOSPEL" BY ANY FREE OR SLAVE BLACK A CRIME PUNISHABLE BY 39 LASHES. THE PLAYING OF DRUMS, WHISTLES AND MUSICAL INSTRUMENTS BY BLACK PEOPLE WAS MADE A CRIME IN SEVERAL STATES. 50 YEARS AFTER THE "REVOLUTION" ALMOST 2 MILLION BLACKS in the U.S., IN 1830, WERE SLAVES.

(1790) — **FREE?** — (1990)

IN TODAY'S PRISONS, the **1**st AMENDMENT TREATS PRISONERS LIKE SLAVES, AS in the CASE *O'LONE VS. ESTATE of SHABAZZ* (1987) WHERE the SUPREME COURT UPHELD A RULE PROHIBITING MUSLIMS FROM RETURNING from JOBS TO HOLD THEIR FRIDAY JUMU'AH SERVICES; "SECURITY" WAS MORE IMPORTANT than "FREEDOM of RELIGION"!

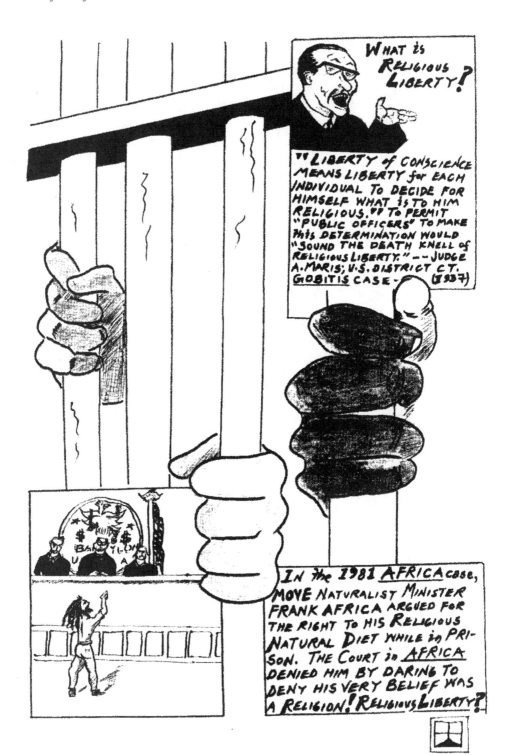

NAT HENTOFF

Death Condemned to Death in South Africa
(A New State Refuses to Kill)

Don't tell me about the valley of the shadow of death. I live there.
—**Mumia Abu-Jamal**
Live from Death Row

In July 1987, a hut in Zululand was burned to the ground. The five people in that hut died. The murderers had been hired to do the job by a man who hated his mother-in-law. She lived—until then—in that hut. The men who set the fire and their employer were convicted of murder and sentenced to death.

This year, the case finally reached South Africa's Constitutional Court. In the new South Africa, and in the spirit of Nelson Mandela, this court of 11 justices is composed of blacks, whites, Afrikaans, and English members. Unanimously, the Constitutional Court of South Africa used this case—the first it has reviewed—to abolish the death penalty in that country. Nelson Mandela is also opposed to it.

Not all murderers in South Africa have been tried or even apprehended. Under white rule, there were covens of secret killers among the police and other scrutiny forces. There have been—and still are—intertribal murders, some of them performed by the horrifying practice of "necklacing." Some of the families and friends of those murdered on all sides of the tribal atrocities have long nurtured dreams of revenge.

So, if the Constitutional Court had taken a popular vote on whether the death penalty should be abandoned, I'm not sure a majority would have wanted to do without state killings, now that the majority *is* the state.

In arguments on the Zululand murders before the court, lawyers making the case for keeping capital punishment said that this is a political issue and therefore the wishes of the public must be respected. That, of course, is the attitude of the American Congress; a predominant majority of the Supreme Court (John Paul Stevens is a partial exception); and our hollow president.

In a recent early television ad for his election campaign, Bill Clinton shouts: "Expand the death penalty! That's how we'll protect America!"

By contrast, Justice Thole Madala of the South African Constitutional Court pointed out that the responsibility of the court is to protect *individual* rights.

That's why the American Constitution could not be ratified until the states insisted on having a Bill of Rights—individual rights against the government.

Interestingly, and rather poignantly—considering the present dismal state of our Bill of Rights—South African Justice Thole Madala quoted from a 1943 Supreme Court decision (*West Virginia State Board of Education v. Barnette*) by Justice Robert Jackson. In all of Supreme Court history, no opinion comes close to Jackson's in defining what this country is supposed to be all about.

The South African justice highlighted this passage:

> The very purpose of a Bill of Rights was to withdraw certain subjects
> from the vicissitudes of political controversy— to place them beyond
> the reach of majorities and officials to establish them as legal princi-
> ples to be applied by the courts... Fundamental rights may not be sub-
> mitted to a vote; they depend on the outcome of no elections.

And there is no more fundamental right than the right to live. Everyone's right to live.

The president of the South African Constitutional Court, Arthur Chaskalson, wrote: "The rights to life and dignity are the most important of human rights, and the source of all other personal rights... . Taking these factors into account—as well as the elements of arbitrariness and the possibility of error in enforcing the death penalty—the clear and convincing case that is required to justify the death sentence as a penalty for murder has not been made out."

On our Supreme Court, this was also the view of Justices William Brennan, Thurgood Marshall, Harry Blackmun (very late in his stay), and Lewis Powell, who came to that decision only after he had left the Court. (Thanks a lot.)

Blackmun—unlike Brennan and Marshall—never did come around to the belief that the death penalty is cruel and unusual punishment, forbidden by the Eighth Amendment. Blackmun finally woke up to the fact that it is exceedingly difficult, often impossible, to be sure that someone on death row has been given due-process rights; fundamental fairness at his trial and afterward.

And in the South African Constitutional Court, Justice Chaskalson—quoted by Anthony Lewis in his June 9 *New York Times* column, "A Culture of Rights"—emphasized that defendants facing death often had had inexperienced court-appointed lawyers and absurdly inadequate funds to prepare a defense.

If you've been watching the O.J. Simpson trial, you realize what it can cost the defense to deal with the overwhelming resources of the state. Along with the very high costs of the "dream team" of lawyers, Simpson's various expert witnesses command huge amounts of money. One of them, a very illuminating witness, Dr. Michael Baden, will have been paid well over $100,000.

By contrast, there was the trial in Philadelphia of Mumia Abu-Jamal. I am not convinced of either his guilt or his innocence, but I am wholly convinced that his due-process rights were wholly, crudely, and deliberately violated by the judge and the prosecutor.

At trial, Abu-Jamal had a court-appointed lawyer who had never tried a capital case. Furthermore, the judge, Albert Sabo, was not only a fan of the police but was also a retired member of the Fraternal Order of Police. Abu-Jamal was charged with the killing of a police officer.

In addition, Sabo has more scalps hanging on his wall than any other judge I know of. Or, as *Time* (August 7) put it: "Sabo holds the national record for sending the most people to death: 31."

Ah, say Sabo's admirers, all that means is that he has presided over thirty-one trials in which the jury decided to send the defendants to eternity.

Okay, but how does Sabo act at those trials? In the July 16 *The New York Times Magazine*, Tina Rosenberg said of some of Sabo's trials: "He made suggestions to prosecutors on how to strengthen their cases, and routinely denied money to defense attorneys to pay for experts, even psychiatrists to examine the defendants."

When Abu-Jamal was the defendant before him, Sabo allowed his defense a total of only $1100 for investigations and experts. So, at his trial—as Leonard Weinglass, his current attorney, points out—Abu-Jamal "didn't have a pathologist, an expert on ballistics, an investigator."

Also, the defense attorney failed to object when the prosecutor used 11 of his 15 peremptory challenges to exclude blacks from the jury. Nor did Abu-Jamal's first attorney say a word when the best friend of a former policeman was chosen for the jury—along with an alternate whose husband was a police officer.

There is much more evidence of the fundamental unfairness of Abu-Jamal's trial. The most damaging witness against him was Cynthia White, a prostitute, who had given a number of conflicting accounts.

What follows is from the Petition for Post-Conviction Relief, Court of Common Pleas, Philadelphia, June 19, 1995. The advocate is Leonard Weinglass, who is one of the most carefully prepared and committed constitutional attorneys I know. This is his account of Cynthia White's role in Abu-Jamal's trial, in which she said that she had seen the defendant shoot the police officer:

"Ms. White's testimony was false.... At the time of the trial, Ms. White was serving a sentence of 18 months for prostitution in Massachusetts. She had 38 previous arrests for prostitution in Philadelphia, and, as readily acknowledged by the prosecution, had three open cases awaiting trial in Philadelphia when she took the stand.

"Although the prosecution maintained that Ms. White had not been offered a deal for her testimony, the evidence showed otherwise. The Commonwealth did not disclose [at Abu-Jamal's trial] that Ms. White had been assigned police 'protection' and continued to work the streets as a prostitute with plainclothes police guarding her....

"Police told another prostitute, Veronica Jones, that [she] would be allowed to work the streets with impunity, like Ms. White, if [she] would testify against Mr. Jamal. The court excluded this testimony."

The judge excluded other testimony undermining the prosecution that I do not believe the Constitutional Court of South Africa would have barred. Not surprisingly, Abu-Jamal was convicted. Next came the penalty phase. Would the jury condemn him to death or give him a long, lesser sentence?

Albert Sabo was still presiding at the penalty phase, and—Leonard Weinglass charges—that Abu-Jamal's attorney at the time failed "to prepare for the penalty phase" and did not "present evidence in mitigation."

The prosecutor, moreover, did not tell the jury during the penalty phase that if they decided on a life sentence, that would be it. There would be no possibility of parole. What the prosecutor did do was give the jury the impression that if they were to vote for death, Abu-Jamal still might not be executed.

Stroking the jury, the prosecutor said that Abu-Jamal would have "appeal after appeal, and perhaps there would be a reversal of the case, so that [the death sentence] may not be final."

The judge did not object to this hornswoggling of the jury. Nor, on appeal, did the Pennsylvania Supreme Court.

Finally, after 13 years, a stay of execution was granted in August of this year by Judge Sabo. Leonard Weinglass thinks it came because of the international support Abu-Jamal has been getting. I rather doubt Sabo cares one whit about the criticism of him by Amnesty International or PEN or the Human Rights Watch or the International Parliament of Writers (Salman Rushdie, president).

My guess is that Sabo decided that even he did not want to go down in judicial history as the judge who hurled a man into the death chamber when his court appeals were far from completed. In all the recent writing about the case, I have seen hardly any reference to the fact that although Abu-Jamal exhausted all his direct appeals, he had only started his habeas corpus appeal in Pennsylvania and hadn't begun his federal habeas appeals.

In the America of Bill Clinton and the current barbarous Congress, consider this attempt, in court, by Philadelphia District Attorney Lynne Abraham—an enthusiast for the death penalty—to prevent a stay of execution for Abu-Jamal:

"Defendant would contend that he will suffer irreparable injury if he is executed, but this argument assumes that the death verdict is an 'injury'.... The carrying out of a valid death sentence cannot constitute irreparable injury for purposes of requesting a stay."

In 1978, Nelson Mandela wrote that he was prepared to die for "the ideal of a democratic and free society." In this country, Bill Clinton and Congress are eager for others to die at the hands of the state.

•••

SAMUEL ALLEN
I Saw the Executioner

I saw the executioner,
ponderous, bloated
but—curious—he was trembling,
could he have been repentant?

Ah yes...clean shaven,
                    check!
his belly full,
              yes, check!
knees buckled
arms strapped
soul shriven
hands clenched,
              yes, check!

legs bound
eyes wild
neck bulging,
        check!
now see him

      —LUNGE—

And at his sucking after gasp, I saw
A countless host issue from that form,
Satisfied—check now!—satisfied at last.

In the big house of history, I saw
Him too stretched out, dead, done,
Cold on the slab of judgment,
Felled by his own cold horror,
His glazed, unbelieving despair.
In his own barbaric rite, the blood cried out
His guilt; and he too, doomed,
Was seized at dawn
And driven into that quickening river
Red from the mangled host he sent before.

•••

GWENDOLYN BROOKS

To the Prisoners

I call for you cultivation of strength in the dark.
Dark gardening
in the vertigo coal.
In the hot paralysis.
Under the wolves and coyotes of particular silences.
Where it is dry.
Where it is dry.
I call for you
cultivation of victory Over
long blows that you want to give and blows you are going to get.

Over
what wants to crumble you down, to sicken
you. I call for you
cultivation of strength to heal and enhance
in the non-cheering dark, in the many many mornings-after;
in the chalk and choke.

•••

PETER LINEBAUGH
Qui Vive?:
The Farce of the Death Penalty

We in the theater are constantly on the qui vive for the humorous side of every situation.
—**Tom Walls**, Aldwych farce actor (1930s)

Why this farce, day after day?
—**Samuel Beckett**, *Endgame* (1958)

"Qui vive?" the sentinel shouted in the olden days to the stranger at the gate. "Vive le roi" was the reply or, as time went by, "Vive la liberté," or even later, "Vive la commune!" History moved on but the sentinel did not sleep, and, as our epoch changes, we, too, must at least ask, Who lives? even if we haven't settled on a name to express our hopes for the coming days.

Who lives, and who dies? It is a question as enduring as civilization and as contemporary as the debate over the death penalty. The connection is not gratuitous, as Newt Gingrich surely understood when, in drafting *his* blueprint for the future, the Contract With America, he pledged to "make the death penalty real." Doltish as he is, Gingrich is enough of a historian to have absorbed a central lesson of governance from the wellspring of Western civilization: the value of death in the maintenance of public order.

Tertullian, the African Christian of the second century, explained in his essay "Of the Public Shows" how in ancient Rome violent death was transformed into a way of life. As part of funeral rites, the Etruscans would sacrifice a few slaves to propitiate the spirit of a dead aristocrat. Their Roman conquerors borrowed this custom and expanded it as military education and character building, instituting games-to-the-death among the legions. Having learned in wartime to kill one another for the common good, during the Pax Romana they established the games as entertainment, war's grief assuaged and deflected by war's simulation. As Tertullian explained, "They found comfort for death in murder...."

Across the centuries we still have much to learn from the ancient fathers of our law, our statecraft, our military organization—not least how the ritual death of the few corresponds to the casual death of many.

California resumed the death penalty by gassing Robert Alton Harris in April of 1992. A week later, L.A. popped in a mega uprising. Sixty were killed. This was followed by the execution of a former coal miner in Virginia. A year later Bill Clinton, who had christened his presidential campaign with the execution of Ricky Ray Rector and his presidency with a bombing of Baghdad, sanctioned the gassing of women, men, boys and girls in the holocaust of Waco, Texas. Meanwhile, the official death penalties mounted: 1993 had the worst record since the reinstatement of the punishment in 1976.

Now Timothy McVeigh, trained by an empire to kill in foreign deserts, may have sought avenging comfort for death by bombing the Federal Building in Oklahoma City on the anniversary of Waco and on the day the white supremacist Richard Snell was executed in Arkansas. "Hail the victory," said Snell as last words, and warned the Governor, "Look over your shoulder." Hours later, after the Oklahoma bombing, the President's *lictor*, Janet Reno, hissed, "The death penalty is available, and we will seek it." She will be assisted by a D.A. who has already sent fifty-seven people to death row.

Thus the metronome of thanatocracy swings back and forth: Harris-L.A., Clinton-Rector, Reno-Waco, McVeigh-Oklahoma. It began even earlier, with MOVE, the anarchic black revolutionaries in Philadelphia whose struggle with the authorities is said to have culminated in the land and air assault that killed eleven people and incinerated sixty houses ten years ago but is hardly concluded, as Mumia Abu-Jamal, an early MOVE sympathizer, sits on Pennsylvania's death row, his execution scheduled for August 17. Tit for tat is the pattern.

In ancient Rome, Seneca the Younger reported of the gladiators, "And when the games stop for the intermission, they announce: 'A little throat-cutting in the meantime, so that there may still be something going on!'" There is the spirit of gallows humor in that; the spirit, too, of farce, which also originated in Roman times, as an interlude, a buffoonish mime of reality, between more serious dramas. Farce shares with the games an essence that Eric Bentley, the seminal modern critic of the form, expressed as "I'll murder you with my own bare hands." Tit for tat. It is the oldest plot of farce.

Farce is derived from the Latin *farcire*, and it means to stuff, as you might a goose. It is still a cooking term, which might explain the ridiculous reviewing of menus in the phenomenology of the death penalty. Governor Pataki of New York made good on his election promise and returned Thomas Grasso to Oklahoma for execution and a double cheeseburger, a can of spaghetti with meatballs, a dozen steamed mussels, a strawberry milkshake, half a pumpkin pie with whipped cream and mango—his last meal. Gluttony makes us forget most anything. Mitchell Rupe of Washington State grew to 400 pounds on popcorn, chips and candy bars, becoming too fat for a hanging, which, he successfully argued, by decapitating instead of asphyxiating him would become a cruel and unusual punishment. Rickey Ray Rector, virtually an idiot, saved his dessert to eat "afterwards." Other appetites distract as well: Westley Dodd, a murderer and auto-eroticist, was granted his request to be hanged in Washington in 1993, probably ejaculating as he swung. Texas abolished smoking in all prisons this past March. Georgia preceded Texas in this, and forbade the condemned Nicky Ingram to smoke until the last few minutes before he was "done," on April 7, 1995.

Once done, they are devoured for the public good. They both "pay" for their crime and "sacrifice" for science. The National Coalition to Abolish the Death Penalty reports that in China, where prisoners are shot according to the location of the organs desired (in the body if the corneas are needed, in the head, if kidneys), a fully equipped ambulance waits at execution scenes so that organs can be removed quickly. In 1993, Joseph Paul Jernigan, denied a court-ordered hearing on commutation, was executed in Texas. A few hours later his body was flown to the Health Sciences Center in Denver, where he was sawed into four and each quarter frozen in gelatin, prior to an elaborate procedure in which he was sliced by a cryomacrotome into 1,878 sections, the cuts then photographed, scanned into a computer and digitized, producing so much data that it took two weeks of uninterrupted time to download it on the Internet. Last November, the National Library of Medicine unveiled this "Visible Man" at the Radiological Society of North America. Can vivisection go further?

Children and dogs are essential to farce, and as any comedian will tell you, there's no competing with either. Last December, a Labrador retriever was ordered executed by lethal injection by Judge T. Ryland Dodson of Danville, Virginia. The dog had menaced three mail carriers. The incident raised an international campaign; forty Italian senators pleaded for clemency, as did Henry Kissinger on syndicated TV (he owns a Labrador). The dumb animal was spared. Had it been known that the retarded Rickey Ray Rector barked like a dog, Clinton's goose might have been cooked.

Or take children. Steve Roach of Virginia turned 19 in April, joining some forty teenagers on the American row. In 1993, the Virginia legislature voted to permit death sentences for 14 year olds; earlier this year in Simi Valley a juror explained why they put the youngest person on death row in California, age 20: "He got what was coming to him. This guy was cold." But it's hard to tell about emotions. Nicky Ingram was on Thorazine during his trial for murder.

As in farce, some canons of taste are maintained to protect the squeamish. Dr. Harold Hillman has studied such deaths in England for thirty-five years. "You cover the face of the person being electrocuted so you can't see them sweating, drooling and vomiting, their eyes sticking out and their faces going blue." A Maryland pharmacist says that pancuronium bromide is mixed into the lethal-injection cocktail to prevent coughing and involuntary muscular contradictions, "which might have made the witnesses to the execution uncomfortable." They find comfort for death in murder.

G.B. Shaw despised farce for its lack of social conscience. Exactly. The pratfalls provide the fun. Ted Koppel goes into the death house and witnesses the lethal injection of Mario Marquez, I.Q. 65. We are meant to keep a straight face. As of February (1995), of 138 lethal injections, at least ten have been botched. In 1988 in Texas, deadly fluids meant for Raymond Landry spurted toward witnesses when a tube burst. In 1985 technicians searched for a clean vein in the arms and legs of Stephen Morin for more than forty minutes. It took them sixty minutes to find a vein in Rickey Ray Rector. Several men have had bad reactions, moaning and heaving. Morris Thigpen, the former Commissioner of Corrections in Alabama, remembers how executioners once turned on the chair and... nothing happened. Later, "the members of the execution team who failed to connect the chair correctly to its power source apologized many times for their error."

We are at the edge of laughter and terror where sense turns to nonsense: that the man lived was a result of "human error," as Thigpen put it. (The error was rectified; the man was killed.) In California the Supreme Court affirms lower-court death penalty sentences with a forgiving legal practice known as the "doctrine of harmless error." In the topsy-turvy world of farce the truth is the opposite of appearances. Justice Clarence Thomas, stalwart hero of the capital punishers, achieved his high dignity via the claim that he was the victim of a "high-tech lynching." "Let the eagle scream," W.E.B. Du Bois wrote after a low-tech lynching in 1911 (a burning), "civilization is again safe."

The first time as farce, and the second time as farce—and whiteface at that. After white people began to complain about the lynching of other whites, Du Bois confessed: "We are taking a mean, almost criminal and utterly indefensible joy these days at lynching, licking, and mob rule in these lawless United States. With our thumbs shamelessly locked in our arm pits we are leaning back at a perilous angle and singing 'I told you so!' in the most cheerful of voices."

Farce begets cynicism. Du Bois, redirecting us to history, suggests a different response. Let us remember two stories.

One. The Holocaust of Waco in 1993, was preceded by the Horror of Waco of 1916, when 10,000 white people lynched a 17-year-old black illiterate hired cotton picker and mule driver named Jesse Washington. His ears, fingers and toes were cut off; he was unsexed; he was chained and dragged around town by a car; he was stoned by the mob until he was bloody. Next to the mayor's office he was hoisted upon a tree by means of a chain around his neck and repeatedly lowered into a fire. Later, his teeth were sold for $5 each. In 1916, 10,000 people killed one person; in 1993 one person killed a congregation. "Which is worse?" may be left an open question, though it is useful to remember that the point about decimation, the Roman military punishment, was not that one soldier in ten was randomly killed, but that the nine others deliberately did it. Murderers are *created*.

Two. Diamond Dick Rowland, an ordinary bootblack, accidentally stepped on the foot of a young white elevator girl in Tulsa, Oklahoma, in May of 1921. A few days later he was indicted for rape, and the newspapers urged lynching. "But when his life was threatened by a mob of whites, every one of the 15,000 Negroes of Tulsa, rich and poor, educated and illiterate, was willing to die to protect Dick Rowland," reported Walter White, the NAACP investigator writing in *The Nation*. In response, the police, National Guard and Ku Klux Klan together besieged Tulsa's Little Africa. Machine guns, armed men in automobiles, and dynamite dropped from planes destroyed 1,000 homes, killed at least 200 and led to the internment of 6,000 black people in "concentration camps." White concluded, "Perhaps America was served sleeping pills."

What do we know about then that we don't know about now? The 1916 Horror of Waco was a punishment of capitalism as well as race; as Du Bois spelled out in the pages of *Crisis*, it was an incident of terror within the political economy of peonage. The Tulsa inferno was the climax to a cycle of repression that began a few years earlier when seventeen Oklahoma Wobblies with Oil Field Workers Union were stripped, tied, whipped, tarred, feathered and threatened with hanging. The NAACP detailed how the inferno re-established a new basis for labor "peace" in the midcontinental oil fields. The cheap oil thus provided was the precondition of "Fordism" and the gasoline culture of twentieth-century America. These stories, described through the social and economic motions of their time, suggest a methodology against farce, and open the way to political resistance.

Qui vive? has a corollary—Who dies?—and the fact is, we know little about the people on death row. It contains people from all over the planet. It's racist too, though statistics such as the following perpetuate the farce:

	Black	**White**
The Row (3,009)	40%	48%
(U.S. death row population)		
Done	38%	55%
(those executed since 1976)		
Hogs (33)	9%	85%
(those forsaking appeal)		
Firstlings (29)	12%	88%
(first to go in each state)		

The volunteers, or "hogs," providing examples of propitiatory contrition, tend to be white. The firstlings tend to be white as well. Is this a fluke, or are we thus to be deceived into thinking that the system is not racist? Jim Crow jumps with laughter. "It is not simply the Ku Klux Klan; it is not simply weak officials; it is not simply inadequate, unenforced law," Du Bois continued, now sober, "it is deeper than all this: it is the in-grained spirit of mob and murder, the despising of women and the capitalization of children born of 400 years of Negro slavery and 4,000 years of government for private profit."

In the search of time that's not so long. Bread and circuses, said Juvenal, were enough to settle the class war in Rome; it was left to Fronto, the tutor of Marcus Aurelius, to explain how. As a palliative, the shows were superior to the bread, he said, since the bread dole was available only to the worst-off of the proletariat and then only individually, whereas the magnificent iteration of murder provided by the games was a collective experience: "By the shows the whole populace is kept in good humor." We call it farce not because Clinton does only one (or a few) while Caesar did 325 in a single show; we call it farce because knaves employ fools and call it justice.

Like farce, the death penalty is built upon a structure of absurdities. It is one among many forms of social and economic morbidity: police assassinations, the institutionalization of AIDS in prison, the casual slaughter of industry and the work machine, the Chernobyls and Bhopals. Then we add the incipient deaths of slower-working diseases in the industrial-medical complex, where triage occurs. From there to the social field of reproduction: the battering of women and the violence of the patriarchal family (94 percent of the murderers on death row suffered child abuse). Capital punishment has become an essential prop of international finance, whose structural adjustment programs impose death on hungry nations. In calling NAFTA a "death sentence," the Zapatistas captured the logic of our period. Violence presents itself as the law of value; social mischief masquerades as fate. Qui vive?

As Wendy Lesser points out, the death penalty is not theater. If it were we would be back in the Colosseum turning our thumbs up or down. There are men like Spartacus, the former gladiator, who refused to acquiesce in the stock roles of farce, or to die like dogs. "I want everybody to know I'm not ready to go," said Raymond Carl Kinnamon last year in Texas. He staged a thirty-minute filibuster to talk his way out of the death warrant; then he tried to slip out of the straps restraining him on the gurney. The warden and prison chaplain strapped him back in. Nick Ingram declined to arrange for a last meal, refused to make a last statement, glared at the witnesses and spat at the warden. Inmates stomped and banged on the walls at Holman prison in Alabama when a man was electrocuted in April, and in Pennsylvania when Keith Zettlemoyer was done the inmates howled, "Killers, Murderers."

The year 1995 began with the execution of Jesse DeWayne Jacobs, whose sister pulled the trigger (she got ten years) for the murder he was done for. Jacobs said, "I hope in my death I'm that little bitty snowball that starts to bury the death penalty." *The New York Times* commented, "This is not the only occasion—merely the worst in recent memory—when a death-penalty case spins out of control because prosecutors, juries and judges share a dispersed responsibility that allows each to duck and avoid blame." Pontius Pilate leaves the court shaking his head in dismay about the banality of evil. The man who shaved the head and gelled the scalp of Nick Ingram, preparing him for the electrodes, said, "It's just a job."

On May 3, in Missouri, the execution machine malfunctioned seven minutes after the poisons began dripping into Emmitt Foster's arms. The authorities drew the curtains—"We have a duty to protect the anonymity of the people involved in the execution process"—and a half-hour later declared the man dead. Some of the witnesses refused to sign off. Zettlemoyer was done by two anonymous executioners paid $300 each. The slogan outside the prison in Pennsylvania that night of May 2, just a few days shy of the tenth anniversary of the MOVE bombing, was "Shame! Shame! Shame!"

Where does it all lead? Telemachus, a monk from Asia Minor, went to Rome in A.D. 325, jumped into the Colosseum and endeavored to separate the gladiators. Although the spectators destroyed him on the spot for interrupting the show, it wasn't long before the games came to an end. Such protest is what the abolitionist Sam Sheppard, whose mother was murdered and father almost electrocuted for it in the notorious Ohio case of the 1950s, is honoring as he walks across America's Death Belt, from Massachusetts to Louisiana. He aims to arrive in New Orleans in August, in time for the National Coalition to Abolish the Death Penalty's meeting.[1] He is pointing a way.

Qui vive? The successive answers of old—king, liberty, commune—alert us to other transformative moments in history. The transition from feudalism brought burning at the stake to untold numbers of women, and genocide to indigenous populations of the Americas. The transition to industrial capitalism brought "Albion's fatal tree," the American lynchings, wars of terror against civilians and, at the fork in the road, the Soviet gulag. We suppose these organizations of violent death were neither "the labor pangs of the birth of a new era" nor "the death throes of the old"—metaphors of inevitability. Rather, we suppose they were part of the political science of government, and thus susceptible to human action. It is no different today, facing a period the ruling class likes to call the New World Order.

"The first law which it becomes a reformer to propose and support, at the approach of a period of great political change, is the abolition of the punishment of death," stated Percy Shelley in 1813, at another time of epochal shift. Hence, reformers, ecologists, autonomists, trade unionists, anarchists, socialists, teachers, organizers, agitators, preachers, feminists, social changers of every kind and stripe—whatever else we do locally and globally—must defy the farce of the death penalty.

Qui vive? Mumia Abu-Jamal answers, "I am we."

---

[1] To support Sam Sheppard, contact Alternatives Walk, Box 167, Arkansas City, KS 67005; (316) 442-8556.

•••

ELIOT KATZ
Lessons from an Uneasy Chair

Through a hazy cloud of violence begetting violence;
amidst confusion of unseen shooters vanishing around thick-aired alleyways;
among a swirl of random bullets ricocheting off unknown origins;
between an emergency room bedside nonconfession nonrecalled for two months
& a gas station owner's nonexistent narratives shredded & tossed into
        a homicide detective's disintegrating can;
only the state executioner's clear desire to murder stands tall & indisputable.
Here lies a robeless hanging judge;
here a fraternal disorder of dysfunctional police;
here autochthonic tragedy gives birth to social calamity;
here the young learn how meaningless a thoughtful life appears still on the
        post-Cold War screen

From this chair lessons look easy:
flick a switch or lethally inject—
then put yr feet up
& watch another nation fall.

•••

TRACIE MORRIS
The Old Days

It ain't necessarily so,
It aint necessarily so.
A Black rights revival we
need for survival,

It ain't necessarily so.
The vestige of fairness
has failed.
The vestige of fairness
has paled.
To be shot on sight and
not be read your rights,
Well, the vestige of
fairness has paled....

Thurgood Marshall got the 'hell-out-of-dodge.'
He was livin' 'large' but tired of the mirage
of fairness via the opinion of dissent.
Frequently forced to vent.
It was a drag he had
to go out that way.
Least now we've stripped
away the facade of equality.

And now we got a
Clarence Thomas situation.
Black face in the wrong place
to represent my nation.
Folks ain't even faking like
we free, and it feels like
the old days to me.

Yes, indeed.

...We'll soon revert to Jim Crow.
'Cause the courts were the last place to go.
We're right back to crisis despite sacrifices.
Our people hit with a death blow.
'Cause it ain't necessarily so.

•••

©1995 GREGORY BENTON
respectfully dedicated to Mumia Abu Jamal.

THEODORE A. HARRIS
The Housing Authority
(A poem based on a collage by John Abner)

I hear cell doors slamming
shut in her screams
in shadows from the bars
cross-hatched split her face

she is a tenant
in a rusted world multiplying
like shanty towns
in South Africa constructed
from a blueprint for destruction
where multitudes are contained
in a social straight jacket
       unfit for human habitation

they stole the music
from her heart
    her mother was arrested
for voicing outrage
against living conditions
in the projects policed
by overseers

that dragged her through
the streets
where there are no covers
on the manholes

•••

PATRICIA J. WILLIAMS
The Executioner's Automat

While walking to work one day, I passed in front of an idling cop car. I glanced at the driver—white with brown hair, and wearing dark shades. He "smiled", put his hand out the car window, and pointed a finger at me, his thumb cocked back like the hammer of a gun; bang-bang the finger jerked, as if from recoil, and the cop gave it a cowboyish blast of breath before returning it to an imaginary holster. He and his pal laugh. Car rolls. Whatta joke, I thought, as I sat down to type up an interview with three women known as the Pointer Sisters, post- "Salt Peanuts" phase. But it was hard to concentrate. There was only one kind of pointing on my mind. And it wasn't those glitzy sisters.

***

On December 9, 1981, the police attempted to execute me in the street. This trial is the result of their failure to do so. Just as the police tried to kill my brothers and sisters of the family Africa on August the 8th, 1978.

—Mumia Abu-Jamal
Live from Death Row

On July 3, 1982, Mumia Abu-Jamal, radio journalist and MOVE supporter, much of whose reputation was built on criticizing the Philadelphia Police Department in the matter of race relations, was convicted of the first-degree murder of officer Daniel Faulkner. Abu-Jamal, who had no prior record, was a Peabody Award-winning radio essayist and president of the Philadelphia chapter of the National Association of Black Journalists. After the conviction, he continued to write from his cell on death row, publishing everywhere from *The Nation* to the *Yale Law Journal*. In 1994, he was at the center of a very visible controversy in which some members of Congress threatened to cut off funding to National Public Radio, which had been set to broadcast a series of his editorials. Amid intense public debate, National Public Radio canceled the broadcasts. "Many believed that NPR was giving a monster a soapbox," reads the legend on the flap of Abu-Jamal's just-published *Live from Death Row*, in which those never-aired commentaries are printed.

Abu-Jamal, who denies killing Officer Faulkner, has become the object of one of those debates that go to the core of the deepest racial divides in this country. Is he the victim of a police conspiracy designed to silence his radical political coverage? Is he, a former Black Panther, in effect a Randy Weaver of the black left? Is he a cold-blooded killer who is now manipulating public sentiment? Does he not deserve a second trial on the substantive merits, given some fairly serious procedural irregularities in the first—or should he be executed summarily in the new spirit of dispatch that swept Pennsylvania's Governor Tom Ridge into power last November? On June 2, Ridge, making good on a campaign-promised "priority," signed a warrant for Abu-Jamal to be executed on August 17, 1995.

Add to this American drama the passionate grief of Faulkner's widow, Maureen, who, with the help of the Philadelphia Fraternal Order of Police, mounted a concerted effort to prevent publication of *Live from Death Row*, and now to prevent Abu-Jamal from receiving any profits from its sale. Other lobbying efforts have been put in motion to redirect any profits to various victims' rights organizations.

It is impossible to sort out the "truth" of this case at the distance from which I write. Nevertheless, weighing the improprieties of Abu-Jamal's trial (including possible suppression of evidence) against the life-or-death stakes for him, I am convinced that Abu-Jamal deserves another trial. Of course, I don't believe that we should have a death penalty at all, and if we must, it ought never to be employed unless there is *no* doubt—not just beyond a reasonable doubt, but none at all—that the defendant committed the crime. Laypeople, certainly not jaded former prosecutors like me, are the only ones who really believe that trials can resolve much more than probabilities; and probably not too many laypeople share that bright faith anymore, a year into O.J. Simpson's eternal, Sisyphean life-sentence of a trial. In the annals of criminology, the passage of a little time has exonerated too many of the convicted for us to be engaging in the headlong rush toward Quick Death that seems so politically popular these days.

That said, it seems to me that Mumia Abu-Jamal's case presents a particularly pressing set of questions for us as a society. The matter of the death penalty is certainly the heart of what we must think about; but the controversy surrounding Abu-Jamal's book highlights the degree to which many people seem to assume prisoners have no right to speak, no right to be heard, no right to publication and thus, in a very concrete sense, no right to appeal.

It is an interesting and dangerous confluence that politicians like Pennsylvania State Representative Michael McGeehan urge simultaneously the limiting of inmates' ability to write journalistically as well as the limiting of the right of habeas corpus. According to McGeehan, Abu-Jamal "believes he is the Donald Trump of death row.... He's trying to get rich by running a little cottage industry while family members of the slain officer suffer." In March, at the urging of McGeehan and others, Governor Ridge signed House Bill 1, which "requires the governor to sign an execution warrant within ninety days of his receipt of the affirmation of the death sentence from the Pennsylvania Supreme Court. If the governor misses the deadline, the commissioner of corrections must schedule the execution without a warrant."

It is striking, furthermore, that the discussion of Abu-Jamal's book is so often put in economic terms, filled with metaphoric turns away from the issue of speech: He-who-is-about-to-die is making a "profit," a "killing," making money, not an appeal. I have heard some justify this sort of suppression by saying that he's in prison, after all—he has no right of free speech (to say nothing of the free market) because he's *lost* his freedom. But this misunderstands the status of prisoners. They do not lose all human rights. And if there ever was a right that is central to our democracy, it is the ability to express, to be heard, to publish, to appeal the matter of state-sponsored life and death. We as a society must be quite careful not to glorify suppression of prisoners' voices in the name of not glorifying violence.

And while, in principle, the idea of using prisoners' profits for victims' funds seems unobjectionable, we must remember that justice in our society is too often obtained at a very high price. "The Simpson case proved one thing about our system," writes Bella English in *The Boston Globe*. "Money talks.... Remember the unemployed immigrant arrested the same week as O.J. and also charged with killing his wife? He was tried, convicted and sent to jail all in a day." In an era when the Legal Services Corporation is on the threshold of Congressional elimination and prisoners' rights organizations operate largely on the charity of the organized bar, the revolving-door justice meted out to the "unemployed immigrant" is unfortunately typical. In Tennessee, for another example, U.S. District Judge John Nixon has come under political fire for vacating the death sentence of a man whose defense attorney had spent only sixteen hours on the case, allowed the defendant to be sedated by jail officers during the trial, failed to raise available defenses and "effectively abandoned representation." In addition to demanding Nixon's impeachment, legislators unanimously voted to eliminate state funding of the Capital Case Resource Center, the organization that uncovered these irregularities. This meant that the Center, overnight, lost nearly 40 percent of its budget.

In a letter of June 6, Abu-Jamal writes:

> *As you no doubt know, I am on Phase II with an active Death Warrant for*
> *Aug. 17, 1995: A Jail w/ in a jail, w/ in a jail... and about to enter another*
> *jail. Yesterday, I rec'd a 5-pp. Misconduct Report (#696776) for "engaging*
> *actively in a business or profession"— as a "working journalist." In effect, my*
> *"misconduct" was writing* Live from Death Row, *and publishing it ... .*
> *They want me to die alone—silently. So much do they fear my words that they*
> *want me muzzled as they prepare to garrote me.*

There's hypocrisy in it, you have to admit: If Sergeant Stacey Koon, convicted of directing the assault on Rodney King, can publish his rambling rationalizations for the glories of excessive violence in *Presumed Guilty: The Tragedy of the Rodney King Affair*, and if ex-con G. Gordon Liddy can stand on the steps of the Lincoln Memorial and rally gun rights supporters by shouting "just don't obey the damn law"— if the First Amendment protects all that, then it ought to protect Mumia Abu-Jamal's description of "Harry Washington," a death row inmate who

> *has begun the slide from depression, through deterioration, to dementia....*
> *The conditions of most of America's death rows create Harry Washingtons*
> *by the score... solitary confinement, around-the-clock lock-in, no-contact*
> *visits, no prison jobs, no educational programs by which to grow, psychiatric*
> *"treatment" facilities designed only to drug you into a coma; ladle in hostile,*
> *overtly racist prison guards and staff; add the weight of the falling away of*
> *family ties, and you have all the fixings for a stressful psychic stew designed to*
> *deteriorate, to erode, one's humanity.*

Abu-Jamal's is hardly an idle "book by a monster" preaching death, teaching death or celebrating violence—it is a book of mourning for the condemned. Mourning the condemned as well as the innocent is something we don't practice a lot in this era. But I think it is central to the project of asking what it is that accounts for the enormous toll of violence at this moment in history. It is a task that requires that we not turn to explanations of genetic inferiority and biological disposition except in the most exceptional of instances; but rather demands that we ask what it is that would make some lives so wildly destructive. It involves seeing even killers as ruined human beings whose potential has been lost to us, and whose loss *means something* to the community, to the increasingly small world we all share. If we feel no loss but only gain, I fear we are indeed on the wrong side of a thin line whose logic leads to the worst kinds of depotism.

We need more writing from inmates, I think, for writing is redemptive for those on both sides of the walls. We need whole jailhouse anthologies. It is worth understanding, this desperation, this cold-bloodedness, this drained hoplessness, this murderous rage. It is worth understanding—a statement that many will read instantly as the equivalent of "worth condoning, worth forgiving, worth being a fuzzy-headed liberal fool."

I appreciate the extent to which my remarks will be interpreted as an apology for nothing less than heinousness. Which surely they are not; I believe in prisons, and in life sentences; too many of us have seen friends murdered senselessly. I recognize the need to confine murderers. No less than Robert Dole and William Clinton do, I sorrow for the violence that grips us as a nation. But I do not believe in the death penalty.

I appreciate how hard my point will be to hear in an age when television stations have sued to broadcast executions as part of our constitutional freedom. How much we want to see but not hear death! (Isn't it odd, when executions occur, that the newspapers always print the last supper of the executed rather than his last thoughts? An altogether peculiar obsession, the advertisement of what he consumed, but not what he was thinking. Like reading tea leaves, the publishable but indecipherable clue, that last hamburger and chocolate milk....)

I appreciate, in short, how unpopular it is to say that even the destructive life bears lessons whose social value we suppress at our own risk. But I think it is an integral part of never forgetting—to be reminded of how seductive murder is as a solution. How close the killer is to the executioner in the search for ultimate resolution. How like ourselves. How appealing it is to control life and death, and how implicated are those who "assist" in death, in overcoming the body's resistance. Thus, I think it is absolutely vital to allow prisoners to appeal as loud and as long as they can—for, as John Edgar Wideman observes, "People are easier to kill if they come from nowhere. If they have no names, no fathers or mothers." We should never be able to kill without that reminder of the body's resistance.

Let me try to press this difficult point by posing the problem as a broad one about the limits of state force. What is, after all, the purpose in refraining from cruel and unusual punishment even for cruel and unusual crimes? Why didn't we just eviscerate Jeffrey Dahmer when we had the chance, for surely one good evisceration deserves another? Why don't we let the families of victims stone criminals, or slice off their tongues? Why don't we officially entomb prisoners alive, in soundproofed little boxes, a hole for air, a hole for drainage, and just wait for them to die like bugs in a jar?

Conventions on human rights and prisoners' rights remind us that casting criminals as subhuman, as animals, as noncitizens, is as much about us as it is "them." They remind us that demonizing wholesale is a risky enterprise. We have not yet reached the point where we are completely unaware of this notion; few politicians could yet suggest that we just stop pussyfooting around and execute everyone convicted of murder, period. O.J. Simpson and Susan Smith. Colin Ferguson and Gina Grant (the young woman admitted to Harvard before it was discovered she had bludgeoned her mother to death with a candlestick). The Menendez brothers. Robert McNamara, for all those war crimes he's now so willing to take responsibility for. Oh, and Timothy McVeigh, should he ever be convicted. We'd all sleep better afterward. Better yet, we could execute them all at the same time. It could be the biggest, best execution in U.S. history. If we want deterrence, what better way, right? We could make it really special and use that big screen that Disney set up on the Great Lawn of Central Park for the viewing of *Pocahontas,* and we could broadcast it live as a public service. The mothers of the victims could step up and throw the first ball, so to speak, by plucking the eyes from the sockets of the condemned. And where once there were baskets into which heads would roll, we could have Dr. Jack Kervorkian with a bucket for the hearts and lungs and livers. (Kervorkian has long been an advocate of "harvesting" the innards of executed prisoners. He wants death row to *move,* shouldn't let all those healthy spare parts shrivel on the vine. What high-tech resurrection potential: death row as the ultimate recycling bin.)

Frankly, the current fashion in calling for what is effectively a public ritual of mockery and crucifixion of criminals is astounding in a nation as largely Christian as ours. It is pagan in form, the call for Death—Retributive Zeus and Howling Hera reborn in Bernhard Goetz and Lorena Bobbit, outlaws no longer but models of the new age of civic virtue, private visionaries of vengeance whose politics have public power these days. When Clinton and Janet Reno invoked the death penalty immediately after the Oklahoma City bombing, it had a hollow, helpless ring—a kind of stunning irrelevance and inadequacy in view of the tragedy already accomplished. The perpetrators will die, we were promised. Why don't I find that comforting? What score could it possibly settle? How futile, how beside the point. Why am I not convinced that a terrorist's date with the gas chamber will do anything but enhance his heroic status to some? And I am absolutely convinced that no execution will do anything to reduce the likelihood of future terrorism.

Yet we have come close to the point, I fear, where all forms of punishment inflicted upon criminals are deemed acceptable as crude but just payback. "Slow bloodletting" is less than what "the criminal slime" deserve, as a law student once put it so succinctly. I suppose we could comfort ourselves with the thought that the clean efficiency of the poison needle, the electric jolt, the quiet waft of gas is ever so much better than they deserve. We could employ the ethics of gang warfare infinitely extended: Kill and be killed. Conceptualizing the suffering of criminals as payback has the extra benefit of removing responsibility from us as voters, taxpayers, fellow citizens, participants in the decision—because, after all, criminals bring it all on themselves. "Automatic" sentencing is an outgrowth of such logic. "Automatic" death.

But it is democracy that dies when we become a nation of heartbroken vengeance-seekers. The seduction of the "string 'em up" mentality is not that it's "frontier" justice in some cruel, cartoonish way. Its appeal is precisely that it is a response of insatiable sorrow, immediate payback; it is heroically grief-stricken rather than reasoned. Moreover, the rage for retribution risks obscuring the possibility of innocence, the need for due process, the presence of mitigating circumstances and the dubiety of crooked informants. And in its most extreme forms, the bloodlust risks being used to justify the state practice of sadism upon all those guilty bodies so *needing* to be beaten, so *asking* to be broken. We despise murderers, we hate. But there is some point at which the despising takes on a life of its own; when the death-dealing actually becomes satisfying and eventually pleasurable. That sense of relief, that rush of goodness is what seems to be growing in this country; what we should resist at all costs; and what Abu-Jamal's essays hold mirrors to with every page.

All this is why we have historically made the prosecutor's role that of representing The People of a state, rather than just the victim of a particular crime. The prosecutor, as surrogate for the interests of the state, is supposed to consider justice in an uninflamed, long-term, social sense.

But the risks of enjoying vengeance too much are troubling enough when we have spectacles like the barbecuing, sun-bathing crowds at serial killer Ted Bundy's execution. If one adds race to the brew, we must take history seriously enough to err on the side of extreme caution. The chain gang has made a comeback in Alabama's largely black-populated prisons. Domination fantasies have become disguised as lessons in work ethic. Writes Mumia Abu-Jamal:

> *In the 1987* McClesky v. Kemp *case, the famed Baldus study revealed facts that unequivocally proved the following: (1) defendants charged with killing white victims in Georgia are 4.3 times as likely to be sentenced to death as defendants charged with killing blacks; (2) six of every eleven defendants convicted of killing a white person would not have received the death sentence if their victim had been black; and (3) cases involving black defendants and white victims are more likely to result in a death sentence than cases featuring any other racial combination of defendant and victim....*

> *Does this mean that African-Americans are somehow innocents, subjected to a setup by state officials? Not especially. What it does suggest is that state actors, at all stages of the criminal justice system, including slating at the police station, arraignment at the judicial office, pretrial, trial, and sentencing stage before a court, treat African-American defendants with a special vengeance not experienced by white defendants. This is the dictionary definition of "discrimination."*

One of racism's many manifestations is the collective wish that blacks were not alive—one can hear this expressed over and over again on talk-radio programs around the country any day of the week. The wish that blacks would just go away and shut up and stop taking up so much time and food and air and then the world would return to its Norman Rockwell loveliness and America could be employed and happy once more. Sometimes it's expressed as an actual death wish, but more often it comes out as a *disappearance* wish. But the sentiment is no less frightening to those of us on the receiving end of such categoric euphemisms. Moreover, the killing wish takes on such public, even joyous legitimacy when blackness is paired with actual outlaw behavior.

There is a relation, I think, between the restraint necessary in law enforcement and the First Amendment cliché about protecting most the speech one hates because it is a test for all the rest of our democratic principles. Should we not, through our government, practice and model the kind of restraint we wish killers could have had? We wish that before they had twisted that knife, pulled that trigger, they had considered the mind they were destroying, the family they were rending, the shattering, spinning loss—the ripped life so suddenly and eternally unrecoverable. Focusing on the crime they have committed reminds us of the need to make sure it never happens again, and we apply varying degrees of punishment, deterrence or rehabilitation. But focusing as well on *who* has committed the crime reminds us that there is a logic in each life. Not so much a logic to be endured or sanctioned, but sometimes a life course that sheds light on what should never have been.

We need to remember that there are prison guards who help prisoners in good and human ways, *and* that there are those who supply them with drugs. We need to know that there are guards who struggle thanklessly to do remarkable jobs under intolerable conditions, *and* those, as Abu-Jamal describes, who put lighted cigarettes in prisoners' ears. We need to know that the sides are not always as clear as night and day—that "Harry Washington," demented on death row, was once a prison guard. We need to consider these as possibilities because some of the people who are in prison will be back among us—we have not yet decided to kill all of them—and if prison ends up spewing out people who are more dehumanized than when they went in, it will cost us dearly.

We need to know because if the officially sanctioned acts of society's guardians turn sadistic, we ought to wonder if there are sadists walking freely among us. We must entertain the unpleasant possibility that perhaps we have lost the ability to distinguish the excess of sadism from the desire for public protection. This does not mean that we have to believe everything every prisoner has to say any more than juries believe every defendant. But *Live from Death Row* pushes the reader to think about the degree to which the death penalty has become a cipher for all that ails us—no longer the ultimate draconian barter-machine. "A death for a death, it's only fair," is how I heard one 11-year-old put it, so childishly, so confidently, so chillingly, in an editorial on a children's radio program. The executioner's automat.

Vengeance is mine, saith the Lord. Vengeance is also the sovereign's, and it is a godlike power. When we send citizens to prison as a way of telling them to go to hell, the state engages in the creation of Good and Evil. It is a powerful art, that magic power over life, a practice that must be approached with care and restraint. For the culture of death is as generative as any life force. Execution is a sacrifice, a religious enterprise. Its unholiness is a powerful agent, never to be approached without a strong sense of taboo. It is a ritual not to be confused with taking out the trash. When the sacrifice of citizens, even reprehensible citizens, degenerates into a bonfire of catharsis and blood feuds, our institutions fuel their own illegitimacy. And when we engage in the public pretense that there are no voices in the bonfires on the other side of prison walls, we conspire only in the ultimate loss of our own.

•••

SALLY O'BRIEN
Interview with Mumia Abu-Jamal

Holding Cell at Sheriff's Department
City Hall, Philadelphia, August 10, 1995
by **Sally O'Brien**, Pacifica Radio, WBAI, New York
Heike Kleffner, for Sueddeutsche Zeitung, Munich, Germany

SO: *We are unbelievably here with Mumia Abu-Jamal, sitting in a little room in the sheriff's holding pen in the court house in Philadelphia. Mumia, it's good to finally talk to you. Let's just begin by asking you, a couple of weeks ago you said that this trial is simply a repeat of what happened thirteen years ago. I am wondering in light of the stay, do you still feel that way?*

MAJ: I probably feel it more now than before. The reason is simple. Many conservative black and white commentators looking at my original trial excoriated and criticized me viciously for my "animalistic behavior." They criticized me, verbalizing my position regarding representation by John Africa for counsel, and they criticized me for criticizing the judge. As many people have seen during this hearing, I have been absolutely silent. I have not criticized the counselors, because for this reason—they are very good counsel, there is no reason to criticize them. What they have shown throughout this hearing is what should have happened throughout the trial. Had they been representing me then, the results would have been astoundingly different. I think that is clear to everyone. But also, what should be clear to everyone is that the behavior of the judge has not changed one iota. I haven't made one peep, I haven't said anything controversial—or uncontroversial for that matter—however, one of my lawyers, Rachel Wolkenstein, was thrown into jail, not far from where we are speaking right now, up on the seventh floor in the sheriff's office, for thirty-five minutes for daring to try to defend her client. Len Weinglass [Mumia's current lawyer] has been threatened with contempt, jailing and a $1000 fine if he doesn't "Sit down and shut up NOW, counsel"—in those words—by the judge. These are things that are happening while I am sitting silently. Which tells anyone with half a brain that had I sat silently at my original trial, then it wouldn't have been very different—either in the result or in the so-called controversy that resulted from the trial and the sentencing itself. It is, as I said earlier, déjà vu all over again.

SO: *Then the obvious question is, how are you holding up? There are a lot of people who have been watching you, who have rallied around you, who have mobilized internationally and nationally and locally, and people really want to know, how is Mumia, how is your head? How are you dealing with this?*

MAJ: I am overwhelmed with the waves and flood of affection, love and support that has been generated both internationally and nationally, and unfortunately, but realistically, to a lesser extent, locally. Overwhelmed is probably an understatement. Considering everything that we have been through, I feel very, very lucky to have that kind of support. I am appreciative to the thousands and perhaps tens of thousands of people. I don't even know their names, but I carry them with me in my heart every day and thank them. It is also interesting when one considers the wide breadth of people who are part of our movement. They are not all radicals, they are not all ex-Black Panthers or whatever. Some of them are people, who are religious like the Bruderhofs (Bruderhof Community), for example, or Christians, or whatever persuasions, or the Academics [Academics for Mumia Abu-Jamal]. No one could have predicted that this movement would have grown and mushroomed as it has among such a broad spectrum of people—but it has. And I am sincerely and deeply grateful to everyone.

SO: *Does it help sustain you?*

MAJ: Yes, it is a flood to be sure. But it is a flood that doesn't threaten to drown me, but it just carries me from day to day, from point to point, from threat to threat, from death to life.

SO: *What was your reaction to the stay? How do you perceive this decision?*

MAJ: Of course, my human reaction to the stay was gratitude. It was completely unexpected. My lawyers would probably tell you in their most honest moments that I was stunned as they were, we never expected this from Judge Sabo. However, when you look at it from a legal, political broad perspective, it seemed as if he was doing what was inevitable. If you read the text of the stay that was released by the judge, he says, it was required by law, because the defendant had a number of appeals that remain. Well, those appeals that remained were there on the second day after my warrant was signed. They were there the first day of our hearing. They were there on the second day of our hearing. They were there on the Thursday before the stay was issued, when my lead counsel Leonard Weinglass respectfully requested a stay. It is not something that just happened in the last ten days. I think it is only fair to say, that it was a legal inevitability. Of course, I am glad that my family would not have to suffer over this period.

I think it is noteworthy also to point out that of all the people on death row in the Commonwealth of Pennsylvania, I spent the longest period of time in Phase 2 (on death watch). But not only in Phase 2— I have spent the longest period of time in Phase 2, and I am the only one, except for Robert Atkins, another brother on death row, to spend DC time (disciplinary custody) while in Phase 2. Robert Atkins spent about a week and a half on DC time, before he got his stay, on Phase 2, because he demanded a phone call to his lawyer who was going to file federal habeas corpus papers the next day, and the jail denied him a phone call, and he blocked the camera that we had in our cell for 24 hours and they went bonkers and wrote him up. I received two write-ups. One for writing *Live from Death Row*, for "participating in a business or profession," i.e. journalism. And the other for writing to the editor of *Prison Legal News*, Paul Wright, a nationally and perhaps internationally published legal publication for and by and about legal issues covering prisoners. Both of these write-ups were directed to make my Phase 2 stay the most horrific in Pennsylvania history. And to a

SHAWN ALEXANDER

large extent they succeeded by isolating me, by holding me to one visit per month, no phone calls and further, tampering with my mail, because I was now in DC. I might add, that even when I was in AC (administrative custody) and not under disciplinary status, we have now learned that for a period of about a year, if not longer, every letter that I have ever sent, that I have ever written to my lawyer, and every letter that he has ever written to me—and I am talking about my criminal lawyer handling my appeals and all of my lawyers—has been intercepted, opened, copied and sent to the government of Pennsylvania. So, I place that in that context.

SO: *It seems that the more they tried to silence you, the further the word gets out about you. So, the more silent they try to make you, the louder your voice becomes, and I am wondering what your analysis is about why your case has drawn such international and national attention. Why the fire?*

MAJ: I think I would like to know that myself. That is not an easy question because I don't pretend to know. I wish I knew, I would do it better, I would do it more. But I have some suspicions and I think part of it is that people see when they look at certain parts of the trial or even the sentence or whatever, in their hearts and in their heads, they know what is fair and what is unfair. I think that the point that I made a few days ago in my note to the Reverend Jesse Jackson was that if I were an Aryan Brother, a member of the Aryan Brotherhood, the white racist prison gang, or a Satanist, a card-carrying member of the Satanic Church for instance, I would not be on death row, even if I were guilty, I would not be on death row. This is not just a hip slick thing to say, for the U.S. Supreme Court has said precisely the same thing. Because in *Dawson v. Delaware* and the *State of Nevada v. Flanegan*— two cases that went up to the Supreme Court—two people from two different states on death row—they had their sentences reversed automatically. Because the First Amendment right of association forbade the state from using the membership of a member of the Aryan Brotherhood on the one hand, and the religious belief of a Satanist in witchcraft or Satanism, etc., —they are forbidden from using that in the sentencing phase of a capital case. However, no court has ever ruled that in the case of *Commonwealth v. Abu-Jamal*, where the Commonwealth has used as a tool for death my membership in the Black Panther Party to convince the jury, this is a reason for that man to die. In fact, if you read the cases coming out of Delaware, if you read the *State of Delaware v. Dawson*, you will find one case cited to support his case because the Delaware Supreme Court, a majority, affirmed his conviction and the death sentence. In its direct appeal to the US Supreme Court, the Delaware Supreme Court couldn't find any cases in Delaware, so they leapt over to Pennsylvania, and they found *Commonwealth v. Abu-Jamal.*

SO: *In essence, it is very much a part of the time we are living in.... How does that make you feel to know that you sit in what is mostly perceived as a powerless position and yet, you are unifying a movement?*

MAJ: I assure you that in the sense that we use the term "power," there are few people who are as powerless as are those people who are on death row. Coming from someone who was on Phase 2—who was under 24-hour watch—every time I slept someone was watching me.

Every time I woke up someone was watching me. Every time I went to the bathroom someone was watching me. Every time I ate someone was watching me. Every step I took, two or three guards were watching me. That doesn't sound like a position of power.

To the extent that there is power, it is people who recognize in my life-experience something of themselves. I wouldn't use the term power, I would use the term that we share something, because we share part of that human experience. And I try to share in my writing, in my everyday experience, things that people recognize in themselves. I would say that is probably the best definition for why some people are motivated to support this movement. Because, when you look at what the state has been doing and has been trying to do for years and years—they are trying to figuratively break my fingers and gag me, shut me up and stop me from writing. I am not the only person [in prison] in Pennsylvania who wrote a book. I am not the only person [in prison] in Pennsylvania who made a tape for broadcasting in radio. I am not the only person [in prison] in Pennsylvania who wrote to a newspaper that is published by a prisoner.

There is a newspaper known as *Inside Journal,* which is published by the National Prisoner Foundation, I think, out of Washington, D.C. Every prison in the United States distributes it through their religious communities, their Christian communities for the most part. The articles in there are written exclusively by prisoners and ex-prisoners, but no one has been written up for writing to this journal, and no one has been written up for writing for any other prison journal—except myself.

SO: *A lot of people are wondering, how you spend your time, especially how you spent your time while you were in disciplinary custody, but also in general. How do you manage to go on day by day?*

MAJ: Well, you know I am gonna do this. I am gonna turn the microphone and ask you, what do you think.... Make a guess.

SO: *I think you spend a lot of time reading and writing, but I don't know, that's why I ask you.... There is a lot of time spent thinking, dreaming and writing. But it would be good to walk through a day.*

MAJ: One of the hells of prison is the sameness of prison. Every day is the same. Every morning is like every other morning. Every night is like the night before. I spent my time on disciplinary custody doing what I do best—talking [laughter]. When I was up in Greene County I spent my time—lucky for me, not lucky for the other guys— there were three other men on Phase 2 with me. We talked for hours. Some of the men I had been around for ten years and we had never talked very much. But when you are next to someone with a date to die, you begin talking. We did human things, we talked. We talked about our children, we talked about the loves of our lives, we talked about jail, we talked about politics, we talked about everything. One guy next to me, we talked about science, all kinds of stuff. So we talked. When I came down to Graterford for the hearing, where they do not have cameras, but they had guards actually sitting there, I talked to the guards [laughter]. We talked like two people. And that was how the experience was overcome and prevailed upon in human ways. I did spend a lot of time thinking, I did spend some time writing. I did not spend a lot of time reading, because I didn't have that much to read. You work with what you have to get what you need. I think the [Black Panther] Party used to call it "juche," back in the Black Panther days. But you work with what you have to get what you need. That was what I did, that's what I had to do. There is no magic to it.

SO: *People are also wondering whether you have been able to see your family at all, have you been able to communicate with them and how is it for you to see them in the courtroom and not being able to walk over to them?*

MAJ: To the extent that the courtroom is, as I call it, the "corridor to hell," the "corridor to decimation," to me it has been a joy to see some of my children and grandchildren. During the period that I was on Phase 2, I only had one visit per month. And because we are so far away in Greene County it is almost impossible. Several weeks before I was placed on Phase 2, in fact in April of this year, one of my sons, one of my daughters, and two of my grandchildren came up to see me and the prison would only let my oldest son in, not my grandchildren and not my daughter. They said that my grandchildren—one at that time age three and the other age seven—were not on my visiting list. So they refused an entry, even after they had come hundreds of miles across the state of Pennsylvania. My daughter, they said, did not have the proper I.D. that they felt was sufficient. I have only recently seen one of my grandsons for the first time. I have never in all of their lives had the pleasure of holding them in my lap or touching them or playing with them. As you see now, there is this barrier between us of *plies* and *Plexiglass*. Those are the kind of barriers that exist in most prisons throughout the state of Pennsylvania.

SO: *Especially abroad, people are wondering why the state is so viciously attacking you. What do you think makes you so dangerous and such a threat that they are trying to silence you while you are still alive, and that they are and have been trying to kill you?*

MAJ: Well, I think here is the perfect place to turn to the ADEX files in the COINTELPRO papers. Recently my lawyers uncovered over 800 pages of FBI documents that were not released during my original trial, which revealed that from the time I was 14 or 15, from the time I became active in the Black Panther Party and in fact even before, FBI agents followed me, talked to informers who were around me, listened in on phone conversations, intercepted mail that I sent to people. This is decades ago. We are talking about the late 60s and the early 70s, and in fact up until 1991, when I got a visit from a delegation of people from a Political Prisoners Convention that was held in New York, that is recorded in my FBI files. All I can say is that this system, this government, does not want anyone objecting to their picture of reality. They do not want anyone resisting their structure, their system, their government, their "authority." It is amazing when you consider that a 15- or 14-year-old boy is being taped, pursued, surveilled by the highest government agencies of America. Not for anything that he has done, but for what he reads, for what he writes and for what he believes.

The FBI documents are heavily censored. Names are struck out, phone numbers are struck out, but what is very, very clear if you read them is precisely that point: They considered me a "threat to national security"—a 15-year-old snotty nosed boy, because I wrote some articles in the *Black Panther Newspaper* that they didn't like. In fact, if one were to review those files, you would find several instances in several states, in fact effecting several countries, where I was named as a suspect in murders, in armed robbery that I had absolutely nothing to do with... when I am in my teens, do you understand what I am saying? If I were not working at the time–and for most of my life I have done different kinds of jobs–then I would have been suspect No. 1 and I would have been in jail when I was 17 as opposed to 27. One of the reasons they couldn't get me back in the 70s was because I had work records which showed that on the weekend, when these murders were said to have occurred... I think they happened in Bermuda... I was at work. So, it was impossible. But if those records would not have been available, I may have been on death row before I reached my 20th birthday.

SO: *Obviously, there are restrictions to the interview which we have to respect, and which we, in fact, personally respect. But, editors being what they are and curiosity being what it is, what are the reasons why you don't want to talk about the case or don't talk about it?*

MAJ: As I said earlier, and what is clear from this hearing, is that I have good counsel for the first time. It is on their advice, an advice that I respect, that I do not do it at this time. There will come a time, perhaps, when a new trial is granted. I think, now is not the time. I agree with that.

SO: *We talked earlier about the attention around your case and the mobilization around your case. I am wondering how do other people on death row react to the attention that your case has drawn? And the other part of that question is: What kind of influence do you think that your case is going to have on the question and the debate about capital punishment in general in this country?*

MAJ: The second one is almost impossible to answer, because I guess, I am right now in the eye of the storm. But like anywhere else, there are differing opinions. I think it is fair to say this. There are hundreds and thousands of Mumia Abu-Jamals on death row and doing life bids in this country. And I think it should be recognized as such. Every day, when I talk to people in my role as a jailhouse-lawyer on death row, I find horror stories that make my hair stand up. There are cases that have been documented in my writings that should give people pause. Those people are not well-known. In fact, in many cases they are unnamed. There are cases in America where people still remain on death row, where unlike in my case where my lawyer was demonstrably ineffective, there are cases where lawyers were drunk. There are cases where lawyers were asleep. There are cases where lawyers referred to their clients as "that nigger." That is in the law books. And those people in Louisiana, in Alabama... . My point was simply that there are many cases that people never hear about and they are just as horrific, if not worse, than mine. I am sure that those are the feelings and opinions of many people on death row. And I think, it is also clear, that when you look at the social and class strata that make up and compose death row in America—there are no O.J.

Simpsons there and that is for a good reason. It is also for a reason that the L.A. District Attorney's office from the beginning and from the outset made it very clear, that even if we convicted this guy of two heinous, slice and dice bloody homicides, he will never see death row. I would bet you, that perhaps three quarters of the people on death row in California are there for one homicide. How do you think they felt? Of course, they didn't have the wealth and the notoriety of O.J. Simpson and they remain on death row for half the crime that the government is trying to convict Mr. Simpson for. That in itself speaks volumes about who comes to death row in terms of wealth and class.

SO: *Are you hopeful yourself? Do you anticipate walking out of here?*

MAJ: It sounds polyannish, but yes, I do.

SO: *No, it doesn't, Mumia.*

MAJ: Well, that sounds good, I like that. Yes, I have to be. I have to breathe for the next day... I also have to dream and plan for tomorrow. I also believe it because it's right. And its time will come.

SO: *Can you just explain why the Black Panther Party and their activities were perceived as such a threat by the U.S. government?*

MAJ: Everything must be placed in its proper context. The Black Panther Party sprung up and came into existence after the Civil Rights Movement had blossomed in America. So as part of that context it can be perceived that the government not only opposed the Black Panther Party or the Black Liberation Movement, of which it was an important part, but it is interesting to note that the Civil Rights Movement's leaders who had completely different perspectives that the Black Panther Party were also the agents (targets) of FBI surveillance, FBI brown-mail, FBI attempts to destabilize and destroy movements that no one could call violent, that no one could call, really, subversive. They went against the power structures that ran America, it is as simple as that. Because it is not in the interest of the power structure of America for black people to be free, when people talk about civil rights and equal rights, that was perceived as a threat to the power structure. When the Black Liberation Movement came about and talked about Black Nationalism, or "All Power to the People," that was perceived at a later stage as a threat to the power structure. Because any people who stand up and demand just their basic fundamental rights as human beings, which they are not getting everyday in America... . When you look around this city of 2 million people—when I was coming down this morning, they drove down the streets, and I was shocked because I saw a man sleeping on the sidewalk, just laying there like he was asleep in his bedroom. He was on a sidewalk and in front of a building that must have cost billions of dollars to erect. What right does a homeless person have? What rights do poor people have? What right do Black people have in this country—except to serve this system or have nothing—to actually live, die, sleep and awaken on a sidewalk of a street.... Well, that didn't answer your question.

Let me try and answer it again: The Black Panther Party was a small group of people that grew into forty-four chapters across the nation. They believed in armed self-defense, self-defense and protection for black people, black political power, black revolutionary political power for black people in America. In the late 60s and early 70s that pretty tame notion was perceived as a threat to the American power structure.

SO: *But then of course, when you look at the Black Panther Party, the movements that sprung up around it, the absolute repression that it got back, the suppression, the annihilation that it got back, and yet, there are offshoots that are still in existence. When you look at the national security state, that is ever growing, where do you see movements growing?*

MAJ: Movements arise out of necessity, not out of a kind of intellectual grasping, but out of necessity, out of a felt, perceived necessity that people feel within themselves. It is the nature of an oppressed people to want to resist that oppression, to resist that repression, to resist that suppression. As long as there is oppression there has to be resistance.

SO: *I have one final question, where do you find your spirituality, the love that is within you?*

MAJ: I find it reflected in a thousand places, I find it reflected in a thousand faces. I see it every day, when I see a blade of grass, when I see something, when I see life. The teachings of John Africa have been very helpful for me as a place to look for strength, to look for love in life in all forms that life takes. And it [the teachings] has helped frame and guide those thoughts and those feelings. But it is not hard to feel that, as I said earlier, when you are flooded with love and affection. And I see it every place, every day, every hour and I am very grateful for that.

SO: *My last question is gonna be: What is your perspective for the next few months, for the future? What are you hoping for? And what is awaiting you?*

MAJ: It is difficult to make predictions, however I think it is a safe prediction that we will not get a new trial out of this hearing under Judge Sabo. We do our best and we try, but I think when you look at our original motion, when we first came in, the motion to recuse, we referred to the judge as a "prosecutor in robes," as a "nightmare for the defense." All of these things that have been referred to by us, he has been proving every day. I don't know if you were listening I think on Monday, or on Friday, Judge Sabo said from the bench that "justice is just an emotional feeling." And I looked around and I didn't see anybody stir. But it seemed like the oddest words to hear in a courtroom. If the courtroom is a room of emotional feelings, then we can have court in a comedy club, we can have court in a church.

SO: *As a matter-of-fact, he said, "When I win a case, I get justice; and when I loose my case, I don't get justice."*

MAJ: I didn't see that quote in any of the newspapers. But I think it's a classic quote that speaks volumes about this courtroom. So, I think it's also safe to say that we won't get justice in this courtroom.

SO: *What would you like to say—and you said such a body of things and continue to write, and of course we receive your writing, which we are grateful for... but what would you like to say first to the people who are building movements around your case—hopefully that will broaden—and secondly to the journalists whom you don't wish to talk to?*

MAJ: I will ignore your second question. I will address the first, only because I think it is a matter of more importance. To those people and the various movements, they have my most profound thanks and gratitude. We could not have guessed or created or had any reason to suspect that such a broad group of people would support us, but we are very, very lucky that they do. I send my thanks and I wish I could do so personally and I thank you. Ona MOVE. Long live John Africa!!!

PART II

Before we present that second interview, conducted August 14, let me take a moment to describe the conditions of it. In a tiny airless room on the seventh floor of Phildelphia's City Hall; Mumia and I sat opposite one another, separated by thick Plexiglass, making it almost impossible to hear one another without yelling. The only mechanism to transport sound was located about waist high and consisted of a round piece of perforated metal about the size of a cat food can lid. Mumia had to bend down to directly speak into this. I, too, bent down to maintain eye contact in our conversation and placed my microphone at the perforations. Despite what can only be described as demoralizing conditions, I found Mumia to be strong, in good spirits, and very clear about the process that was going on. For the purposes of this second interview, we spoke only of journalism, and I must say , to me, as a journalist, I find it important to note that the harder they try to silence Mumia Abu-Jamal's voice the louder it becomes.

SO: *Let's talk about the journalist in present-day society.*

MAJ: The role of journalists, as long as there's been mankind...I mean, in ancient Africa, the role of the Griot was not just to sing praise songs to the king, which is the present role of journalists, I guess, but to tell the tale of the people, to tell the story of people from their perspective. It appears that half of that message, half of that role has been lost in today's journalism. It is still the full role of journalism to tell the story of the people and to tell it from their perspective and not from the perspective of the rich and powerful, not through those who can afford your access. That is a role that is not popular today, of course, but that does not mean that it is not necessary today.

I think to a large extent, many people remember me, if at all, by my work. Many of the people who sign the petition or come out to a demonstration have never met me before, but they remember the work that they heard. And there was a distinction in that work that was different from the work of others, and they sensed that it wasn't about money, it wasn't about prestige. It was about speaking not just to the people, but for the people, speaking from that reality, from that ground level.

We use the word radical and use it descriptively to say radical journalism. Well, a lot of people get afraid when they hear that: "Ooh, radical!" Radical justs means, 'from roots,' and that means we should be in touch with the roots of our people, to speak their truths, to reflect their realities and to give their voice to the world.

SO: *Giving a voice to the voiceless. It's ironic that I have to interview you this way and to put the political prisoners in a place where they could speak. There's been a lot of criticism over the years of Pacifica (Radio) for our programming for that. I stand very much in defense of radical news. I think the bourgeois press does forget something called advocacy journalism. To take it further, do you think the ancient concept of bearing fair witness comes into play here?*

MAJ: Again, we go back to the Griot, speaking of life in the way that reflects the real, heartfelt interests of the people. When we talk about advocacy journalism, the suggestion, kind of inherent within your question, was that bourgeois or corporate is not advocacy journalism, that the two are distinct. Well, I don't think so, because bourgeois journalism is advocacy journalism. It advocates the system. It advocates corporate life and reality. It advocates capitalist excess.

Every journalistic organ on the planet has a perspective. Oh, they hide it. They hide through guidebooks. They hide it through journalism schools. But their interest can be reflected in what they do, who they speak of how they do what they do, who they speak of, how they do what they do, who they're speaking to, and from what perspective. I think they are the premiere advocacy journalists on the planet. That's just my alternative phrase.

SO: *It's amazing how afraid the powers-that-be are of the process of thought and verbiage of that thought. You said in our first interview how you were under surveillance at the age of 14 and how they were afraid of, as you put it, a snotty-nosed kid. It really is true that in someways they are more afraid of that than the Aryan Nation, for instance, or the people who are out there in training camps. In the Everglades. In fact, they utilize them. I'm wondering, as attacks go more and more on progressive information what we, as progressive journalists, can do to safeguard that, to try to keep the information flowing and to keep the editors of the powers-that-be in our institution brave.*

MAJ: I don't think you'll ever keep them brave. You can make them respect you just by the tone and tenor and perspective of your work. If your work touches people and embraces their lives, they will see that as distinct from the other work that's out there and demand it and fight for it. The people are the power. We used to say, "More power to the people." But that reality has not changed.

All it comes down to is perspective and acknowledging the simple fact that everyone has a perspective. The foolish illusion that only leftists or people on the right have perspective, and the mass media as a whole doesn't have a perspective, is illusion. They have a perspective, and their functioning perspective is the preservation of the system, and the preservation of the system requires the domination of people in the system to keep things quiet, so to speak, stable...or the appearance of the same.

People must fight and build and protest. I was thinking of Imbana Kintango, the blind brother who built his own radio station, a small unit that goes a few blocks. There's going to be more and more Kintangos. When you consider the kind of repression that was visited upon him and his family because of that small, tiny four- or five-block radio station, that then gives you some inkling of the power of thought, the power of the word if that word is in resistance to the system. They wanted to destroy him, because he was an example of what is rare in America, truly rare...free radio.

SO: *In terms of the press coverage that's been happening around your case, have you seen change and gradual shift in the way that the media is looking at your case? It ebbs and flows, but there is a certain pattern to it.*

MAJ: Well, I think your parenthetical comment about it ebbs and flows is the truest reflection of it. Some days it ebbs, some days it flows. To the extent that it has been not as negative or derogatory as usual, I think is a reflection, again, to the power of the people, and the inherent bourgeois media bent to appeal and sell. They want to sell newspapers to anybody. That's their objective.

I'm not really impressed by the ebb and flow, because I understand their function. For example, I was thinking about, as I was preparing for these sets of interviews, a brother in Philadelphia. They've done small articles, one or two. It no longer makes news. The brother's name was Jalil Glenn Thomas. About a month ago, he was shot to death after he and his family were stopped in Phildelphia. According to police, he came out to his car and ran and reached for a gun. According to people who were witnesses from the community, who were nonpolice, they said he got out of his car and ran and was not armed. He had his arms up. What both agreed to was that he was shot in the back of the head. I mean, you gotta be a rare person to be threatened by someone's back. Either you have to be a rare person or that back has to be a rare back.

The point is, no one called for this cop to be fired. No one called for him to be sent to prison. The [term] "death row" is never used in conjunction with that. No one really gives a damn about Jalil Thomas' wife and children. He is a nonentity.

Again, I come back to perspective. If all was as they say it is—fair and impartial for all, journalism is an equal reflection, everybody's equal and nonsense like that—then we would have (some) front pages demanding justice for Jalil Thomas. Well, you're not going to see that. And it's only radical journalists who will speak his name and make people remember.

•••

BAHÍYYIH MAROON *

Fire Keeper

for Mumia Abu-Jamal—political prisoner

i save your grace inside
pamphlet shrines/ thin books/
the skulls of our dead
i speak to your legend often
and wonder what you think about
pissing on the prison toilet
bleeding your pencil hung words
in exile

you printed the move
exhaling charcoal graffiti
through the narrow tubes of journalism.
dissecting cointelpro strategies into spit factions
insisting conspiracy theories at every printing
until they made you a part of one
now, only you can recount your story
one sprawled out on the oil drive
in a bloodied night.
there are casualties
some of whom still breathe
and sweat puss from blindfolded eye jams

you are centered in this excrement bathed hole
we call America - a periodical
of our new age bondage
the fiber optic chains on your mind
popped open/ your tongue becoming
a finely serrated blade/ you pierce
the lies

sometimes, i dream you
knotty dreads screaming with the tightly blown wind
fire strapped across the backdrop
this is battle
our hands are wet with the liver and kidney of our tormentors
i see you

JOHN ABNER

hunter truth/ heart of human animal in hand
raging/ AMANDLA!!!/ AMANDLA!!!
you dance vicious/ unlocking Winnie
calling a nation of unbordered Zulus to war

and we love/ in this boiled summer/ you
21st Century warrior in graying locks
redeemer of printed language
you taste the precious finite reality
life is/ each these numbered days
knowing death to be inescapable
that injustice feeds on that truism
and plays the chords of our reaper often
in the auditorium of this decorated concentration camp

i see you Mumia
in that flat coal space
running/ conjure and
write firmly/ in stone/ we will strike matches
against the hemorrhaged visions you bear
and set the cities to drown in our blaze

•••••

v. Look who watches

GEORGE "GEO" SMITH

(the international scene)

NGÙGÌ WA THIONG'O
Prison Without Trial

In a neo-colonial country, the act of detaining patriotic democrats, progressive intellectuals and militant workers speaks of many things. It is first an admission by the detaining authorities that their official lies labelled as a new philosophy, their pretensions often hidden in three-piece suits and golden chains, their propaganda packaged as religious truth, their plastic smiles ordered from abroad, their nationally televised charitable handouts and breast-beating before the high altar, their high-sounding phrases and ready-to-shed tears at the sight of naked children fighting it out with cats and dogs for the possession of a rubbish heap, that these and more godfatherly acts of benign benevolence have been seen by the people for what they truly are: a calculated sugar-coating of an immoral sale and mortgage of a whole country and its people to Euro-American and Japanese capital for a few million dollars in Swiss banks and a few token shares in foreign companies. Their mostly vaunted morality has been exposed for what it is: the raising of beggary and charity into moral idealism. There is a new-found dignity in begging, and charity for them is twice-blessed; it deflates the recipient and inflates the giver. Nyerere once rightly compared those African regimes who dote on their neo-colonial status to a prostitute who walks with proud display of the fur coat given to her by her moneyed lover. Actually the situation of a comprador neo-colonial ruling class is more appropriately comparable to that of a pimp who would proudly hold down his mother to be brutally raped by foreigners, and then shout in glee: look at the shining handful of dollars I have received for my efficiency and integrity, in carrying out my part of the bargain!

But recourse to detention is above all an admission by the neo-colonial ruling minority that people have started to organize to oppose them, to oppose the continued plunder of the national wealth and heritage by this shameless alliance of a few nationals and their foreign paymasters.

Thus detention more immediately means the physical removal of patriots from the people's organized struggles. Ideally, the authorities would like to put the whole community of struggling millions behind barbed-wire, as the British colonial authorities once tried to do with Kenyan people. But this would mean incarcerating labour, the true source of national wealth: what would then be left to loot? So the authorities do the simpler thing: pick one or two individuals from among the people and then loudly claim that all sins lie at the feet of these few 'power hungry,' 'misguided' and 'ambitious' agitators. Note that any awakening of a people to their historic mission of liberating themselves from external and internal exploitation and repression is always seen in terms of 'sin' and it is often denounced with the religious rhetoric of a wronged, self-righteous god. These agitators suddenly become devils whose removal from society is now portrayed as a divine mission. The people are otherwise innocent, simple, peace-loving, obedient, law-abiding, and cannot conceivably harbour any desire to change this best of all possible worlds. It is partly self-deception, but also an attempted deception of millions. Chain the devils!

But political detention, not disregarding its punitive aspects, serves a deeper, exemplary ritual symbolism. If they can break such a patriot, if they can make him come out of detention crying 'I am sorry for all my sins', such an unprincipled about-turn would confirm the wisdom of the ruling clique in its division of the populace into the passive innocent millions and the disgruntled subversive few. The 'confession' and its corollary, 'Father, forgive us for our sins', becomes a cleansing ritual for all the past and current repressive deeds of such a neo-colonial regime. With a few tidbits, directorship of this or that statutory body, the privilege of standing for parliament on the regime's party ticket, such an ex-detainee might even happily play the role of a conscientious messenger from purgatory sent back to earth by a father figure more benevolent than Lazarus' Abraham, 'that he may testify unto them (them that dare to struggle), lest they also come into this place of torment'. The forgiving father sits back to enjoy international applause for his manifold munificence and compassionate heart. But even when they find that such a detainee is not in a position to play the role of an active preacher against the futility of struggle (they may have damaged him beyond any exploitable repair), they can still publicize this picture of a human wreck or vegetable as a warning to all future agitators: he could not stand it, do you think you are made of sterner steel? The former hardcore patriot is physically or intellectually or spiritually broken and by a weird symbolic extension, the whole struggling populace is broken. All is now well in imperialist heaven for there is peace on neo-colonial earth, policed by a tough no-nonsense comprador ruling class that knows how to deal with subversive elements.

The fact is that detention without trial is not only a punitive act of physical and mental torture of a few patriotic individuals, but it is also a calculated act of psychological terror against the struggling millions. It is a terrorist programme for the psychological siege of the whole nation. That is why the practice of detention from the time of arrest to the time of release is deliberately invested with mystifying ritualism. My arrest, for instance.

N.B. The above piece is an excerpt from Ngugi's prison diary, *Detained*, written while he was detained without trial (from December 1977 to December 1978), by Kenyan authorities, for his anti-imperialist, anti-colonial, and neo-colonial writings. Ngugi's detention in Kamiti Maximum Security Prison, like Mumia's death sentence, gained international attention and outrage.

•••

DAISY ZAMORA

Message to the Poets
to Ernesto, Julio, Vidaluz

*and if we want to fight there are numerous
enemies on the other side of the barricades...*
–V. Maiakovski

Forever in secret confabulation, chameleons,
undercover agents, the masked among us,
they rode the turbulence of waters,
defying the ebb and flow of tides
with their buoy-like bodies, inflated heads,
more duly established than any of us.

They've had their fun with craft,
been skilled at the art of poison
all the while protected
by their shield of multiple servility.
They've had mountains of tribute,
awards from one side and the other.
Let us not envy them, my noble comrades,
unconditionals to Poetry alone!

In their speeches they proclaim themselves immortal
but like disguise artists, when the curtain falls,
take off their makeup and must gaze
upon their own true, unbearable faces.

They, who got fat telling lies,
now thrive once more in familiar waters
as they attempt to steal the voices of our heroes.
Let them spew their stupidities,
their bread of every day.
The galloping power of life
will erase their words.

Translated by Margaret and Elinor Randall

•••

JESUS PAPOLETO MELÉNDEZ
A San Diego/Southern African Night

(O i have no opinion
    of What My Eyes See!...)

:There's a black man,
    A man whose skin is black
      — the color,
    BlacK!
    Running across The Street
    in the middle of the night;
      BlacK NighT!
      Only the flickering lights of business buildings
        ,still
      burning in the night(
        like the eyes
        of obese monsters)
    And the stars,
      of course   — They
        in their distance
    are out tonight;
      Quietly know ing,
      Unsaying a word.

THE TRAFFIC LIGHT CHaNGeS —
    So Now, The Color RED is Against
    HiM — WHO crosses The Street!
    POLICECAR
    cruises   by.... And
      SeiZe HiM!
      (BlackMan)
      & FLaSHeS
      itS LiGHtS
       BRiiiiGhHtTtT!!!!!!!!
    ¡¡¡In the Middle of the Night
    RED&OrANGe/BlUe&WHiTE!!!
    LiGHTS!!
!!!!!!!!!!!

THEY cut HiM off at the pass
Of the corner of a sidewalk/UP
Against!
TheCARRRR!!!MOTHER!!!!!!!!!!

HiS Hands on the hood
He is forced to spread his legs A/ParTWIdE—Like this
THEY Dare call it Eagle!
So THEY could search him up good, To make sure
There's nothing up his sleeve
The/re/s/no/thi/ng/u/p/hi/S/m/i...... n/D!
:THEY take his wallet ,from out of him/
Removing the papers ,from the person
:THEY tell him to go sit in the car/
In the memory of the back seat,
Looking out the window like that, perhaps
resembling a bird
And He obeys THEM,
HE does
What HE believes that THEY say/
It is dead night.
The night is dead.
There are not too many people around,
walking
,with their opinions on hand
:"Art!
for Art's sake!"
(And i think;
How difFerent this is
from, "SomeWhere Else"
where, a Soldier would demand
or the same kind of rights
In a foreign land,
dressed in camouflaged fatigues
with an Uzi
slung over his shoulder,
say
ing
"YOUR PAPERS! YOUR
PAPERS! LET ME SEE YOUR PAPERS!!!"
,except
for those ,mostly
in cars

going home
from the long days
they've just lived
in the lengths
of their lives
              /tired
from the things
that they do
with their lives,
And/ThereForeTheyAreInGreatHurries(
              Be....lieveIt!
              Be....lieveIt!
              YouBetteRBe....lieveIt!
              Be....lieveIt!)
Nonchalantly tossing
lighted cigarettes
from out their
open windows
              watching
the world go
down the drain(
              bye)
stepping harder
on the gas
when they see
the lights
turning
from yellow, to red,
              They
already traveling
beyond the speed
of anybody walking,
trying desperately
to be
the first to
get
to
the other side
of a brand new street
which they've seen
before,
at the corner
of which

are
2POLICE
& 1 blacKDude
imprisoned in a trance
& a light
turning
from yellow, to ReD!
    (My little sister says
      about her visit with me here
        :"The lights don't give you enough ti)me
        to
        chew yo
        ur gum
        &cross the
        street!"
        ,She
    coming from a real Cool/CRUeL Metropolis
    having thus acquired an acute UNderstanding
    of the danger of crossing a simple street,
      for a girl, She says
    "As soon as you step out to cross it
    The lights start blinking for you to go back!
    It's a car's world out here!
    Pedestrians should drive!"
    TheBlack peDestrianMan
      sits
    In the POLICEMAN's CAR
    with his BiGBlacKHanDs
      down
    in front of HiM
     moping,
    sort of
    For TheCAUSE! of his BlacKsKiN
    — THaT
    though it blended with
    the color of this NiGHT,
     It failed
    to cloak HiM from THEIR SiGHT!

And
THEPOLICE,
WoMan,
LaDy,

CoP,
is sitting in the front seat
          (preTending)
            that it is Her duTy
              to be doing her nails
                ,While
          holding on to the leather of herGun,
          touchingIt,
                    ListeninG..
          To Every ThoughT that HE has
          To Think
           :This BlackMan,
          HiS Black Pride, Fuming
          within
          hiS BlackMan's Feelings
          (sitting
          in the back
          seat
          of a
          STraNGeMaN's
          CaR!)

Outside,
          The Air is Cool ....   :Thus is San Diego,
          A City most noticeable for
          Its Lovely Days
          of
          Perfect Skies
            (iF
          you ignore the factories
            where BomBs are born
          & ,Therefore, THE TARGET
            That carpets the floOR)
              ,And ToNighT....
                is a beautiful night
                To Be Lived
          & enjoy in your being.............!

THEMANCoP
            rests languidly,
            leaning against the
            roof of his car
              ,Observing the tranquility

of a RedLightDIstriCT's ACtiVity
ReMarKing,
"How smoothly America funCtions
free from Crime,
   at
   Peace" (
while, POLItICIans seek Votes
in the childish arms
of
loving prostitutes)

THEMANCoP calls
   THEBoYS
   ,Back at the Ranch
   To see how the BallGame is going
   — & if anybody thoughT
   to leave him a sandwich
   for when things go BORinG
   ,And while he's at it
     (& picking his teeth with a knife)
   He asks THIS COMPUTER
    THEY'VE got over there (with a VoICE like a woMan
   of aNAnDRoGyNous souND)
   If sHE'S
   Ever Heard of this WiseGuy
     HE'S got
      in the backseat of the Car/
     If "HE" EverEver
     ,Ever Did
    AnyThing!
    AnyThing, WronG
   In HiS Whole Loving Life/
   AnyThing/AnyThing!
   As aBlackMan/Child
   in this World
   WITHaCRIMINALMIND!
  —Anything, Anything!
   "Are You Sure?!
   —What's The Score?!"

THE ANSWER IS:.....   NO!!!.... /&/SO!!!....

THEMANCoP must   write HiM a ticket, According to
        'TheProPerProCeDurE'
          (Thinking)
            :If this were a windy city
            HE'D run HiM in
                for spittininthegutter!
                    ....&TOHELL!
        WITHtHEWoMEN
        SCReeeEEEEaMINGGGINALLEYS(
          some)
        Reluctantly,losing,virginities
            ,while
        the blood of their taxes
        pays
        the way
        forthewagesofSin
        &Preachers
        are left
        to argue
        withtheMeanFaceoftheWind!

Now, THEMANCoP calls
        TheBlacK, bOY
to come out
from out
of the car,
            realeasy, like slow
And sign Here
On the line
To say
That I
Gave yoU
This,
And ThaT
YoU
Took IT
And, Now

U
N
D
E
R
S
T
A
N
D
ThaT
YoU Owe
"The
Good
PeoPle"
Of
This
Fare
City,

       Truly
       America's Finest
       Fair City,

35 Bucks
Of
Your
Hard Earned
How
Ever
It
Is
That
YoU
Get
IT
Cold
Cash,
BECAUSE!!
!!!!!!!!!!!!!!!
YoU DiD
Cross
The
Street
While

The YelloW
LighT
Was
A-BlinK-InG
And, Then
DiD
Turn
A-ReD
By
The Time
YoU-A-GoT
To
The
Other
Good Side!
And, So HE Signs
HiS NaMe!....
On
The
Paper:
The NaMe....
HiS Mother
Gave
To HiM,
The NaMe!....
By Which
He Is
KnowN
On
The
Face
Of
This Earth,
The NaMe!....
By
Which
GOD
Will Know
HiM
As Well:
CAPITAL X!
And HiS Fingers
are All on the pen!

O!HiSBlacKFinGer'SPrinTS!
Are On
The Piece of Paper
And On
The Hood of The Car
And On
The Back of The Seat
Where HE WePT
HiS TeaRS
And
HiS TeaRS
Are NoW LeFT
Where
HiS ShAdOW
Once Sulked
And, For This
Even IT!
Refuses
to
walk
with
him
just now, No
not now
It fades
in
the
depth
of
This Night,

"OH! WHERE IS HOME?!"....
THEMANCoP
gives HiM
TheTickeT
withPride
like a piece of ArT
but itaint
TearingiT
from out of a book
of them.

And, NoW, "THE COMPUTER"
Has Devoured HiS NaMe!....

And, *"SomeWhere," "SomeWhere!"*
　　No One Knows Where
　　　– It is smacking its lips
　　　& waiting for dessert!

AND IT WILL NEVER FORGET!
NO! IT WILL NEVER FORGET:
The NaMe!....Nor/the/Height/of/Said/MaN
Nor the Weight of HiM
Nor the Color of HiS Eyes
Nor the Color of HiS Hair
Nor the Color of HiS Skin
Nor the Number that isHis
Nor The Age of This MaN as He Ages
Through Time
　　　　— This BlacKMaN
　　　¿WHO?
　　　...at 2-30 in the morning/ One
　　　　　dark and lonely, Good Morning!
　　was detained by THEPOLICE
!!!
!!"The 'DistinCtive' Color
!!!of a LighT
!!was
!!!AGaINST/HiM!"

We Must Be Thankful ThaT
　　　ThE DiFfErEncE, HeRe
　　　　,from AnyWhere ElSe
　　　　In This World (is)
　　　ThaTThisBlacKMaNis
　　　　,Finally set,
on the leash of his f , reedom to go about,D,oing　his bu,si, ness　in pursui, t　of　　the
ha,pp,y,n,es,s he dreams, in his　w i d e　o p　e n,d　mind
　　　— *AnyWhere ,ElSe*
HE WOULD HAVE BEEN SHOT • RIGHT ON THE SPOT • FOR BREAKING THE
LAW!!!

So, TheNicePOLICEMANWoMANCoPs
　　　having, Thus
　　　　Completed Their DuTy,
　　　　　drive away, with their lights
　　　　　　swallowed up

       in the eyes of the monster
         ,Whom(?)
     They've Sworn:
      ToProTecT&ToSerVe
      WithTheirLives................Owns
  the
  world
  going
  round
&TheBlacKMaN, goes
    slowly, across the street
      (contemplating ,This)

AndTheLightsHaveNoMoreOpinionToUtterInHisFace!
BuT NoW!!!—HE IS CURRRRRRRRRRRRRRRRRRRRRRRRRRSSSSSiNG!!! ....
POuNDING theAiROfTheNIGhT—————————————————with HiS VoICE!:
I-KNOW-I'M-NOT-WHITE!!!-I-KNOW-I'M-NOT-WHITE!!!-I-KNOW-I'M-NOT-WHITE!!!-I-
KNOW-I'M-NOT-WHITE!!!-I-KNOW-I'M-NOT-WHITE!!!-I-KNOW-I'M-NOT-WHITE!!!-I-
KNOW-I'M-NOT-WHITE!!!-I-KNOW-I'M-NOT-WHITE!!!-I-KNOW-I'M-NOT-WHITE!!!-I-
KNOW-I'M-NOT-WHITE!!!-I-KNOW-I'M-NOT-WHITE!!!-I-KNOW-I'M-NOT-WHITE!!!-I-
KNOW-I'M-NOT-WHITE!!!-I-KNOW-I'M-NOT-WHITE!!!-I-KNOW-I'M-NOT-WHITE!!!-I-
KNOW-I'M-NOT-WHITE!!!-I-KNOW-I'M-NOT-WHITE!!!-I-KNOW-I'M-NOT-WHITE!!!-I-
KNOW-I'M-NOT-WHITE!!!-I-KNOW-I'M-NOT-WHITE!!!-I-KNOW-I'M-NOT-WHITE!!!-I-
KNOW-I'M-NOT-WHITE!!!-I-KNOW-I'M-NOT-WHITE!!!-I-KNOW-I'M-NOT-WHITE!!!-I-
KNOW-I'M-NOT-WHITE!!!-I-KNOW-I'M-NOT-WHITE!!!-I-KNOW-I'M-NOT-WHITE!!!-I-
KNOW-I'M-NOT-WHITE!!!-I-KNOW-I'M-NOT-WHITE!!!-I-KNOW-I'M-NOT-WHITE!!!-I-
KNOW-I'M-NOT-WHITE!!!-I-KNOW-I'M-NOT-WHITE!!!-I-KNOW-I'M-NOT-WHITE!!!-I-
KNOW-I'M-NOT-WHITE!!!-I-KNOW-I'M-NOT-WHITE!!!-I-KNOW-I'M-NOT-WHITE!!!-I-
KNOW-I'M-NOT-WHITE!!!-I-KNOW-I'M-NOT-WHITE!!!-I-KNOW-I'M-NOT-WHITE!!!

•••

NANCY MERCADO *

On My Return from Puerto Rico to the U.S.
(or The Idleness of It All)

    It's yesterday wasting away behind our backs
    Ducking at our every twist
    Imploring us to return
    From this cold casket where time flies robbing youth,
    An alienating stare,
    A decrepit course of a life time

Shown through the eyes
Of a middle-aged black woman,
Through a young Puerto Rican man
Riding the subway arguing with some imaginary figure,
An ice box shuttling people nowhere for years
Sending them off to their graves before time,
Icicle days fooling us,
Mesmerizing even the keenest of minds
Into believing time does not run out,
Rows and rows of steel and concrete,
Chemical plants and train tracks
Laughing at our misplaced sense of life,
A shivering view of barren trees
And soot-wrenched grass, defying all odds,
Standing there, daring man,
A bad joke leaving us here
In knee-deep oil slicks
With barbed wire memories of childhood ignorance
Joys of family life almost forgotten.
We're misplaced in this lifeless machine
Trying to construct homes out of straw pieces in the snow,
Speaking foreign languages to those
Who run off on their way to work
To contribute to valleys that lay in waste,
We're dangling from a noose
Between epochs and conversations never begun
And, dressing up wrong,
And using chopped up words: manufactured phrases
Invented to describe a manufactured life,
We're the living dead
Idly speaking, mindlessly racing through our existence,

Aimlessly hurrying from one stage to the next
Like volunteer slaves onto the auction block
Donating to their own demise,
Supporting toxic dumps and empty faces
Combing playground sides
In search of future O.D.'ed addicts,
Withering away in housing projects:
Neighborhoods used as toilets for the rich.
It's MTV across America!
Delusions of stardom!
As you sidestep all those crack vials past your doorway

Your mother, suffocating on a baseball field, a landfill
Approved for little league games
Where your little brothers play
All their days away,
A cold solitude, mute and still
Like everything beyond that sheet of ice covering your window,
A bird's petrified song in the air,
A frozen tear stopped in its tracks.
It's haunting memories of an era abandoned:
The dazzling sun on mother's tiled-kitchen floor
Adding the final touch to our afternoon meal,
Father's laugher just beyond a caress,
Mother's last kiss,
My nephew's bewildered glance,
Will I return again—

•••

IAN WILLIAMS
Non-swinging Europe

It was at a conference on Bosnia in Washington, D.C. that I first realised that the U.S. was in an atavistic time warp, one that is different from Europe's judicial perspective. A hall full of liberal, caring, sensitive Americans almost howled in outrage when they discovered that the War Crimes Tribunal could not impose the death penalty on the accused.

It was almost inconceivable that a similar group of West Europeans would have had such a reaction. While it is true that in the eighteenth century Britain had over three hundred capital offences, we have become more civilized since then. Perhaps even more strikingly, looking at the present U.S. Congress, British politicians of all parties, from right to left, had consistently voted against the death penalty even when the polls indicated that a majority of voters wanted to retain the death penalty, i.e., hanging.

United States' politicians seem to be trapped in an eighteenth century time warp, when any populist cause could have a noose attached to it in parliament. (Among the capital offences in Britain then were arson in naval dockyards, pissing off Westminster Bridge, and impersonating a Chelsea pensioner). In fact, even in the eighteenth century, juries were reluctant to convict criminals when they felt the penalty was inappropriate.

The reasons for the abolition of the death penalty in Europe after the Second World War were mixed. As Mao Tse Tung once said, "It is easy to chop off someone's head. It is very difficult to put it back on again when you find that it was a mistake." There were indeed several notorious mistakes. However, the main reason is, I suspect, that Europeans feel that if society takes the life, even of a murderer, then we collectively put ourselves on the same low level of morality as the killer. In addition, delighting in the death penalty was a trait we associated with the repressive regimes of the 1930s and 40s. The piano wire nooses, the bullet in the neck, not to mention the death camps, created seriously bad public relations for state-mandated capital punishments.

Yet strangely enough, most of us in Europe still think of the state as "ours" and are not that unhappy about paying taxes to it, since we trust it to deliver the services we pay for. However, in the U.S.A., most voters have such a visceral suspicion of government that they

RENALDO IMANI DAVIDSON

seem unwilling to trust it to spend their tax money. So why do they trust it with the lives of the accused?

While Europeans abolished execution on the moral grounds of not seeking retribution, subsequent experience suggested that capital punishment had little or no deterrent effect on would-be killers. The death rate from crime did not rise in the majority of European countries that abandoned execution. Most British police are still unarmed. And the state's absence from the macabre and grotesque ritual of execution has undoubtedly made the whole society more civilized.

Looking at penal policy in the United States, keeping prisoners of questionable guilt like Mumia for decades and then trying to kill them; its execution of mentally deranged and juvenile offenders; its short shrift with minorities and the poor, remind me of Ghandi's quip when asked what he thought about Western civilization. He said he thought it would be a good idea. I could only add, one that is two hundred years overdue, here in the U.S.A.

•••

ROSEMARI MEALY
Cuba - In Defense of Mumia

One immeasurable dimension to the United States' history of vicious incursions into Asia, Africa, and Latin America are the marks of destruction brought on by war, famine, and environmental plunder. There are bomb blasts so powerful that outlines of human bodies remain carved into sidewalks. The aftermath of "their" conventional warfare battles leave entire water supplies poisoned. Once the gun fire ceases, after the scorching flames have raged across the lands, everything is made uninhabitable . Years after the Marines, Special Forces, and the CIA depart from the killing fields, the booby traps continue to explode, maiming and extracting limbs from the innocent—suddenly refugees in their own lands.

The World Bank, like a rear guard, moves into place siphoning off the remaining wealth, while demanding that governments borrow and negotiate loans that impose austerity programs on their starving and devastated people. Later, we read—in the business sections of *The New York Times, The Times* of London, and *The Wall Street Journal*—money market reports of failed programs where neo-colonial rulers were forced to mortgage their entire countries to Wall Street. Once a nation becomes an economic hostage of U.S. imperialism, that nation has lost its sovereignty; its people's dignity forfeited.

The Cuban Revolution, however, represents the one nation where people and leaders continue to remind us of the tremendous growth that can be achieved when there is an emphatic rejection of that which belied the so-called advantages of capitalism. This was best understood by the descendants of African slaves and Spanish colonialists, whom forty-two years ago on July 26, 1953, were led by Fidel Castro to attack the Moncada Army Barracks in Santiago de Cuba. This daring feat signaled the begining of a new stage in the independence process, which eventually led to the triumph of the Cuban Revolution on January 1, 1959, proving not only to the people of Latin America and the Caribbean—but also to the world—that human-ity's destiny was not locked into a perpetual state of submission and oppression despite the hegemony of capitalism.

In assuming responsibility for their own destiny, the Cubans unabashedly appropriated—to some extent—the destiny of all of humanity in the quest for freedom and justice. For their bold actions, Washington has shown nothing but outright contempt for Cuba's leaders and its people through the imposition of a more than 32-year-old economic blocklade.

A major strategy of the U.S. blockade has been to reverse the gains of the Cuban people by attempting to deny them life and prosperity, and to isolate them from the people of the United States much in the same way as proponents of the death penalty in the U.S. attempt to craft campaigns to destroy the life of Mumia Abu-Jamal.

The voices of Mumia Abu-Jamal and Fidel Castro are harmonious. As a brilliant young lawyer, orator, and writer, Fidel penned from prison—after the Moncadea attack—his own defense plea:

> It is curious, the very men who have brought me here to be judged and condemned have never heeded a single decision of this court. [W]hat I say here, will perhaps be lost in the silence which [Batista's] dictatorship has tried to impose on me, but posterity may often turn its eyes to what you do here.

Similarly, Mumia, in an essay entitled "Death March and Lessons Unlearned," wrote:

> There is a quickening on the nation's death row as of late—a picking up of the pace of the march towards death. The political prod is sparking movements, and judges in death cases are beginning to find themselves under increasing pressures to make the final judgement; as murder rates rise in America's cities, so too does the tide of fear. Both politicians and judges continue to ride that tide that washes toward the execution cham-bers. Many of the condemned, with constitutional errors rife throughout their records, will soon be executed without meaningful review.

Fidel voiced similar sentiments when he wrote from prison to his accusers:

> Remember that today you are judging an accused man, but that you your-self will be judged not once, but many times, as often as these days are sub-mitted to criticisms in the future. What I say here will be repeated many times, not because it comes from my lips, but because the problem of jus-tice is eternal and the people have a deep sense of justice above and beyond the hairsplitting jurisprudence. The people wield simple but implacable logic, in conflict with all that is absurd and contradictory. I know that imprisonment will be hard for me as it has ever been for any-

one filled with cowardly threats and wicked torture. But I do not fear prison as I do not fear the fury of the miserable tyrants who took the lives of seventy of my comrades. Condemn me. It does not matter. History will absolve me.

Since the birth of the Cuban Revolution, the humanity of the Cuban people has been expressed through gestures of international solidarity. These expressions of solidarity have been far reaching, while taking many forms. In recent times, nowhere has that expression crescendoed more than in the Campaign to Free Mumia.

During those frantic weeks in July and August, when we were demanding that Pennsylvania stay the execution of our Brother, and that a new trial was in order, Cuba responded immediately. From Havana to Las Villas, from Oriente to Camaguey, the message upon the lips of the Cuban people echoed: *"¡No Ensombrezcas, Philadelphia!"* (translated: "Don't Put a Death Shroud On, Philadelphia!")

In the forefront of the campaign coming out of Havana were the organizing efforts of groups such as the Federation of Cuban Women, Casa de Las Americas, Union of Cuban Journalists and Writers (UPEC), the National Union of Cuban Writers and Artists (UNEAC).

Nowhere were the efforts more diligent than those of the Organization of Solidarity with the People of Asia, Africa, and Latin America (OSPAAAL). The General Secretary of OSPAAAL, Companero Ramon Pez Ferro, communicated in a letter on August 7, 1995, to U.S. Attorney General Janet Reno, denouncing and condemning the order to execute "Afro-North American Journalist Mumia Abu-Jamal." Ramon Pez Ferro also conveyed the same message in a subsequent letter to Governor Thomas Ridge of Pennsylvania. Ramon Pez Ferro also sent letters, written on behalf of Mumia, to The Center for Human Rights in Geneva, Switzerland, Sub-Commission on the Prevention of Discrimination and Protection of Minorities, the Special Commission on Human Rights; and to José Ayala Lasso, president of the High Commission for Human Rights. The message to each of the leaders documented the most scathing denunciations of Judge Albert Sabo's role in Mumia's trial, while appealing to these international bodies that," in their authority and high responsibility of the Center for Human Rights, OSPAAAL requested that "it intercede to save the life of U.S. citizen Mumia Abu-Jamal, by echoing the swelling universal outcry against his execution on August 17, 1995."

Meanwhile, at the International Youth Festival held in Villa Clara, Cuba, August 1 - 7, 1995, Cuban journalist Carlos Castro Sanchez of the Cuban magazine *Somos*, initiated a petition with an open letter attached. In beautifully written prose, each stanza rang out, "Cuba Lives" while "Black Journalist Mumia Abu-Jamal, the victim of political persecution because of his ideas and his writings, faces execution in the United States."

Carlos Castro Sanchez's writing voice hauntingly warns the international community that it should not have any illusion regarding the propensity of the United States when it comes to violating the human rights of its own citizens. Castro Sanchez invoked the international community to call for an immediate stay of Mumia's execution. More than 125 signatures were submitted representing journalists from more than 24 countries.

SANDRA MARÍA ESTEVES

As a broadcast journalist, it was significantly important that I was able to contribute feeds to Radio Havana's English language broadcast regarding Mumia's trial proceedings, in addition to the station's regularly broadcast news notes on the trial. On August 7, 1995, the Cuban broadcasters jubilantly announced to the world that there had been a stay of the execution. Radio Havana's broadcast was beamed throughout Europe, North America, and the Caribbean and translated into other languages as well.

The August 23, 1995 issue of *GRANMA International,* (in its Spanish, French, and English editions), carried a photo of Mumia with the headline: "Execution of U.S. Black Activist Postponed."

Cuba has been consistent in its support of our political prisoners and prisoners of war. The Mumia Campaign in Havana was coordinated by our Sister and freedom fighter in exile, Assata Shakur, who stated: "I think that the act of soliciting the help of international bodies will be one of our most important organizing tools to ensure that Mumia lives and eventually is set free."

And we thank you, Cuba, for

<blockquote>

When powerful nations threaten us
with their demagoguery and war machines,
when our freedom fighters face death at the hands of the state,
We listen to Cuba when she pierces the walls of propaganda
with truth—
while challenging without fear
her enemy.
We have observed Cuba reaching out to the world
through acts of active solidarity.
It is understandable how a Cuban child
would hold my hand and tell me emphatically—
"Mumia will be free!"

</blockquote>

•••

MARGARET RANDALL
A WORD, BOSNIA

A word not at home in our handled memories
dances on prime time. Images
sting the eyes, dismantle reason.
Ethnic cleansing: will we
reach for translucence of other voices... bodies...
or is it always a new word
descending from wooded hills, scaling walls,
this history of arched stone?

Bosnia: some would say it is your turn now.
They would be wrong. Picture
held by remote control, stopped by
a magic switch of channels.
Generous upper screen offers bodies
—ceaseless count—while the leaner bottom strip
moves Major League results across
our numbered response.

Headline News tugs at the corner of my mouth.
What is that flash of color sandwiched
on periphery? One lost birthday
my heart reaches to swallow

and disguise.
One-on-one works here: last child out today
is five, his face
a permanent question mark.

Our four old women starved in their nursing home.
Too quickly they are arranged
then rearranged to reap our charity
but never explain the word cut through
by sudden heave of shoulders,
eyes averted, smile misplaced
beside the 30-second byte.

This new word parts sirens, creeps into my language,
will not sleep.

•••

FRANK M. CHIPASULA

We Must Crush the Parasite
after Pablo Neruda

We must hunt that parasite, the pest,
until we crush him under our boots;
smoke him out of his hill-hewn palace
into which his desire for death has driven him.
Either stone him down his self-made prison
Down the luminous dungeon or snuff him out,
And let him writhe in the scorching sun.
We must spray him with terrible bullets of verse,
This skunk who has made dark and shady
Transactions with the enemy and sold our land;
Bombard this thing till it is tattered like a rag:
This flea, this swollen jigger, this parasite
lodged between the immense toes of our land,
filled to the neck with our pilfered blood.
We must fearlessly dig our own flesh
and root him out of his secret hide-out;
Hook him out by his shriveled wasp legs
Swaddled in the London worsted;
Flush out this parasite that wears the image

of a benevolent lion stained with our blood:
Grab his false tail and chop off
his long claws that have strangled our land,
that have reached every hut and snuffed out the fire.
We must grab him by his false tail
and brain him against Mulanje mountain.
We must be ready with our sharpened pens and inkwells
filled with the blood he has siphoned from our veins
and splash his huge sin all over his overcoat.
We must be ready with hard-hitting couplets
angry with double hatred, furious with love,
tercets exploding with thrice the violence
of this terrible lion.
We must load them with monstrous images
of fierce grotesque lizards always ready to strike.
We shall train our polished steel muzzles on him,
let the hand grenades of flaming metaphors
get him right in the gut, and ravage this handful of dust.
We must rout this terrible Chitute[1] today;
We must crush this parasite today.

---

[1] Chitute: the ugly mouse that amasses food.

•••

AMMIEL ALCALAY
A Stitch in Time

The following text was written in 1987, in Jerusalem, following the arrest, abduction and imprisonment of Mordechai Vanunu, an Israeli nuclear technician who "revealed" the "secrets" of Israel's nuclear capabilities to the world. Vanunu remains in prison in Israel; far from being embraced by the liberal left, he has been abandoned, left to cope with conditions created to make him insane. When charged with "exposing state secrets," Vanunu said: "The individual can compel the establishment, can say to it, You are accountable to me. The individual can expose the dark machinations of any regime in the world, in any sphere, by means of civil disobedience. An action like mine teaches citizens that their own reasoning, the reasoning of every individual, is no less important than that of the leaders. They use force and sacrifice thousands of people on the altar of their megalomania. Don't follow them blindly." When asked to contribute to this collection, the circumstances of this piece seemed fitting. The specific politics also seem quite apt, even at the remove of eight years, even despite the agreements reached between representatives of the Palestinian and Israeli people.

A few days after getting back from Cairo, I found myself in bed reading the paper and listening to the radio. I was recovering from a case of laryngitis, the germ of which, I suspect, had been planted by a mean wind coming out of the Libyan desert in Saqara; the germ was then nurtured by the bitter March cold of Jerusalem. Radio Jordan was on the tail end of a twelve part series called 25 Years of Rock. After Lyndon Johnson's fateful words, "I regret the necessities of war have compelled us," a song I remember well came on, "The Eve of Destruction," by Barry McGuire. The song reminded me of the strike my brother had helped organize to shut down our high school during the bombing of Cambodia in 1970; it reminded me of the older students we saw teargassed and beaten by the cops in the afternoons in Harvard Square or around the Boston Common, of the Black Panthers I used to talk to as they sold the party paper on streetcorners. Everything that had been a way of life for kids from Roxbury or Dorchester slowly entered our lives. We didn't have to be black: Having long hair or hanging around the park after dark was as good a reason as any for the cops to flip on their searchlights, invite you in for a ride, and start asking funny questions.

In the paper I was reading, under the bold headline, "He's No Traitor, He's My Brother," two dark, resolute faces stood out against the silhouette of buildings and TV antennas. It must have been the end of another long day. Asher, who looked a little more like his older brother Mordechai, seemed a bit wearier than Meir Vanunu. Neither really had the time to shave. Whatever their worries, something else came through their eyes: a look that surfaced from a deeper source, the place where feeling and conscience unite in action. The caption under this stark image said it all. In Hebrew the literal phrase was, "He went in the light of day." "He came clean," I'd say, in good American. I was glad at least someone was their brother's keeper.

An Israeli paper had asked me for a contribution to a special issue devoted to twenty years of occupation. I must confess that my first reaction was one of extreme cynicism. Fine, I thought, they'll have a cocktail party, maybe even a barbecue. Many Israelis and foreigners, myself included, seemed guilty of institutionalizing the terms of oppression through subsidized research, ideas, and finally, talk and more talk about a simple unadorned question of power that remained as clear as the light of day to any stone-mason, prisoner, taxi-driver, short-order cook or right-wing politician. Meanwhile, olive trees continued to be ripped out of Palestinian earth and placed cosmetically along the flowered paths of Israeli institutions for the benefit of Hadassah ladies or visiting artists and academics. Land continued to be confiscated; houses blown up; people imprisoned, expelled and tortured; families kept apart; students teargassed and shot. Daily. Weekly. Monthly. Like the rent. Or taxes. Just part of life. At least Vanunu had done something dramatic. Then I figured, why not write about him? After all, speaking your mind never hurts. Maybe there was more light in Meir and Asher's eyes than I'd bargained for. So I wrote something, but they didn't publish it.

I've never been one to subscribe to what I call the liberal "dream deferred" theory that once there was a pure Zionist dream that went askew: for some, in 1948; for others in 1956, 1967, 1973, 1977, or even 1982. More like a rotten apple, I thought, or the fig of good and evil. A description of Albert Entebbi, one of the more important Palestinian Jewish leaders in the early 1900s, kept coming back to me during Vanunu's capture and the disclosure of his diaries. They called Entebbi an "arrogant, haughty, capricious, perverse, irascible, violent, despotic, ruthless," and, finally (in my mind, at least), the key word: "Asiatic." Entebbi had repeatedly argued that Palestinian protest was generated by the practices of the new settlers and not the "violent" or "despotic" nature of anyone. Has anything really changed? Or were the slurs against Vanunu simply the same prejudices, with subtler methods? In remembering how he grew up in Marrakesh, Vanunu said: "The rich lived outside, but most of the people lived in the *mellah*. There were Jewish schools in the Quarter, but I studied at the Alliance School, with about an hour a day in Hebrew. I used to go around quite a bit, I remember there was a place called the Jamaa'l-Fnaa, people would come from all kinds of places outside the city, and there were all kinds of performers there—snake charmers and acrobatic cyclists, someone reading from the Quran, musicians, and everyone used to sit there and I used to go there myself, a little kid, by myself, and wander around." Later on, after being bound and gagged in court, he managed to describe the way he was kidnapped in Italy and brought back to Israel: "They brought me here like Kunta Kinte, chained up like a slave."

In contrast to the reigning rhetoric, I thought of a New Year's sermon I had been studying, given in 1942 by Moise Ventura, the chief rabbi of Alexandria: "After the lamentable failure of Western civilization, the Orient is again called upon to play an important part in the cultural life of Nations. The Orient means Egypt, Palestine, Syria, Iraq; more specially, the Semites—Jews and Arabs—are again called upon together to play a vital role within the scene of history. Everyone whose mental capacities are in free working order must recognize that today the enemies of the Jews are as well the enemies of the Arabs—that is, the enemies of civilization." In the long run, Jews will always remain a minority in the world, and in the Middle East. The choice remains to either keep building the ghetto walls higher and higher and thicker and thicker, or to start picking and chipping and breaking them away—to look at the light of day and see that there is no Palestinian problem but an Israeli one; that "security" can only be measured by how one reacts and acts against continuing oppression. The memory of a suffering people, as Jews know only too well, is long and both good and bad deeds are inscribed in everyone's remembrance. Moreover, true relationships are always reciprocal, and relations between people have always outlived those between states.

In 1945, Rabbi Ventura delivered another sermon in Alexandria, entitled "An Echo of the Atomic Bomb." It began like this: "The state of the discovery of the atomic bomb marks the historic moment of the most spectacular explosion of materialism, that world system founded on the principle of the eternity and indestructibility of matter." The monotheistic concept of god, as delineated by both classical Islamic and Jewish theologians, projects a spark of brilliance into the nuclear age. Yet the authorities continue to act as if they were in the vanguard not of the twenty-first, but of the nineteenth century—still living as if this world will last forever, still thinking in colonial, positivist, materialist, and determinist terms. Maybe the decision of Mordechai Vanunu's brothers to initiate a public campaign on his behalf; to refuse the terms and implications of his imprisonment, and to attempt to throw those terms back in the face of his accusers as a challenge is part of a deeper critique, a deeper revolt, part of the way back to another vision of things that can break down the ghetto walls. The choice? To mix mortar and cover the bricks that will seal our eyes from the light of day; or to retrieve forgotten and buried chapters left out of official and received history, alms against oblivion that can be turned to knowledge and used in the only place they might have any possible bearing on the future.

•••

MARTÍN ESPADA
The Meaning of the Shovel

Barrio Rene Cisneros
Managua, Nicaragua 1982

This was the dictator's land
before the revolution.
Now the dictator is exiled to necropolis,
his army brooding in camps on the border,
and the congregation of the landless
stipples the earth with a thousand shacks,
every weatherbeaten carpenter
planting a fistful of nails.

Here I dig latrines. I dig because last week
I saw a funeral in the streets of Managua,
the coffin swaddled in a red and black flag,
hoisted by a procession so silent
that even their feet seemed
to leave no sound on the gravel.
He was eighteen, with the border patrol,
when a sharpshooter from the dictator's army
took aim at the back of his head.

I dig because yesterday
I saw four walls of photographs:
the faces of volunteers
in Catholic school uniforms
who taught campesinos to read,
bringing an alphabet
sandwiched in notebooks
to places where the mist never rises
from the trees. All dead,
by malaria or the greedy river
or the dictator's army

swarming the illiterate villages
like a sky full of corn-plundering birds.

I dig because today, in this barrio
without plumbing, I saw a woman
wearing a yellow dress
climb into a barrel of water
to wash herself and the dress
at the same time,
her cupped hands spilling.

I dig because today I stopped digging
to drink an orange soda. In a country
with no glass, the boy kept the treasured bottle
and poured the liquid into a plastic bag
full of ice, then poked a hole with a straw.

I dig because today my shovel
struck a clay bowl centuries old,
the art of ancient fingers
moist with this same earth,
perfect but for one crack in the lip.

I dig because I have hauled garbage
and pumped gas and cut paper
and sold encyclopedias door to door.
I dig, digging until the passport
in my back pocket saturates with dirt,
because here I work for nothing
and for everything.

•••

JORGE MATOS VALLDEJULI

From the Cordillera to the Altiplano[1]

Yuisa
woman chief
of ours
look who watches
over your Cordillera
Creoles and those
wealthy from the north

that have not respected
the "cemis"
still waiting for their liberty

Look Yuisa
at the disgrace
of the Caribbean
that you saw
from Mt. Duarte
a Balaguerian lighthouse
Dominican shame
denounced by Guillen
"Shout your black soul poet"
denied and exploited
in Latin America
Cuba will be proud
of your indigenous
guerilla insurrection
Rise Chiapas
and send fear into the
mansions of
Mexico City
struggle for your
roots that
Guatemalan generals
want to exterminate
along with peasants that walked
with machetes by Sandino
beautiful Nicaragua
assaulted by American flags
robbing bananas
from your land

Take a look Yuisa
at the Andean barbarity
your daughters dead
from Cuzco to Lima
Tell me Neruda
who was oppressed
in the peaks of Macchu Picchu
Come down from the heavens
Allende and rescue
those assassinated
in Pinochet's conscience

Return Guevara
to your Buenos Aires
to cry with the
mothers of the disappeared
in cemeteries made by
Peronists, Videlaists, Galtierists
Resurrect Tupac Amaru
and save your
miners of tin
forgotten in Potosi
Bolivian people in struggle singing......[2]

.........Fin

---

[1] This poem, originally written in Spanish, was translated by the author.

[2] Lines of a Bolivian folk song (usually sung during reading).

•••

SUHEIR HAMMAD *

Patience

I await you tonight
with my spirit sharp as a blade
ready to slice

I await you in silence
my people's screams & cries of horror
mixing with the sound of the crickets

I await you in sunlight
my soul kissed by the warmth
shiny as the blade I carry
I wait in silence

I play with butterflies
while cleaning my blade
I clean in the rivers
enjoying the fish fly
while I await you

I await you in the dark
the moon playing a game of
shadows with me

the night flowers opening
while we await you

for these flowers & butterflies
these rivers & this soul
belong to this land
you cannot own them

I await you forever
to laugh at your
official documents, legal treaties

the fish & butterflies & flowers laugh
we laugh at your tanks and bombers
we carry our spirits
sharp as swords
We await you
shoulder to shoulder
our soldiers in the battlefield
our grandparents in their graves
our future in their wombs
shoulder to shoulder
sharp as the tall grass
strong as the morning tide

our dancer's sweat... the dew on the leaves
our mother's cries... the soaring birds above

We await you
know you will come
for it seems your nature
we smell your greed
taste your money
while I crouch in the fields
I wait for you

These fields & shadows
this spirit & life
belong to this land
and you cannot own us

And for you we wait

•••

NGÔ THANH NHÀN *

Mumia - Con Ròng Và Nhà Tù
(Mumia - The Dragon and The Prison)

Nhà lao mó cúa át ròng bay...
nhú nhât ky Cu Hò[1] còn ghi lai dâu dây
nhú chúng nhân cúa thê ky lúu dày...
và thê ky cúa phong trào giài phóng
và thê ky cúa dâu tranh giành dôc lâp
cúa con ngúòi vùng dây vói lúóng tâm!

When the prison gate opens
The dragon flies out!
This verse of Hô Chí Minh[2] still resounds today
like a witness to the century of exile
to the century of the liberation movements
to the century of the struggle for independence
of the people arising with a voice of conscience.

Chúng bát anh
khi anh bi thúónng nàm mê trên vung máu
Chúng bày trân hành quyét anh bang nhung ngon dòn thù
Chánh án
      toàn quyen
          canh sát
             luât pháp
                nhà tù
Chúng to chuc giet anh bang luât hình thâm dôc!

They captured you
when you were wounded, lying in your own blood
They meditated the execution process
   with all their weapons of hatred
The judge
      the governor
         the police
            the laws and the prisons
They schemed to execute you
      with their laws of crimes!

Chúng bit miêng anh
tuong loi anh mãi mãi chon vùi
nhung tieng nói anh van vang dong dat troi

They muzzled you
thinking they would bury your words
but your voice still rings loud throughout the sky

Chúng xu tu anh
tuong rang anh se chet
Anh chua di ma bão noi dien cuong...
The gioi bên anh voi loi buoc toi
voi tieng thét gao doi công ly cho anh!

They signed your death warrant
thinking you would surely die
Yet you have not gone
the angry storm of the people has struck
The world is by your side with an indictment
and the call for justice!

Anh Mumia
Abu-Jamal–môt dung si da den oanh liêt
Anh Mumia
Abu-Jamal–môt con nguoi khí tiet
truoc su that dau lòng trong xã hôi vong thân
truoc lòng tham không dáy vô cùng
truoc bô máy dàn áp dân nghèo khon kho
truoc xã hôi ca tung dong tien khong mac co
trouc môt bay tu ban quy su luu manh...
                              rao giang nhân quyen!

Brother Mumia
Abu-Jamal–a valiant black fighter
Brother Mumia
Abu-Jamal–a courageous human
in the face of the society of the disenfranchised
in the face of the insatiable greed
in the face of the oppressive machine

                                    against the poorest
                            in the face of the societal system
                                    that worships money shamelessly
                            in the face of the satanic capitalists...
                                    who dare to preach human rights

Anh Mumia
Abu-Jamal
Loi anh nói thiet tha tình nghiã
Anh dang nói
            cho nhung dong chi Báo Den
                    dã bo mình trên chien dia!

                            Brother Mumia
                            Abu-Jamal
                            With your words of love and justice
                            You speak
                                    for your Black Panther comrades
                                        who sacrificed in the battlefield!

Dau phai chi o Viêt Nam
            thoi tien cách mang
Chúng dung nhà tù Chí Hoà, Tam Hiêp, Côn Son, Thua Phu...
200,000 tù chính tri
            trong môt nuoc thât nghèo...
Dâu phai chi o Phi luât Tân
            El Salvador
                    Chilê
                            Colombia
                                    Guatemala
Không nuoc nào
            chúng không giet nguoi, hãm hai nhieu tù chính tri
Dung bô máy sát nhân
            de cho chúng làm giàu...

                            It's not only in Vietnam
                                    before the revolution
                            where they built prisons and guillotines
                            like Chi Hoa, Tam Hiep, Con Son, Thua Phu
                            with more than 200,000 political prisoners
                                    in a country tiny and poor
                            It is not only in the Philippines
                                    El Salvador

Chile

Colombia

Guatemala

where they freely kill people and political prisoners

to become even wealthier

Nhung o My chúng diên cuong

nhieu lan hon môt triêu

Canh sát, FBI, CIA, luât pháp, quân dôi, nhà tù

Khap moi noi...

ngang nhiên...

nhu bánh mì cua cuôc song hàng ngày

dông dao tù nhân chua tung thay trên doi!

But mind you, in the U.S.A.

they are a million times more vicious than

elsewhere

The police, FBI, CIA, the laws,

the army and the prison system

are everywhere...

standing tall...

like part of the people's daily bread

with the largest number of prison inmates

ever to be found anywhere on earth!

Nhà lao mó cúa át rông bay

Anh Mumia,

môt dáng viên Báo Den anh dung kiên cúòng

Anh biên thành pháo lênh tiên công

bói anh không còn là môt ky giá dón thuàn

bói anh dã biên thành môt ti con nguòi cam giân

ram râp xuong duong không chi o Phila

New York, Boston, Frisco và nhieu tinh nua

Paris, Hambourg, Viêt Nam cho chí Cuba

When the prison gate opens

The dragon flies out!

Brother Mumia,

a glorious Black Panther Party member,

You have become our call to battle

Because you are not merely a journalist

Because you have become a billion people strong

marching on the streets not only in Philadelphia

                    but also in New York City, Boston,
                    San Francisco, and more
                    from Paris, Hamburg, Vietnam to Cuba

Dâu phái chí ó Viêt Nam
Chúng bi dánh võ dâu tan tác!

                    And it is not only in Vietnam
                    that they were smashed to pieces
                            even before they left!

Anh Mumia
Ròng den bay khói nhà lao!

                    Brother Mumia
                    The black dragon is flying out of prison!

_____

[1] Ho Chi Minh. 1966. *Prison Diary*. Hanoi, Vietnam: Foreign Languages Publishing House.
[2] Poem translated by Ngô Thanh Nhàn & Merle Ratner.

●●●

vi. My eyes wide open

ERIC DROOKER

(statements)

SAFIYA BUKHARI

COINTELPRO & Philly Cops Conspire to Kill Mumia

Mumia Abu-Jamal, former member of the Black Panther Party, MOVE supporter, internationally renown revolutionary journalist, husband, father, grandfather, is on death row in Pennsylvania. On Thursday, June 1, 1995, Pennsylvania Governor Tom Ridge signed a warrant of execution and ordered Mumia to be put to death by lethal injection on August 17, 1995, at 10 pm despite knowing that Mumia's legal team was filing his Post Conviction Relief Appeal (PCRA) on Monday, June 5, 1995.

The ostensible reason the Commonwealth of Pennsylvania plans to execute Mumia Abu-Jamal is because of the death of Police Officer Daniel Faulkner, the night of December 9, 1981. Mumia was arrested on the scene, tried, convicted, and sentenced to be executed for Daniel Faulkner's death. The real reason Mumia is on death row is because of his political beliefs and affiliations and the fact that his life is a testimony to those political beliefs. Mumia did not just verbalize what he knew to be the inequities and oppressive nature of Philadelphia specifically and this society in general. Mumia internalized the problem and then used his journalistic skills and political education to pull the cover off the corrupt government in Philadelphia, its police, and its police state, exposing them for who and what they were/are.

Mumia understood the purpose of journalism. He understood that he had a responsibility to tell the truth and expose corruption and injustice to the people. The people could not be expected to act on this corruption without the facts. Mumia not only exposed the corruption but uncovered the facts and made them known to the people in a manner the people had no problem understanding. He also spoke out in defense of the people who had no one else to speak for them. A case in point was that of the MOVE organization, which had been continuously victimized by the government of Philadelphia and the Philadelphia Police Department. Women and men in the MOVE organization had been continuously victimized by the police department to the point where the brutality women suffered had led to miscarriages and stillborn babies. The baby of one MOVE sister had been beaten to the point that the baby died in her arms as a result of the sister being knocked to the ground. No one but Mumia reported on these atrocities.

But Mumia's standing up for truth did not just start with MOVE. The record of his quest for truth and speaking out began in 1968 when he was fourteen years old. He knew which side he stood on in the struggle between the oppressed and the oppressor, and from that day forward he worked to educate the people and expose, by example, the nature of the state.

This constant barrage of information exposing the Philadelphia Police Department's history of police brutality and police violence made him a thorn in the side of the Philadelphia Police Department and someone to be dealt with. The Black Panther Party, which had helped him develop his journalism skills, in addition to his political education, had been destroyed by the FBI's COINTELPRO war against it and the inability of members of the Party to internalize some very basic principles of the protracted struggle.

Many Panthers—left out there on their own, without organizational backing and support—became vulnerable to the police departments of their various cities and states and to the FBI because of their revolutionary political stances while they were members of the Black Panther Party.

•••

WILLIAM M. KUNSTLER

Death Row Writer Deserves New and Fair Trial

To the Editor:

Re "Mumia Abu-Jamal, Celebrity Cop Killer" (*The New York Times* Op-Ed, August 13, 1995): Philadelphia's District Attorney, Lynne Abraham, who seeks the death penalty in virtually every murder case in that city, is just as grotesque when it comes to telling the whole truth.

In seeking to blunt the worldwide outcry for a new trial for Mumia Abu-Jamal, she labels all of his defense theories as "falsehoods," and attempts to destroy them by her version of what she calls "the truth."

I do not want to add the slightest veneer of legitimacy to any of the arguments advanced by her in her effort to controvert those put forth by what she calls "a well-financed propaganda machine" with its "shrill chorus" of "lawyers who will say anything, no matter how false, to attract publicity, and by attention-seeking celebrities and spin doctors who attract it all too easily."

However, a few examples should reveal the intensity of Ms. Abraham's desire to placate the Fraternal Order of Police and enhance the reputation of her office.

She maintains that Mr. Abu-Jamal was represented at trial "by an experienced former prosecutor" when she knows that the latter, who was later disbarred, insisted from his appointment that he had never tried a capital case and was not prepared to do so, an appraisal he repeated under oath just weeks ago.

Although the jury was informed that Mr. Abu-Jamal had confessed to the crime, the arresting officer, who was present at the time such admission would have been made, wrote in his report that the defendant made no statements at all.

This officer conveniently took his vacation at the beginning of the trial, and a defense request for a short continuance to await his return was summarily denied by the judge, a former Philadelphia undersheriff.

Lastly, Ms. Abraham struggles to downgrade Mr. Abu-Jamal, whom she labels "a high school dropout," as a radio reporter, omitting that, at the time of the incident, he was president of the Philadelphia Association of Black Journalists and an outspoken critic of Mayor Rizzo's police force and its brutal vendetta against the members of the black radical group MOVE.

In 1985 an incendiary bomb was dropped by the authorities on the MOVE house, incinerating 11 people, including several infants, and destroying 62 black homes in the area.

Ms. Abraham does herself little credit by slandering concerned people who are interested in nothing more than a new and fair trial for a man who may well have unjustly spent almost 14 years on death row.

•••

HERB BOYD
An Award-winning Journalist Denounces NABJ A Letter—August 7, 1995

If the National Association of Black Journalists (NABJ) insists on having its annual convention in Philadelphia on the date scheduled for the execution of Mumia Abu-Jamal, then this is one member who will respectfully resign from the organization.

Moreover, the award the association gave me in 1992 for excellence in journalism, which to date I have cherished, will be promptly returned. There is no way I can, with integrity, be affiliated with an organization that seems so insensitive to the plight of a fellow journalist.

While there is no way for any of us to determine with certainty whether Abu-Jamal is guilty or innocent in the death of a police officer in 1981, we do know that his *Constitutional* rights were abrogated, and that alone is compelling enough for me to side with him as he awaits execution August 17. It should be noted, too, that there are at least nine examples of why Mumia did not get a fair trial, including denial of counsel of his choice.

It is incomprehensible that the NABJ's board of governors is so firmly committed to hosting a convention on such an inauspicious date. Are we to assume that the reports are true that the association is capitulating to the Philadelphia Fraternal Order of Police (FOP)? Or worse—that the decision has more to do with a board that has no empathy or regard for a black journalist who stepped across the so-called lines of objectivity in his position on MOVE?

Neither of these reasons is overwhelming and of such critical import to leave a brother to a merciless state poised to take his life.

Should you hold to your course, I am sure that there will be others who will take umbrage at your despicable resolve, which bears all the earmarks of a collection of spineless, gutless careerists. If anything, the NABJ board should be joining those interested in the pursuit of justice.

Mumia's situation is reminiscent of hundreds of cases where black men have been framed and railroaded to prison and death on trumped up charges. The savage, unfair executions of Willie McGee, the Trenton Six, and the Martinville Seven come quickly to mind.

It is all the more reprehensible that the city of your planned convention is Mumia's home and the place where he headed one of your chapters.

Finally, I find it disheartening that such callous disregard, such cold indifference can be found among black journalists. There is time yet to show your true colors, to dispel the notion that NABJ—with apologies to Elombe Brath[1]—does not mean NEGROES AGAINST BROTHER JAMAL!

The appearance of this letter was soon followed by a number of responses from NABJ members, including sharp condemnations from K. Maurice Jones and Glen Ford, a founder of the organization. These responses, however, did nothing to move the board to change its mind. Although as the date neared for the convention, there were rumors of differences among board members and some assertions that the intransigence should be placed on Dorothy Gilliam, the president.

A week before the scheduled convention, Judge Albert Sabo ordered a stay of execution, and this decision took some of the heat off the NABJ. Now they could proceed without facing the possibility that some of them might have had the ignominious task of covering an execution in which, in my opinion, they were complicit.

JUAN SÁNCHEZ

While I was elated by Judge Sabo's decision, which was a cynical move on his part to save face, it still did not alter my stance on the NABJ and the convention. I had no intention of attending, particularly after learning that a panel I was scheduled to be on had arbitrarily been canceled. To this day I am convinced that my opposition to the board was instrumental in this cancellation.

From several close friends I received reports of the convention. The panel devoted to Mumia's case, according to one participant, was interrupted by people from the audience who demanded to be heard. I was also told that the Fraternal Order of Police had formed a counter demonstration against those protesting the convention. And this support from the FOP indicts the whole affair better than any critique from this writer.

No, I have not returned the award—I don't know who to send it to anyway—but there is no intention on my part to renew my lapsed membership. Until the NABJ, as an organization, declares it is more than a body of careerists who place their jobs above integrity and conscience, I will remain a nonmember. If the mission of the organization is one that contradicts salvaging a journalist in need, then it is of little use to this reporter, who finds it impossible to be "objective" about the plight of Mumia Abu-Jamal.

---

[1]Elombe Brath, chairman of The Patrice Lumumba Coalition, has defined NABJ as Negroes About Bullshit and Jive.

•••

STANDING DEER

Fast for Survival - August 6th thru 17th, 1995
for Hiroshima - Nagasaki - Mumia Abu-Jamal

If we are to vent our riotous anger
let it be before they try to murder
Mumia Abu-Jamal, not after.

—Michael Parenti,
Martin Luther King H.S., Berkeley, California
June 25, 1995

I am honored and overwhelmed that there are three sisters fasting for Mumia in my name. I send my love to Rosemari Mealy of NYC, Anne Meegan in Chicago, and my dear friend and long-time supporter from Seattle, Gavin Greene. To these sisters and to the organizer of Political Prisoners Unite, I extend the left hand of my left arm, which is closest to my heart.

Each August 6th, for over a decade, I have fasted and prayed for four days for the victims of Hiroshima and Nagasaki, and for the survival of Mother Earth and the creatures who find sustenance at her breast. This year, because the State of Pennsylvania has plans to legally lynch our brother Mumia Abu-Jamal, he is foremost in my prayers; we must do everything in our power to save him.

My religion is against the law in this Iron House of Greed, but fasting is one aspect of my religion my jailers are powerless to stop. So my fast this year is twelve days, from August 6th thru the 17th. The extra eight days are for Mumia.

I am fasting and praying for all the peoples of this world, for all the little animals of the woods, for the gilled people of the waters, for the winged creatures of the air and for all living things such as the flowers, trees, and grasses. I pray that our Mother will not be destroyed as was Hiroshima and Nagasaki. I pray for the victims of those atrocities both living and dead. I pray that the politicians of this world will quit building these life-taking weapons of mass destruction, and instead begin dismantling them so that our unborn generations may know a life in harmony with our Mother. I pray for those who daily suffer the knowledge of hunger because they cannot find even a crust of bread to feed themselves and their starving children. I especially pray for the little ones who in their innocence have inherited a world intent on destroying itself, because of the greed of a tiny minority of criminals like Tom Ridge and Judge Sabo who lust for power and privilege and will kill poor people without number to get and keep it.

I am praying for Mumia Abu-Jamal and my brother Leonard Peltier, and for all of our sisters and brothers who are imprisoned throughout the world. But most of all I am praying that some of our people will come to realize that this is about our brother's life. HIS LIFE!!! and it only takes a few of us who don't want him dead. Think of sister Assata. In the words of Ray Luc Levasseur: "We are at a point beyond candle vigils that reflect little besides moral indignation."

We don't need another martyr. We need our brother Mumia breathing, smiling, laughing; alive and well among us, talking that talk and writing those words as only he can do.

FREE MUMIA ABU-JAMAL!!!

•••

LEONARD PELTIER

Statement in Solidarity with Mumia Abu-Jamal
June 20, 1995

Greetings, my friends,

When I heard the awful news that Pennsylvania Governor Thomas Ridge had signed a death warrant for our Brother Mumia Abu-Jamal, setting an execution date for August 17th, two thoughts hit me simultaneously. One was absolute heart break for this man who has sacrificed, since he was just fourteen years old, so much of himself in his struggle within the African American Movement and for his family, friends, and supporters. The other was: What can I do to help? How can my network become involved in saving his life?

Nearly two decades in prison for a crime I did not commit, my sense of solidarity with Mumia is great. We are men in similar situations, men who fought for justice only to be persecuted by the system, a system that could not silence us. We have both been targeted by the

FBI for neutralization. We are both the victims of COINTELPRO. So many African and Native brothers and sisters have been victimized. When does it stop? What kind of a world are our children facing?

Today I take this stand, that the African and Native struggles unite in solidarity, that members of all races, of every sacred color unite. There are many good people in the world, but we are spread out and working on our own issues. If we join hands, mountains will move. We must force Judge Albert Sabo from this case by supporting Mumia's Motion for Recusal, and we must pressure Governor Ridge to grant a reprieve.

There is no more time to waste. We must forget our differences, make the effort to work harder, and save the life of Mumia Abu-Jamal.

There are few human beings with the eloquence and effectiveness to be the voice of the struggle for civil and social rights. Mumia is one of that handful. The world cannot afford to lose him.

In the Spirit of Crazy Horse...

•••

FEDERATION OF CUBAN WOMEN

To: The Coalition to Free Mumia Abu-Jamal

Queridos amigos:

En nombre de la Federación de Mujeres Cubanas, deseamos expresar nuestra satisfacción por la suspension de la ejecución de Mumia Abu-Jamal, conocido periodista afronorteamericano y luchador por los derechos de sus hermanos negros. Unimos nuestra voz a las de miles de escritores, artistas, periodistas e intelectuales en general, así como a cientos de personas prograsistas, que reclaman en distintos países del mundo la realización de un juicio justo que impida la condena racista e inhumana de Mumia Abu-Jamal.

Reiterándole nuestra solidaridad en esta lucha por la libertad del reconocido periodista, así como por la justicia y el verdadero respeto a los derechos humanos, llegue a él y a ustedes nuestro mensaje de aliento y amistad.

Federacion De Mujeres Cubanas
La Habana, 17 de agosto de 1995

Dear Friends:

In the name of the Federation of Cuban Women, we wish to express our satisfaction for the suspension of the execution of Mumia Abu-Jamal, well-known Afro-American journalist and struggler for the rights of his Black brothers and sisters.

We join our voice to that of thousands of writers, artists, journalists, and intellectuals in general, as well as that of hundreds of progressive people who are demanding, in countries throughout the world, the realization of a just trial that would overturn the racist and inhumane sentence of Mumia Abu-Jamal.

We reiterate our solidarity in this struggle for the freedom of this renowned journalist, as well as for justice and true respect for human rights. We hope our message of support and friendship reaches him and you.

Federation of Cuban Women
Havana, August 17, 1995

•••

PAN AFRICAN CONGRESS OF AZANIA
Statement in Support of Mumia Abu-Jamal

The Pan African Congress of Azania condemns in the strongest language the racist elements that wish to embark upon the execution of this great son of the soil, Africanist, and humanist: MUMIA ABU-JAMAL.

African blood will not continue to flow in vain. We stand with MUMIA ABU-JAMAL, just as we stand with our political prisoners here in Azania who have yet to be released from the sewers of prison cells in Pretoria, Cape Town, Johannesburg, Durban, and many other cities across Azania. We stand with political prisoners in Peru, Mauritania, Gambia, Nigeria, and the United States of America. We serve a reminder to all lovers of freedom that October 11 must not only be a day of solidarity with political prisoners, but a day when we demand and indeed fight for their release all over the world. The fight for MUMIA's life is the process of liberation of African people worldwide. It is a fight for our national dignity; it gives true meaning to the struggle for bread and social dignity. This internal relation is one of the roots of the immense solidarity that unites oppressed peoples to the exploited masses all over the world.

The Pan Africanist Congress of Azania and the Azanian people commit themselves to the peoples engaged in struggle, who today are convinced that Africans share their combat and are ready to intervene directly at the first call of the directing bodies towards a FREE MUMIA. We reiterate what Dr. Nkrumah said, Africans have nothing to lose but our chains, and we have an immense fight to win. We are brothers and sisters in the same struggle. We in Azania are not willing to accept the lie that we are free, the lie that Apartheid and colonialism are over. We are not willing, as a consequence, to accept a renovated but continued colonisation. The occupation of the settlers, through collaboration within the government of national unity, is the perpetuation of minority rights and freedoms on Azania. The masses go on scratching out a living from the soil, and unemployed men—now at 50%, who never find employment do not manage, in spite of public holidays and flags, new and brightly colored though they may be—cannot convince themselves that anything has really changed in their lives. The masses have no illusions, the struggle continues. They realise that they have been co-opted by those who have refined specialised opportunism. They can no longer believe that demagogues are the answer to freedom.

It is the allies of the same settlers who show contempt for all African people by planning MUMIA's execution on the birth of one of the true great Pan-Africanists, Marcus Garvey. It is imperative that Africanists everywhere join up, not only to condemn this action against

MUMIA, but to have a plan of action that declares to the world: touch an African; touch fire! The truth is that we ought not to accept this contempt. Our challenge to all the oppressors of MUMIA and African people worldwide is not a rational confrontation of point of view. It is not a negotiated settlement, but the untidy affirmation of an original idea propounded as an absolute: MUMIA MUST BE FREE! It is not enough for the imperialist executors of MUMIA to be reminded that their ability to delimit us through the use of their army and police force shows their cowardice. But we must remember what a corrosive element they are, destroying all that comes near them. They are the deforming element, disfiguring all that has to do with beauty or morality; they are the depository of maleficent powers, the unconscious and irretrievable instrument of blind forces. MUMIA must not be allowed to be prostituted by these poisoned and diseased executors for their own imperialist aims. MUMIA MUST BE FREE!

Our aim continues to be the same: to put an end to settler occupation, to give the land to the Azanians, to establish a policy of social democracy in which men and women have an equal right to culture, to material well-being and to dignity. WE the people of AZANIA stand with MUMIA towards the triumphant freedom from his executioners.

IZWE LETHU I AFRIKA (THE LAND IS OURS!)

Issued by Z.B. Moore,
Secretary for Publicity and Infromation
The Pan Africanist Congress of Azania

•••

INTERNATIONAL ACADEMICS FOR MUMIA ABU-JAMAL

Canadian Journalists Support Mumia

The co-chairs of the Racial Minority Writers' Committee (RMWC) (of The Writers' Union of Canada) join individuals and organizations in the international writing community to protest the death sentence of Mumia Abu-Jamal.

Hiromi Goto and Ashok Mathur, co-chairs of the RMWC, are calling on the other Canadian writers and concerned individuals to join this protest, demand a new trial, and force the removal of Judge Sabo from the case.

In Calgary, Mathur said, "This is not just a matter of guilt or innocence, nor simply a case for debate over capital punishment; this is about an abusive legal system, one that carries out the will of systematic racism in all its ugly manifestations."

Abu-Jamal, an African American journalist and activist, convicted of the 1981 murder of a white Philadelphia police officer, has gained a worldwide network of supporters who consider him a victim of a racist judicial system. His execution date of August 17, 1995, has been stayed indefinitely.

•••

PEN-International

The PEN-International Writers Union Parliament met in Paris on August 1, 1995, to condemn the trial process which has convicted Abu-Jamal. Among those writers voicing their demand for a new trial are Jacques Derrida (France), Günter Grass (Germany), Peter Handke (Austria), Patricia Williams (USA), Cornel West (USA), and Harold Pinter (Great Britain).

•••

Academics for Mumia Abu-Jamal

More than fifty professors and teachers, representing at least twenty-five universities and colleges, have now signed on with Academics for Mumia Abu-Jamal (AMAJ). Moreover, AMAJ now has a coordinating council that includes Professors Ann Fansworth-Alvear (History and Latin American Studies) and Ann Evans Guise (Education), both of the University of Pennsylvania in Philadelphia.

The enlarged group has released the following:

Declaration for Mumia Abu-Jamal

Across our many differences as scholars and citizens, we, in unity, declare our concern that full and deliberate justice and fairness be extended to Mr. Mumia Abu-Jamal.

As faculty of the tri-state area of Pennsylvania/New Jersey/New York, and increasingly throughout the nation and world, we protest Governor Ridge's signing of Mr. Abu-Jamal's death warrant. We demand Judge Sabo's removal from the case. We call for a new, speedy trial.

AMAJ Members' Sample Statement:

• *Manning Marable, Columbia University:*

"I have followed this case with considerable interest, and I deeply regret that Pennsylvania Governor Tom Ridge has signed the death warrant for Abu-Jamal."

• *Cornel West, Harvard University:*

[After witnessing the hearing before Judge Sabo on July 12, 1995.] "I'm here to support a fair trial for Mr. Abu-Jamal. But we've got to talk about the atmosphere here. This is a Jim Crow court. It is Mississippi, 1995."

• *Henry Louis Gates, Jr., Harvard University:*

"This is clearly a miscarriage of justice."

• *Patricia J. Williams, Columbia Law School:*

"It is impossible to sort out the truth of this case at the distance from which I write. Nevertheless, weighing the improprieties of Abu-Jamal's trial (including the possible suppression of evidence) against the life-and-death stakes for him, I am convinced that Abu-Jamal deserves another trial."

Photos by DEBORAH POHL

Academics for Mumia Abu-Jamal

Rebecca Alpert, Temple U. • Buzz Alexander, U. of Michigan • Houston A. Baker, Jr., U. of Penn. • Dennis Brutus, U. of Pittsburgh • Eduardo Cadava, Princeton U. • C. George Caffentzis, U. of South Maine • Sheila M. Contreras, U. of Texas • Joanne Cunningham, William Paterson • Michael Eric Dyson, U. of North Carolina • Silvia Federici, Hofstra U. • Ann Fansworth-Alvear, U. of Penn. • Henry Louis Gates, Jr., Harvard U. • Everett Green, SUNY • Ann Evans Guise, U. of Penn. • Victor Goode, Columbia School of Law • Sarah Griffin, U. of Penn. • Michael Hamm, Rutgers U. • Obrey Hendricks, Drew U. • Carolivia Herron, Harvard Div. Schl. • Alan Howard, Rutgers U. • Walton Johnson, Rutgers U. • Jung-Ha Kim, Georgia State U. • Bill Lawson, U. of Delaware • Paul Lefrak, U. of Michigan • Linda Longmire, Hofstra U. • Antonio McDaniel, U. of Penn. • Manning Marable, Columbia U. • Jim Marsh, Fordham U. • Alamin Mazrui, U. of Ohio • Howard McGray, Rutgers U. • Elsie McKee, Princeton Th. Sem. • Christopher Morse, Union Th. Sem. • Jack Nelson, Rutgers U. • Lucius Outlaw, Haverford College • Peter J. Paris, Princeton Th. Sem. • Janie Paul, U. of Michigan • Joyce Penfield, Rutgers U. • Marcus Rediker, U. of Pittsburgh • Yvette Richards, U. of Pittsburgh • Ellen Ross, Swarthmore College • Leong Seouw, Princeton Th. Sem. • Earl Shaw, Rutgers U. • Robert Stone, Long Island U. • Paul Surlis, St. Johns Univ. • Mark McClain Taylor, Princeton Th. Sem. • Mark Wallace, Swarthmore Coll. • David Watt, Temple U. • Cornel West, Harvard U. • John Edgar Wideman, U. of Mass. • Patricia J. Williams, Columbia U. Law

•••

U.K. Journalists Honour Death Row Black Activist

The National Union of Journalists (NUJ) in the U.K. and Ireland has thrown its weight behind the campaign to save the life of U.S. radical black journalist Mumia Abu-Jamal. The NUJ has made Abu-Jamal an honorary member—the first such member in its 87-year history.

The NUJ has involved scores of politicians in protests calling on the U.S. Federal Government to intercede to ensure a fair retrial for Abu-Jamal. The Union has also initiated a similar campaign among the 93 journalist unions all over the world affiliated to the Brussels-based International Federation of Journalists.

In the wake of the announcement of the stay of execution, the NUJ is organising a public meeting to renew the campaign to save the life of Abu-Jamal. The meeting is supported by the Anti-Racist Alliance and Amnesty International.

•••

MUMIA ABU-JAMAL
Letter to asha bandele

Long Live John Africa!

Ona Move, Asha—

Thanx for your kind and warm letters; I'm sorry I've not written sooner; I've been meaning to, but it seems as if there aren't enough hours in the day; I say "it seems," because there's always time to do what you want to do— yes? Of course.

I want to thank you for your invite to Pam and Ramona; My Sisters are true rebels: Revolutionaries of John Africa's Revolution who have battled this system for years and years, and are still rumblin'! Long Live John Africa's Revolution!

Thanx for your work on my behalf, and on the behalf of all political prisoners—I do appreciate it;

I once lived in Oakland, back when I was a teenager in the Black Panther Party; I found it a town turned cold to the party by the time I got there.

I lived there very briefly, spending most of my time in Berkeley, California, and some in Frisco—

I even did some time out there.

Our Elder Brother and teacher, Dr. Frantz Fanon said (I paraphrase) that "each new generation must discover their destiny, and either act to fulfill it, or betray it."

I know that as a young person, a teenager, and a high school student, you, and many of your colleagues, feel somehow out-of-the-flow of what's going on, ineffectual, and perhaps not "plugged in"!

In truth it is young people who are "natural revolutionaries";

Think of South Africa; The struggle in South Africa would've perished were it not for the youth of Sharpeville—whose sacrifice, whose sweet, young blood, watered the tree of freedom of the

LONG LIVE JOHN AFRICA!

5/11/94

Ona Move, Asha —

Thanx for your kind and warm letters;
I'm sorry I've not written sooner; I've
been meaning to, but it seems as if
"there aren't enough hours in the day!"
I say "it seems", because there's always
time to do what you want to do — yes?;
Of course.

I want to thank you for your invite
to Pam and Ramona; My sisters are
true rebels; Revolutionaries of John Africa's
Revolution, who have battled this system
for years and years and are still rumblin'!
Long Live John Africa's Revolution!
Thanx for your work on my behalf, and
on the behalf of all political prisoners — I
be appreciate it;

I once lived in Oakland, back when I was a
teenager in the Black Panther Party; I
found it a town turned cold to the party by
the time I got there.

I lived there very briefly, spending most of
my time in Berkeley, California, and some in
Frisco —

I even did some time out there ☺ ;
Our Elder Brother and Teacher, Dr. Frantz
Fanon said (I paraphrase) that 'each new
generation must discover their destiny, and either
act to fulfill it, or betray it.'
I know that as a young person, a teenager, and
a high school student, you, and many of your
colleagues, feel somehow out-of-the-place or remotes
going on, ineffectual, and perhaps not "plugged in!

My best to you —

Ona Move!

Mumia

rebel movements in S.A.

The "comrades"—young kids who refused to learn the hated language—Afrikaans—took to the streets and Energized a Movement that was virtually moribund;

The youth, Asha, are true revolutionaries. Once they challenge the repressive world of their elders, they literally can turn that world upside down.

This is Truth; If the youth of South Africa did what their parents said, and "shut up," and "sat down," and did what the Boers told them, Blacks would still be under the thumbs of the racist Afrikaaners; Mandela would still be in jail; and the ANC would be in Moscow, Oslo, N.Y.C., D.C., Dar Es Salaam; everywhere but in South Africa.

So, teach your fellows, your brothas and sistas, that they have Power; The Power of Youth; The Power of Will; The Power of Saying "No."

Reread Fanon's saying...

My best to you—

    Stay Rebellious!

    Ona Move!

    Mumia

•••

KALAMU YA SALAAM

my eyes wide open:
an open letter to my executioners

if you
catch me, so be it

my dark face knows
bush joys
i laugh at your square world
alternatives, everything you offer
smells like jail

my hair has been clipped
many, many times
but i continue to let it grow
choosing my beard over the edge
of your razor

track me with your dogs, spy
my toe prints on the mud
where i ran, where i danced

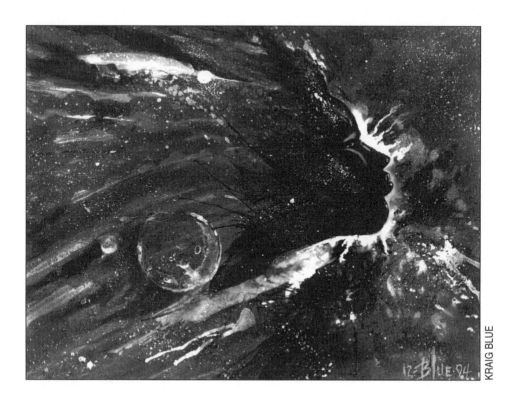

KRAIG BLUE

catch me if you can
and if you do
so be it

but before i'd dine on your
stolen feasts
i'll drink rain,
wash myself in the streams of life
and keep steppin'
keep steppin'
keep right on steppin' down the road
past my people's martyred bones
broken and stacked in irregular piles
by the wayside, past skulls
perched on poles, cruel totems
which i decline to heed
even if i have to go

totally nude to fight your dragons
you will not detour me
i will go
i will live while i'm alive
  refuse

i will even go to your white wall
place my firm handprint on the
  damp stucco darkened by body
   fluids siphoned from murdered comrades
reject the charity of your blindfold
wink as i stare down your bullets, and
greet sweet death with
my eyes wide open

catch me if you can
and if you do
so be it

•••••

VII. In the land of confiscated dreams

MAC MCGILL

(literary expressions)

JOHN EDGAR WIDEMAN
Ascent by Balloon from the Yard of Walnut Street Jail

I am the first of my African race in space. For this achievement I received accolades and commendations galore. Numerous offers for the story of my life. I'm told several unauthorized broadsides, purporting to be the true facts of my case from my very own lips, are being peddled about town already. A petition circulates entreating me to run for public office.

Clearly my tale is irresistible, the arc of my life emblematic of our fledgling nation's destiny, its promise for the poor and oppressed from all corners of the globe. Born of a despised race, wallowing in sin as a youth, then a prisoner in a cage, yet I rose, I rose. To unimaginable heights. Despite my humble origins, my unworthiness, my sordid past, I rose. A Lazarus in this Brave New World.

Even in a day of crude technology and maddeningly slow pace, I was an overnight sensation. A mob of forty thousand, including the President himself, hero of Trenton and Valley Forge, the father of our country as some have construed him in the press, attended the event that launched me into the public eye.

The event—no doubt you've heard of it, unless you are as I once was, one of those unfortunates who must wear a black hood and speak not, nor be spoken to—the event that transformed me from convict to celebrity received the following notice in the *Pennsylvania Gazette*:

> *On January 19, 1793 Jean-Pierre Blanchard, French aeronaut, ascended in his hydrogen balloon from the yard of Walnut Street Jail in Philadelphia to make the first aerial voyage in the United States. In the air forty-six minutes, the balloon landed near Woodbury, New Jersey and returned the same evening to the city in time for Citizen Blanchard to pay his respects to President Washington, who had witnessed the ascension in the morning.*

Though I am not mentioned by name in the above, and its bland, affectless prose misses altogether the excitement of the moment, the notice does manage to convey something of the magnitude of the event. Imagine men flying like birds. The populace aghast, agawk, necks craned upward, every muscle tensed as if anticipating the tightening of the hangman's knot, its sudden yank, the irresistible gravity of the flesh as a trap door drops open beneath their feet. Men free as eagles. Aloft and soaring over the countryside. And crow though I was, my shabby black wings lifting me high as the Frenchman.

I was on board the balloon because little was understood about the effect of great height upon the human heart. Would that vital organ pump faster as the air grew thinner? Would the heart become engorged approaching the throne of its maker, or would it pale and shrink, the lusty blood fleeing, as once our naked parents, in shame from the Lord's awful gaze? Dr. Benjamin Rush, a man of science as well as a philanthropic soul well known for championing the cause of a separate Negro church, had requested that a pulse glass be carried on the balloon, and thus, again, became a benefactor of the race, since who better than one of us, with our excitable blood and tropically lush hearts, to serve as guinea pig.

The honor fell on me. I was the Frenchman's crew. Aboard to keep the gondola neat and sanitary, a passenger so my body could register danger as we rose into those uncharted regions nearer my God to thee.

Jean-Pierre Blanchard was not my first Frenchman. Messrs. De Beauchamp and De Tocqueville had visited my cell in the Walnut Street Jail on a humanitarian, fact-finding mission among the New World barbarians to determine whether this Quaker invention, "the penitentiary," reformed criminals and deterred crime. The Frenchmen were quite taken with me. Surprised to discover I was literate. Enchanted when I read to them from the dim squalor of my cage the parable of the Good Shepherd, the words doubly touching, they assured me, coming from one who was born of a degraded and outcast race, one who, they assumed, had experienced only indifference and harshness.

No. Beg pardon. I'm confusing one time with another. Events lose their shape, slide one into another when the time one is supposed to own becomes another's property. An excusable mistake, perhaps inevitable when one resides in a place whose function is to steal time, rob time of its possibilities, deaden time to one dull unending present, a present that is absolutely not a gift, but something taken away. Time drawn, quartered and eviscerated, a sharp pain hovering over the ghost of an amputated limb. Too much time, no time, time tormenting as memories of food and blankets when you lie awake all night, hungry, shivering in an icy cell. No clocks. Only unvarying, iron bars of routine, solitary confinement mark your passage, your extinction outside time.

I would meet De Tocqueville and De Beauchamp years after the flight with Jean-Pierre Blanchard. By then I'd been transferred from Walnut Street Jail to the new prison at Cherry Hill. There, too, I would have the distinction of being the first of my race. Prisoner Number One. Charles Williams: farmer; light black; black eyes; curly black hair; 5' 7 1/2"; foot, 11"; flat nose, scar on bridge of nose, broad mouth, scar from dirk on thigh; can read.

First prisoner of any race admitted to Cherry Hill. Warden Samuel Wood greeted me with no acknowledgment nor ceremony for this particular historic achievement. Later that day, when I complained of dampness in my cell, he reminded me that the prison being new, on its shakedown cruise so to speak, one could expect certain unanticipated inconveniences. The good Warden Wood allowed me a berth in the infirmary until my cell dried out (it never did), but unfortunately the infirmary was also dank and chilly, due to lack of sunlight and ventilation, the cold miasma from marshy soil sweating up through the prison's foundation stones. So I began my residence with a hacking cough, the subterranean air at Cherry Hill as thick and pestilential as the air had been wholesome and bracing in the balloon.

I'm complaining too much. All lives a combination of good times and bad, aren't they? We all suffer under a death sentence, don't we. Today I wish to celebrate the good, that special time rising above the earth. So up, up and away then.

A cloudless morning. In minutes we drift to a height that turns Philadelphia into a map spread upon a table. The proud steeple of Christ Church a pen protruding from an ink well. After the lazy, curved snake of river, the grid of streets laid straight as plumb lines. I pick out the State House, Independence Hall, the Court House, Carpenters Hall, the market on High Street. And there, the yard of the Walnut Street Jail, there at 1, 2, 3,...count them...4, 5, Sixth

Street, the Jail and its adjacent yard from which we'd risen.

People are ants. Carriages inch along like slugs. Huge silence beats about my ears. A wind clean and safe as those rare dreams that enfold me, slip me under their skirts and whisk me far from my cell.

But I must not lose myself in the splendor of the day until I execute the task that's earned me a ride. Once done, I can, we can, return to contemplating a world never seen by human eyes till just this unraveling, modern instant.

I place the glass on my flesh, count the pulse beats 1, 2, 3,...as I practice courting rungs on the ladder of streets rising, no, sliced one after another, beginning at Water Street along the Delaware's edge.

Near the end of that momentous year of the balloon's ascension, a plague of yellow fever will break out in the warren of hovels, shanties and caves along the river and nearly destroy Philadelphia. My Negro brethren, who inhabit that Quarter in large numbers, will perform admirably with enormous courage, skill and compassion during the emergency. Nursing the afflicted, burying the dead. One measure of the city's desperation in that calamitous year, a petition that circulates (unsuccessfully) suggesting we, the inmates of the jail, be allowed to serve and, thereby risking our lives, purchase freedom. This is the year that famous prisoner, the French King, is beheaded, the year my bretheren will build their separate church, the African Episcopal Church of St. Thomas at Fifth and Walnut, a location empty at the moment, though cleared and ready. See it. From this elevation, a mere thumb print opposite the jail.

The Quakers, with their concern for the state of my soul, their insistence I have boundless opportunity to contemplate my sins, to repent and do penance, arrange matters in the jail so I have ample time to consider things consequential and not. I've often pondered late at night when I cannot sleep, the connection between two events of that busy year, 1793: the establishment of a Negro church, the plague that took so many citizens' lives. One act, man's, an assertion there is not enough room in the house of worship for black and white; the second act, God's, making more room.

During the terrible months when the city teetered on the brink of extinction, when President Washington with other Federal and City officials decamped to more salubrious locations, various treatments, all futile, were prescribed for the deadly fever. Among the treatments, phlebotomy, the opening of a vein to draw blood from a victim, was quite popular until its opponents proved it killed more often than it cured.

My brethren, trained and guided by the ubiquitous Dr. Rush, applied his controversial cure: an explosive purge of mercury and calomel, followed by frequent, copious bleedings. Negro nurses became experts, dispensing pharmaceutical powders and slitting veins with equal dexterity. Out with the bad air. In with the good. I couldn't resist a smile when I pictured my brethren moving through white peoples' houses during broad daylight as freely I once glided through the same dwellings after dark.

Emptying purses, wallets, pockets, desk drawers, I, too, relieving my patients of excess.

In prison also, we must drive out bad blood. Though all of us infected by the fever of lawlessness, some prisoners incurably afflicted. One such wretch, Matthew Maccumsey, Number 102. His crime: speech. Too much talk and at the wrong times and often in an obstreperous, disruptive, disrespectful manner, threatening the peace and economy of the entire system of absolute silence.

Ice water ducking, bagging with black hood, flogging, the normal and natural deterrents all applied and found wanting in lasting effect, the iron gag was prescribed. Number 102 remanded for examination and treatment to Dr. Bache, the nephew, I've heard, of the famous Dr. Franklin, the kite-flyer.

A committee, convened a decade later to investigate continuing complaints of questionable practices at the prison, described the gag in these words: a rough iron instrument resembling the bit of blind bridle, having an iron palet in the center about an inch square and chains at each end to pass around the neck and fasten behind. This instrument was placed in the prisoner's mouth, the iron palet over the tongue, the bit forced back as far as possible, the chains brought round the jaws to the back of the neck; the end of one chain was passed through the ring in the end of the other chain drawn tight to the "fourth link" and fastened with a lock.

Rousted out of sleep before first light, groggy, frightened, I knew by the hour, the hulking stillness of the figures gathered into the narrow corridor outside my cell, I was being summoned for a punishment party. Seeing the faces of other prisoners of color in the glaring torchlight, I rejoiced inwardly. This night atleast I was to be a punisher, not the punished. The guards always enlisted blacks to punish whites and whites to punish blacks, by this unsubtle stratagem, perpetuating enmity and division.

We forced No. 102's hands into leather gloves provided with rings, crossed his arms behind his back and after attaching the rings to the ends of the gag chain drew his arms upwards so their suspended weight pulled the gag chains taut, causing the chains to exert pressure on jaws and jugular, trapping blood in the averted head, producing excruciating pain, the degree of which I could gauge only by observing the prisoner's eyes, since the gag at last had effectively silenced him.

Niggrified, ain't he, a guard exclaimed, half in jest, half in disgust as 102's lifeless, once pale face, now blackened by congealed blood, was freed of the gag.

Again, I'm muddling time. The pacifying of 102 came later at Cherry Hill. My job on the balloon was to record the reaction of my own African pulse to heavenly ascent. Higher and higher it rose. The striped French balloon. The stiff, boat-shaped basket beneath it, garlanded with fresh flowers, red, white and blue bunting. Inside the gondola the flags of two great republican nations. We intended to plant them wherever we landed, claim for our countrymen joint interest in the rich, undiscovered lands far flung across the globe.

Watching the toy town shrink smaller and smaller beneath me, all its buildings and inhabitants now fittable on the end of a pin, for some unfathomable reason as I rose irresistibly to a heretofore undreamed-of height for any person of my race, as I realized the momentousness of the occasion, all the planning, sacrifice and dumb luck that had conspired to place me here, so high, at just that fantastic, unprecedented, joyous moment, as I began to perceive how far I'd risen and how much further, the sky literally the limit, still to rise, a single tear welled out from God-knows-where.

From my swaying perch high above everyone I watch our shadow eclipse a corner of the yard, then scuttle spider-like up the far wall of the Walnut Street Jail.

Observed from the height of the balloon I'd be just another ant. Not even my black hood pierced with crude eyeholes would distinguish me as I emerged from the night of my cell, blinking back the sudden onslaught of crisp January sunlight.

My eyes adjusted to the glare and there it was finally, the balloon hovering motionless, waiting for someone it seemed, a giant, untethered fist thrust triumphantly at the sky.

From the moment it appears, I am sure no mere coincidence has caused the balloon to rise exactly during the minute and a half outdoors I'm allotted daily to cross the prison yard, grab tools, supplies and return to my cell. If Citizen Blanchard's historic flight had commenced a few seconds sooner or later, I would have missed it. Imagine. I could have lived a different life. Instead of being outdoors glancing up at the the heavens, I might have been in my cell pounding on the intractable leather they apportion me for cobbling my ten pairs of shoes a week. In that solitary darkness tap-tap tapping, I wouldn't have seen the striped, floating sphere come to fetch me and carry me home.

How carefully I set the pulse glass above a vein. Register the measured ebb and flow, each flicker the heart's smile and amen.

•••

EUGENE B. REDMOND *

Mumia's Air/Mumia's Rainbow
(Refractions: Schomburg Open Mike Reading)

Harlem Becomes Mumia, I think, totin my East/Saint Louis "baggage" & steppin into W.C. Handy's "evening sun"; then descending the steps of Augusta Mann's brownstone—just a few doors, Amiri has reminded me, from the birthplace of Harlem's Black Arts Movement of the 60s—I go left to Malcolm X/Lenox Ave. & left again at the corner (overseen by Legs & Eyes Cocktail Lounge) to the Schomburg Center for Research in Black Culture: facing Harlem Hospital across 135th Street & M/L Blvd. The 5-block sun-stroll is crammed w/storefront Jesuses, money-changers, fish-mongerers, construction crews, liquor labs, grinning grocers, deals-on-wheels & "Free Mumia" posters/flyers. Harlem is inundated by Mumia, I'm noticing, just as Mumia must be inundated by Harlem in his Pennsylvania prison cell. [Tomorrow, I muse, a bus—or 2—loaded w/Free Mumia people will leave Manhattan for Philly & a "Free Mumia" Rally—hopefully laying the groundwork for a permanent "Stay" of Assassination/Execution.]

Inside Schomburg's hallowed American Negro Theatre, there is, first, Chair Room Only, then SRO, then H[all]RO, then Jammin by the Poetic/Performance Rainbow: begun when Sam Anderson bears witness to the Pantheon of incarcerated-activist-literati: Mumia/Malcolm/George Jackson/Angela Davis/Eldridge Cleaver. Then "colored blood" from voices of color—& others—flows: a river of stalwarts steeping in the belly of the Schomburg: Mumia...om...Mumia; & on to D. Prime: "kickin the Black Facts." Yo, now, Eunice Townsend's paradigm of racism: Santa Claus descending chimneys on/w a lynch rope to claim the "dead body of Affirmative Action." The late Audre Lorde is also here in her student Cheryl Boyce Taylor's: "shoe laces too loose to run": "wearing uniforms of the enemy." From the "scream[s]" of participants "in this slow dance of torture" to Cheryl's "sons' bleeding backs," WordUp: "Free Mumia!"

She Taylors into the Vietnamese voice of Ngô Thanh Nhàn: "but mind you, in the USA, they are a million times madder than elsewhere." He also hurls a prophecy: "Brother Mumia: the Black Dragon flying out of prison." From 'Nam, we segue into Louis Reyes Rivera's "makeshift baracoons" where, lo, we "celebrate even the look of Mumia"—"this branching baobab"/"roots of Rastafari": Roots to strangle those whom Carolyn Peyser warns: aim to "keep the tribes tame."

If the Rainbow signals the storm's end, the struggle to free Mumia begins at the "Bottom of the Storm," as Mike Ladd declares: "I want my own aircraft carrier w/Bed Sty for a crew": "It's on America. It's beyond the government's ass; it's eating it's stomach. It's on America!" On?...: Vanguard surgeon, Mumia, "dissecting cointelpro strategies," Bahíyyih Maroon notes, adding: Sometimes I dream you—"knotty dread screaming" & "I see you hunter of truth"/"decorated concentration camp." Now Rashidah Ismaili textifies from *Missing in Action & Presumed Dead*, yielding to a world of Bluesography, i.e. a New/afrkian Chorus of Barakans: Ras chanting, "People want freedom like Sojourner bare-chested on congressional floors"; Amina crooning "in the spirit of Ida B. Wells & Billie Holiday"/"Free Mumia" & "Strange Fruit"; & me, EBR, suddenly seeing a white rose growing from Amina's hair. Then transbluescendent Amiri urges "2 dollar books & 100 dollar movies"/"where are your garage galleries?" Kimako's Blues People, yall, "50 people in the basement: better than a blank or begging your enemy."

Fire & song: Sandra María Esteves singing, "Sometimes I Feel Like a Motherless Child"/asking "Who says I can't kill away my pain?"/"Lay foundations that orbit the sun & movement of stars?" Sister Nancy Mercado identifies: "The Puerto Rican contingency is in the house, Mumia!" And for Peter Adams, Mumia is a "Black Star" propelled by "invisible fire." Willie Perdomo's blues-itchings are followed by an implosion of video-poetics orchestrated by a brother who parallels South Africa & the US, Mumia, he assures us, told the "Truth" about MOVE!

Yet another young blues/scribe calls for A New Black Poet!: "A new poetic anthem"/"new & improved crack poems." Then he seems to challenge Michael Jordan to cross the River "Jordan" ["the revolution could use his help"]. Five def-song Sisters follow suit: one confirms "Mumia's defense of hip hop." Another—dreaded one—announces: "I am the daughter of Eshu." A 3rd, acoustically reminiscent of Wanjiku, intones: "Brother Amiri & Brother Mumia"/"Making Revolution a household word." Stephanie Johnson cautions: "No matter what your address there is no place you can call home." A 5th Sister spins this: "Mother is nature"/"Please don't tell me how to raise my son"/being one who knows "Mike Tyson, Tupac & Central Park in the dark."

"Lumumba! Mumia!" And, yes, Glenn Stupart is clear in his clarion acoustics: "The New World Order is predicated on the extinction of the African"—"Rally w/Reality!"/"Mumia!"

Jabbing from the cultural insides, a Brother Shariff Simmons—in dreads—waxes hypothetical to nail home a point: "Ask the Jews if they would attend Hitler High or Herman Goering U." The "remedy" for Black Folks, Mumia, Oppressed people & the Vulnerable?

Tony Medina has the last word: "I want people to breakdance in the streets"/"Turn my passing into a collective deliverance from evil."

Continuum? Bridges? Linkages for Mumia? Yes, Henry Dumas, the Circle Will Remain UnBroken!

•••

TED WILSON

TAKE IT AGAIN... this time from the top
for Larry Neal

Both space and motion can be manipulated rhythmically,
Existence can also be manipulated in a like manner.
—**Larry Neal**

1/7/81

Twinkle twinkle little star
No need to wonder where you are
Because your brilliance shines so bright
We'll never want for any light

I regretfully announce the passing of my brother....the star
at approximately 11 p.m. last night, after transmitting creative
information in a presentation of dramatic art at Colgate University
The machine that pumped energy to the star_____ceased
Without prior warning or mechanical difficulty_____zap
Pronouncement____Larry Neal has passed to another state...the Cosmos
Upon breakdown of the energy-pumping machine the star switched to
emergency—automatically the light shined brighter
Flashzzzzzzzzzzzzzzzzzzzzzzzzzzzzzzzzzzzzzzzzzzzzzzzzzzz LARRY NEAL LIVES

Twinkle twinkle little star
No need to wonder where you are
Because your brilliance shines so bright
We'll never want for any light

Larry Lives... in the tradition
the tradition of
Frederick Douglas and Sojourner
Harriet Tubman and Monroe Trotter

Kid Ory and Booker T.
Du Bois and Leadbelly
Van der Zee and A'Lelia Walker
Langston and Zora
Blind Lemon and The Scottsboro Boys

              Larry Lives Larry Lives
                        with
Satchmo and The Signifying Monkey
Jelly-Roll Morton and Father Divine
Lester and The Lady
Art Tatum and Bud Powell
Bird and Elijah
Clifford Brown and Brown vs. The Board of Ed.
          yes indeed He Lives, Lives, Lives
...with
Backstage Sally on cold nights with
The Sidewinder and Mingus' Moods on a
Trane with Malcolm blasting into our very soul
these weird looneymoon changes prodding and pushing us
to action - the continuation of struggle and hipness
... in the tradition of
Shine and Uncle Rufus and
the Blues God like being Yoruba with
Oseijeman embracing Orishas the
embodiment of our ancestors touching the land
tasting fruit being all that is
hip (AFRIKAN) encompassing centuries...
all that is sacred

              Twinkle twinkle little star
            No need to wonder where you are
          Because your brilliance shines so bright
              We'll never want for any light

He placed me on the wings of Bird
carried me through space waves
                  and
guided me to places(spheres) beyond the planet

He introduced me to the Spirits of Muntu
                    and
birthed awareness of the black ethos - titillating
my sensibility - an Afrikan sense of things
like him might say—
"Virgin land is like Afrika. It's a reservoir of energy and everything
born from it charged with powers. When you walk in a forest or on
a land of power, you feel a great radiance enter into you. It's the
force of Ossae."

Twinkle twinkle little star
You are among the best by far
Because your brilliance is so bright
We need not ever fear the night

N.B. Larry Neal was one of the founders of the Black Arts Movement of the 1960s. He died in 1982.

•••

FRED HO

The Climbers

I say
Don't be afraid, you haven't got it made

I say
Don't be afraid, you haven't got it made

Calling all tragic mulattos
Calling all tragic mulattos
Calling all model minorities
Calling all model minorities
Calling anyone who's a credit to their race
Calling all role models
Calling all role models
Calling the talented tenth
Calling the talented tenth

It's easy to forget about the forgotten
But can the forgotten forgive the forgetters?

In the good ol' days of equal opportunity
It was convenient to be a minority
But now with the open attack on quotas
You hear:
"I got to where I am because I worked hard."
You're now middle class
the beneficiaries of affirmative action
a whole career ahead of you with law degrees, medical school, MBAs.
You pleaded not to be bothered
by minority student organizations, coalitions, demonstrations
so you could do more
later
and now it's later
for us

Some are honest about their cop out
their politics having stood still
they stand there with a diploma in hand and
gracefully excuse themselves
"sorry, I'm too educated to know what to do..."

Some just skipped out and quickly became
superstar signifyin' monkeys justifyin' 2 Live Crew's doo doo

the 1970s me-generation
turned into the '80s megabucks generation
and going out together meant getting
matching gucci briefcases
she got a perm but her mind got stuck in the hair dryer,

We heard it before:
climb to the top to help the trickle down
trick us down
trip us down.
New Black Aesthetic For Sale!
New Black Aesthetic For Sale!
Get your New Black Aesthetic while it's HOT
Mo better than the ol' Black Aesthetic:
no revolutionary politics, just folks of color making it, being made;
no revolutionary raps calling for the redistribution of wealth
in America:
no art that says Fuck Mapplethorpe, Fuck self-indulgent performance
art, Fuck the NEA, the Rockefeller Foundation with Art that

has working class men and women, people of color, gays and lesbians, youth pissing, vomiting, shitting and farting on George Bush and CEOs of Fortune 500 Corporations.

Don't be afraid, you haven't got it made.
Don't be afraid, you haven't got it made.
Join us. Join us.   Join us.

Turn Pain into Power.

•••

BRENDA WALCOTT

Asylum
after Tony Medina

The only refuge
For the black
Artist todayyyy
Is the insane asylum

ASYLUMMMM

There's no hidinggg
Place down here

The only Refuge
For the dark
Truthsayer
Today
Is in the insane
ASYLUM

Wretched Poets
of the Earth
RUNNNN
into the streets
with your chants of beauty
of the glory of our past and
you'll be pacified
Classified.....*DELUSIONAL*

Run in the streets chanting
ALLAHHH

and the gate keepers,
the blacks with white masks
the whites with guns, memos, forms, drugs
will put your ass
in the psycho ward

Yell: "SHANGO BURN MY ENEMIES!
TURN MY CHILDREN INTO
UNDERGROUND FIGHTERS!"

You will find refuge
in the insane asylum
as fast as the Haitians
were drowned in the
sea

Run chanting
LET MY PEOPLE GO
HALDOLLLLLL
will be the answer

Refuge is refusal
to be washed "whiter than snow"
Refuge is in keeping our babies alive, alert, aware
Refuge is knowing that we are painting liberation poems
on the walls of the real crazy house *all around us*
Refuge is knowing that we are all living art treasures

Those walls must be scaled

Asylum is in the sweet strength of
  Struggle for our convictions
Asylum is on the
  Brave battlefields for human dignity
Refuge is refusing to resignate, vacate our reparations—
40 Acres+Mule

•••

MICHAEL S. WEAVER

Improvisation for Piano
after Mood Indigo

freshly lit cigarette in his mouth,
his collar turned up in the cold,
his face turned wry, and the question,
the awful question hidden beneath.
It is so difficult to see the baby
I sent scooting over to my mother.
laughing out, "He can walk, see."
It is difficult to look in my arms and
remember how he once fit there, how
I could keep the word away from him
if it threatened to hurt him, to rob him.
When I admit that he has been hurt,
that he has been robbed and that I was helpless,
I wonder what register there is for pain.
He is leaving home, and I am sending
another black man into life's teeth and jaws.
All that I know about being black
is some kind of totem knotted with the prints
of my fists beating out a syncopated pain.
I can't begin to tell him how to carve.
I can cry. I can counsel other black men,
but love is its own resistance in
the eye a father shares with his son.

The storm window glass sticks to me
with its cold, and I watch him go under
the big tree up the street and away.
The night is some slow rendition of
Mood Indigo, and the blues takes me
away to some place and frightens the shit
out of me, as I think of how my son will live.
What life will he have without proper
attire, I wonder. I think to run after him,
catch him, and say, "Here, another sweater."
And I know the other sweater is the first time
I saw "nigger" in a white man's eyes.
I know he needs gloves, too, for his hands,

when they stiffen, as he wonders how
blackness colors his life. I close the door.
There is a silence like dead flesh
in the bedroom. My son has left home,
a big, black manchild. I pull my cold feet
under the comforter and swallow sleep medicine.

I slip away hoping there are angels.

•••

STEVE CANNON

Mysteriousa
Who Be Do Be Do

Round midnight, on that Friday night, at the Disco Do Be Who Be Do
sat at the far end of the bar, into the house music overlaid with
John Coltrane's Saxophone, riffing, first on Giant Steps, and
later, A Love Supreme, with a heavy blues bass bottom located in
the backbeat.

Suddenly a young lady's presence was felt standing beside him,
sayin, in a melodious, half talkin half singin:

You say you want heaven?
I am your heaven!

You say you want love?
I am your love!

You say you want freedom?
You are your freedom!

And away she went, into the darkness of the disco, swayin her hips
as she sashayed deeper into the room, the music. And Do Be Who be
Do Be do Be Who sat there, at the corner of the bar conjuring her
words, lost inside the music, the sound of Trane's Saxophone, his
highs and lows, his medium range, dat backbeat, his mind in search
of images   of Heaven,   Love, and   Freedom, tryna figure out in
figures, exactly what she meant, Nobody came and went, it was just

him and the music, the words, lost inside his thoughts! Deep. What had she really meant??

•••

CLAIRESA CLAY
Much Ado About Nothang?

Did I say I was in this for life? And, Blood? Mumia Abu-Jamal. My indifference left a man in jail. I neither tore down the rock system or contested chain gangs, once again in Alabama.

On a trip set for Europe, right before the national march for the destruction of institutionalized man killings, I took off to a place to find my being which already exists wherever I go.

Innocent until proven guilty is our constitutional right. The document never said anything about framing us by governmental officials and the local police department. Again, the black race is on trial—Case: Mumia; Case: O.J. Who'd know that destiny laid in their hands?

I am a poor black woman. Do I know my rights? Do I know my power? I need to stand for something, not just my own insecurities, but stand erect toppling mountainous fears.

I watched a professor at Brooklyn College debate himself about Mark Fuhrman, "Are there other cops out there that did this, *a hideous act of manipulating state evidence?*" (Emphasis mine.) I wanted to shout, "Larry Davis, Angela Davis, Assata Shakur, Fred Hampton—any Black Panther, Paul Robeson, Richard Wright, Atallah Shabazz, Mumia Abu-Jamal, the corner drug dealer, the lawyer in the fancy suit, the mother from the projects working her second job, the teenager out of a cut-back summer job. Hell, yes! Cops do frame people.

Is Mumia's fate any different from my own? Should I divorce myself and forget that I'm intertwined. Question simply answered with action. Do what must be done to survive for myself and for my people.

Yesterday, my young cousin, Juakiem, was arrested while playing in the Brownsville Projects. (Juakiem, 16 years old, and I still did not arm him for life.) Juakiem and his friends stood in front of a dilapidated building shouting, "Yeah, we sell drugs! PCP. Coke. Crack." While the cops' Sting Program was in action—to try and catch people selling drugs by looking down from the roof—they, instead, stormed down on the youth's naïve exuberance. They are now fingerprinted, computerized, listed as criminals, with a sidebar called Disorderly Conduct. A charge usually filled out on a high school report card.

These boys/men took power. They wanted to torment, to antagonize the police; to strip the police powerless, immobilize the dark blue head hunters the way they usually make young African American boys/men feel, trying to survive in a fascist society. A heartwrenched feeling to immobilize. Stop at the period. These teenagers wanted the police stopped from acting, from action.

Juakiem's needs altered into a pursuit to be a part of the sickening power and powerless, the yin and yang, the systematic denigrating, trickle-down, knee-bent, genuflecting, God-praising, social idolized, lying, scheming system that made him, my cousin—male, black and poor, and by virtue, powerless. Stop at the period. Powerless. (Let the games begin.)

(NO, I don't want this rat-trap of a system to keep the keys of escape from him, which limits and kills off the Mumia's of the world.)

A farce, I say. The world's a farce. Can the players come out and take a bow: New World Order members, the World Bank, Federal Reserve System, American Dollars, United Nations Peacekeepers, the Armed Forces, and our local cops—Mark Fuhrman, Sr. and Gooliano Mobsters, the paid-off status quo keeping judges—Ito and talking Sabo. "Capital Punishment. More Arrests. More Arrests. More Capital Punishment," they void the world. I say, Can the crime of injustice have a color? Isn't a human being innocent until proven guilty?

Once again, Americans believe in printed and televised made-up Democracy; and, I, a tax-paying citizen, buy literally into it. Planted Evidence?!! I demand that every person be let out of jail. The L.A. Police Department kills! The New York City Police Department kills! Philadelphia, Chicago, Detroit Police Departments kill!!!

Now hear me through the bullhorns of American stench: "All political prisoners within two minutes, around the world, are decreed free. Jails are to be taken away rock by fist. Blood by chain."

1995—irony reigns supreme. People of the conservative left, right, and center—who exclude people of color regionally—want to dismantle the government. Wait a minute, didn't political activists say the government and the police "got to go." Now there is a slight difference of word terminology that the congressional members, state, and city officials used. "Government is too big." Al Sharpton's slogan, "No Justice, No Peace," works. There is no justice, and we are still at war with each other.

Brother Mumia will never die. All over Europe I saw slogans, graffiti, and posters to rally people to stand against this atrocity. American journalists and other like media representatives ponder as we ask from the Atlantic Ocean to the Pacific Ocean, can a man be sentenced to death for planted evidence? Orange Juice squeezed produces pulp fiction, which is lying all over the justice system.

The rage of Bigger Thomas lives on. I couldn't help him as a Native-born Son, I feel like I can't help him now.

Rage builds up. We re-act upon it. I am enraged! I stay in it. I eat in it. Jails. I live in a jail called the United States of America. I ask for the freedom of Mumia to come into a bigger jail system?—What do you think?

The police stopping me from going inside a store. A policeman standing on the corner, awaiting my stepping routine to dance over me. He's trying to figure out my game. Landlords and real estate agents policing me to stay in run-down apartments charged at an exorbitant rate. The local bodega spinning that nightly, encased Fiberglas window for my needed provisions, as I spin back the money for a swollen quart of milk, a pack of cigarettes, a 25-cent stale cake. My local supermarket chain policing the quality foods to other neighborhoods, and shoveling the garbage to me. Medicare, Medicaid, HMO's are all policing me to overcharged doctors whose business it is to keep me standing on one good leg. I grow lean as Juakiem locked into the lies of a corporate education system bent on policing and mishandling him.

Somewhere deep inside, I think of The National Anthem. Ain't no stoppin. It's been far too long. Ain't no stoppin us now. Every protest, every effort, written poem, essay, word pushes the system back. Our power. Visionaries are what we have to be. Visionaries.

•••

ZÖE ANGELSEY

Commit to Continuity
for Andrew Salkey

When you draw close to
the one who wears black
does it mean she's mere sorrow?
Walk into the pull of her eyes
like you do the Carib Sea.
She promises Abeng horns
that made the night sound free
from Quaco Hill to Montego Bay.
Accept her invitation
to a Village jazz spot.
Listen in that refulgent blackness.
See how the flash of blue and silver
spark a rythms climb.
Away from this mountain
no one sees the fire.

•••

VICTOR HERNÁNDEZ CRUZ

If You See Me in L.A. It's Because I'm Looking for the Airport

Even without Hollywood
It would still be an invention,
An imperialist drama from the
Spaniards to the Gringos,
Some automobile Hap Along Cassidy,
Arty hillbillies doing 90
On the San Berbardino
Its like a baker drop you

In the middle of the dough
Of the rising Angel cake.

What is it, just a script in motion.
A performance,
Cameras rolling without text
So far through Sunset Blvd. to get
To an idea—
A Russian corner
A certain Gorky that salvaged beer.

What city,
A wiring of freeways, suburbos,
Only when you turn the TV on
The news convinces you that
There might be an attachment.
Bill boards
So that perhaps if you're doing
80 you could look at them.

The relationship of people to
Their TV is a perversion
In the pocket of some
Beverly Hills cat psychiatrist—
Lap cats forced to sit with
Owners dizzied from remote control.

Don't get me wrong:
There are great literary geniuses
Practicing dialogue for be cool movies
Try reading that evoro/mental snarl
From a Caribbean balcony
Things people say down the street
In spontaneous coconut drops
Finds parking in the lot
Next to proverbs
And the rhythms.
More than cheese burgers
Gay or those that drive straight
Off Maliboo
Speed I can't get to,
I am still depraved by distance,
A Barbarism that Jajuyas
So far from Rome—

An Immigrant eternity
Should that make it unique,
Is that a third of the planet
Outside of the doors of San Juan

L.A. is constant May Day
Residential barns
Off of constantly circulating
Traffic—
Wide enough so that you are
Not crowded by the slave
Quarters of looney tunes,
Utility living in mind,
Just keep the body running
Like a 57 Chevy.
Every ten years everything
Starts all over again.
If it were not for the oldies
What landmarks would there be,
The place would only have a future,
Nothing happening yet
It's coming,
Can I park your car,
Can I take your order.

Car flirting
Car sex
Ah, if I get that chrome
What gets out of them
Diminishes.

I have found memories of L.A.
Getting lost stories on a pile,
The kind of off the track
Where you run out of gas
And can't find a gas station.

What would the Mexicans want
L.A. back for
They got Mexico City
And can give lessons
On how to perfect
The pollution.

So if you have survived
The image of your own image—
Perhaps you see something
Walking outside your windshield,
A mural surprising Huichol
Giant Mayas up on project walls,
A Guatemalan woman carrying
A bag balanced on her head down
Pico Street climbing up some stairs
To a blue coated apartment
Where Mayan corn
Hangs like framed Saints.

A chanting that is old
In a du-wop radio,
The palms of the hands
Playing eternity upon
Tortilla flats,
A bridge over a river
That refuses to die
Linking what is not lost,
With what will not survive.

Now I see it in the rear
View mirror
La Virgin of Guadeloupe
I gave my flowers to
Upon a wall
Like a gate into the East Side
A little brown boy and girl
Holding hands
Clutching tamales
As they walked towards Brooklyn
Of the urban Michoacan,
Now the ultra new buildings
are smaller
Than the shine of the
new world eyes
Beholding the distance
Of the smog.

•••

asha bandele

4:15 in the a.m.
a jailhouse love story

You enter from a door across the room
steady walk
caribbean confidence &
a hint of an 80s bop
Your smile
parading ahead of you like a victorious soldier
is a lie.
There is no reason to smile here in the land of confiscated dreams
plastic plants
state-issue clothes
roaches
murder &
Blackmen.
I rise to meet you
hold you /
& we lock, perfectly together, like found pieces of a lost puzzle.
We stand like this for 45 seconds, but no longer.
Longer might mean a police will come over or yell on the p.a. system:
NO EXTENDED EMBRACES!! EXTENDED EMBRACES ARE A VIOLA-
TION! RESIDENTS WILL BE WRITTEN UP!

You run your hands through my hair, ask me perfunctory questions:
how wuz the ride up?
did you sleep okay last nite?
can we get business out the way first?
still
luv
me
baby
?

I never sleep the nites before i come to see you
all these years later & i still can't relax
I read
watch television
fantasize
masturbate

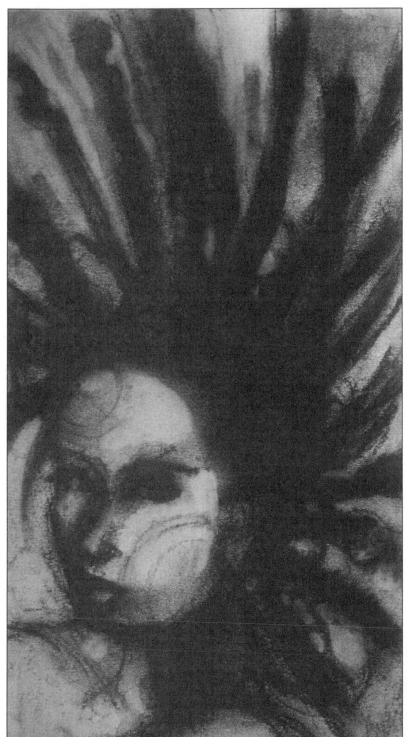

DIERDRA HARRIS-KELLEY

but at 3:00 i'm always wide awake waiting for the alarm.
4:15 in the a.m. it'll beep
& i'll shower, drink coffee, figure out what to wear, wait for the van
say a prayer.

You look so pretty today you whisper past my ear
& something inside me shrinks away from your words
i wonder if you mean i looked shitty the last time
& you can't believe i really hooked myself up
This place makes me hostile, defensive, mean & scared
The truth is these crackers could keep you forever
or more likely,
they'll find a way to damage you forever
What have i taken on i wonder
but don't say.

It's easy to love in 6 hour intervals,
twice per month.
It's easy to love without bills to pay,
responsibilities to share.
In this institution that is rank with the bizarre & vicious odor of
    annihilation,
we have only ourselves to hold up as light and possibility
And i hold you up & i hold you in as
People tell me i am crazy,
loving you across barbed wire & time
But i believe in our love because you struggle with me
lean close to my words,
respect our differences,
honor my mind,
challenge my ideas,
think i can make qualitative change in the lives of our people.
You
take me
real muthafucking serious.

We talk about your case, the one against the state,
where some cracker police set you up with drugs
& had you thrown in the box.
Convicts are the easiest people to frame.
Who believes a convict or these days
even thinks they are human?
But we thank God for the arrogance and stupidity of police.
they couldn't even do this simple shit right

& you proved it was a lie.
Now you just wonder how much the state will have to pay you.
Now i just wonder why this is relevant.
10 or 10 million or all the money in the world,
you'll still be in prison.
I'll still be in pain.
I suppose in some broad, political sense
a case like this has serious implications,
but sitting here beneath the shadow of your eyes
& the haunting of our future,
i am narrowed & confined to my own sorrow & needs.
I luv you momi
you say & pull me into a kiss
This type of thing has taken getting used to for me
Public affection was never my thing
& as much as i need the insistence of your tongue, part of me numbs
knowing we can be seen.
These crackers
the Black & Puerto Rican ones too
have unlimited entry into our intimacy & what does that mean?
It means
We are their porno
    their 16mm 2-minute flash of the kinky & forbidden.
We're their gyrating bitches in revolving cages on 8th avenue in n.y.c.
We're their filthy talk on a coffee break
    We are their dirty joke.

Stop it
i say.
Let's get back to our discussion.
In a minute momi,
you insist
& pull me back into your mouth.
Your fingers brush my nipples & i moan
Don't do that, & my voice is stunted
& separated from the rest of my body, an exposed nerve pulsating desire.
After all
i need you too.

Your eyes are on the police now,
sitting at the desk.
He's eating a foul-smelling sandwich from the vending machine.
We are shielded by a pole
& your hand slides down my belly, down between my legs, pushes them

apart, pulls my panties to oneside all
in one motion.
In spite of myself,
i am wet.
i
am open &
this could be two lovers at a restaurant,
a movie,
a dinner party,
an office.   This could be sexy / exciting
a memory to cherish   a knowing glance   a private grin
this could be a scene from your favorite erotic movie but instead it is
prison.
The sweat is from fear not lust or raw pleasure.
In 20 years we will not remember these as
the hazy crazy bold days of youthful sex.
We will remember what we risked.
We will remember that if we were caught
i would have to visit you through glass for at least a month maybe two,
however long they think it will take till we learn the lesson:
suppress everything you are
& have been
& will be.
No love
No passion
No hunger
No sensuality
No connection
No bonding
No humanity   No Humanity NO HUMANITY NO HUMANITY!

You murmur
Oh momi your pussy is so sweet
baby you feel so good
Goddamn i need to make love to you....

Your fingers on my clit are magic brown butterflies.
i try to be still but cannot stop myself.
I

          shift.
Moan.
Almost come out my seat.
& i am the rapid waters of the Delaware now.

I am the Mississippi river,
the Amazon,
the Nile.
I crave you.
Thirst you.
Love You.   Love You Deeply.
Love you like Isis loved Osiris.
& like Isis,
when we are separated,
i spend my days searching for pieces of you
in Soweto Havana San Francisco BedStuy.
i pull these broken parts of you together from corners of the Earth
stitched in blood.

I cum
unbelievably
in the warmth of your hands.
The police is still eating
The other visitors & prisoners are still locked
in their own discussions
embraces
card games & arguments.
The world is the same.
Except for me.
i have changed,
once again,
i
have
changed.

•••

LESLEY-ANN BROWN

Listen

When you were here
I felt your breath
just a second away
when you said things like
I love you... come here,
let me see how pretty you are
just like your mother,
you would say.

I want to feel the rope
of your hair
in my fingers,
twirl it & twirl it
and feel the coarsness
that reflects experience
& experience
all wrapped up
in twisted & knotted hair.

And they ask me how hard it is
to live without you.

I answer:

Read into the soul
of our history
and ask every fatherless
ghost-child how she felt
when they dragged her father away,
forced him to work,
whipped him,
shot him,
burned him, or...

I answer:

Read into the Soul
of our history,
because it begs
to be studied
and to be heard.

And I answer:

     Listen.

•••

MICHAEL S. WEAVER

A Black Man's Sonata

for John Dowell

Here in West Philadelphia,
one of my neighbors was
a black man just released from jail.
Home again, he imposed
a frigid order on his family.
He staked his territory,
crossing the street to threaten
a woman with his gun.
He tried his bravado in a bar,
and a man angrier than him
put a bullet in my neighbor's brain.
His house was hushed and solemn
as relatives came and went.
I think he wanted to die.
He threatened people and strutted
like a tiger because a bundle of hurt,
a mess of dangling threads, rags,
and curses had replaced his heart.

If I ever wonder where
America's heart is, I have only
to come to my neighborhood,
black homes of the poor and working poor.
The country radiates out from them
in history's circle where wealth
is built on poverty. If I ever
wonder whether to be poor
and black is to be exempt from evil,
I have only to watch the eyes
that watch me as I walk home.
They look for a weakness,
like tigers in the grass.
They look to see if I am a tiger too.

The young boys, the hip hops,
are all about respect.
Respect me, and I'll respect you.
They were born after Aretha Franklin
sang out respect between man and woman.
The hip hops say, *don't dis me man.*
Many of them will not live
to be men, to go creaking along
in the streets with old bones.
Many of them will not know
the fear an old black man fears,
of death, of not seeing grandchildren.

I walk the streets slowly, heavily,
knowing my wife hates the streets,
praying the young will not devour us.
We sleep under the sun's needles,
our deep black stripes in a fire yellow.

•••

BETHANY JOHNSON (AGE 16) *

My Synopsis of the World Aspects of a Jejune Mind

The righteous and wicked
Dopeless
voodoo gurus
Prodigies, aqua sea foam, shame
in a sea of stress
I'd say just another southern fried freak on a crucifix
Aphrodite euphoria
crack fiends awaiting another hit
Lume and Slang giving it to you strictly Beth
unimpressed by immaterial access
Blackness is anger
Whiteness is fear
Star Spangled Banner–a blanket acne'd with cigarette burns
held in white eyes as dear
Manic depression searching my soul
no matter what your address
there is no place you can really call home
I lie in the soil and fertilizer mushrooms in my brain

Lume
Duke of my domain
The herb put a spell on me
It had me kiss the sky all around the world
Will it be tomorrow or till the end of time

•••

AMIRI BARAKA *

I AM

for Addison for his Black Aesthetic

We are being told of the greatness
of Western Civilization
Yet Europe
is not the West

Leave England and headed West
    you arrive
        in Newark

The West is
The New World.
            not Europe

The West is
        El mundo Nuevo
        The Pan American
        Complexity
        As diverse as the routes
        & history
        of our collection

The West is The Americas
    not Europe

It is the America that the home
    boy tells, the sister we can
    see, yr wife, husband & children

Yr mama
Yr friends
Yr family
Yr closest enemies

Are West, The Quest
The Search
for Humanity
still goes on

But of the Euro White Supremacists
The Slave Masters
Conquistadores
Destroyers of Pharaonic Egypt
Carthage

Invaders. Destroyers of Moorish Spain
Of African and Asian world,
Creators of the Inquisition
Christ Killers
Murderers of thousands of Christains
in the Coliseum
Murderers of Spartacus
Vandals
Germ Mens
Ditch Men
Boers

Destroyers of Mohodarenjo
Tenotchitlan
Killed Montezuma & Emiliano Zapata
Malcolm X, Martin Luther King, even
the Kennedys, Bobby Hutton, Fred Hampton
Medgar Evers,

The Aztecs
The Incas
The Mayans
The Taino
The Arawak

Conquerors
of
America

Enslaving

Humanity
in
Cannibal
Menus

Bush men living on human
flesh as public
ritual
ideology of predators
& blood covered claws

Murderers of Iraq, wd be destroyers of
the ancient Mesopotamian culture

Assassins of Sandino
Toussaint Louverture, Patrice Lumumba

Enslavers of Women
Overthrew Mother Right
Killed Socrates, Copernicus, Lincoln
John Brown & Nat Turner
Amilcar Cabral & David Sibeko

Who claim Civilization & Christianity & Philosophy
as Crucifiers
who worshipped statues
till 300 AD

Who destroyed the libraries of Alexandria
the University at Timbuctoo
Who thought the wind made babies

Who say now they are the creators of Great Civilizations
plagiarists, ignorant imitators
claiming Geometry & the lever

which existed 1000 years before
they was even here
whose great minds are thieves like
Aristotle, Con men like

Democritus & Anaximander
whose Gods' are the Vanilla Ice
of Ethiopian Originals
half dressed cave dwellers
painted blue

Anglos (knife wielding) Saxons
Sackers (Robbers) of Ancient Civilizations
Vikings whose Gods were drunk and rowdy
robbers like Conan & Woden

Punks like Napolean who
got run out of Haiti
by Toussaint & Dessaline

who got bum rushed out
of Russia
wacked out
racist monsters
shot the nose & mouth
off the Sphinx
so sick &

anti-life & history were they
who put Mali & Songhay &
all Africa
in Slave Ships

for money, whose profits
were numbers not visionaries
Life as a low thing
worshippers of Mines not Minds
War Lovers not Peace Makers

Aint instead of Art
(Death instead of Life)

Dog they best friend
Ice & Snow
Not We & Know
Blood Suckers &
Mother Fuckers

Love War
so much
call the history
of their civilization

The Canon!

in honor of Marco Polo's
trip to China

Should we praise them
for Dachau, for the poisoning
of David Walker
the Genocide of Native
Americans
or concentration camps
for Japanese
Americans

Perhaps 700 years of Irish Colonialism
or Gandhi's
murder
The Conquest of India
The Opium Wars
TB Sheets for
Indians
or the trail of tears

So how should we praise them?
And what should we call them?
Who style them selves God
Whose New World Order
Seems old & Miltonic in that they rule
& do not serve

But somehow the term Satan seems too narrow
The word Devil is too limiting

But there must be some description, some appropriate
horrific
we can coin–

Something that says liar, murderer, maniac, animal
something that indicates their importance.

•••

RAYMOND R. PATTERSON
A Black Thought

If the Black
dead took back
their dust,
if the living
Black refused to give
their dark refractions
to your pale lust,
what wastelands
would be left,
America? —what
deserts show?
We know.

This is a
Black thought.

•••

CHERYL BOYCE TAYLOR *
House of the Un Natural World
for Mumia

I

Before this is over
I want to know
how many of us will be cold   hard
filled with cement poured into us
while our bodies are still soft   warm

How many of us will die
gold teeth stolen from our mouths
shoe laces too loose to run
unidentified   designer labels strung
around big toe

Before this is over tell me
how many of us will be bound
gold chains shackling bodies
our locks stuffed in our mouths
silent

How many of us will die
wearing uniforms of the enemy
our guns aimed at our children's heads.

Lord let this plague be lifted
in heart and mind.

II

One new leaf has sprung
on winter rock
lord let this plague be lifted
in act and deed

O Oya let Mumia's homecoming be
red   black   green   kites
waving victory in the sky

III

Unshroud the dismembered limbs
beheaded with insults and fury
that ceased to die 400 years and more
preserving secret wrongs white men do

Oya   yyyyyyaaaaaa   Shangooooooo
unleash the voices scream bloddy Christ
bloddy christ   this must stop   this must stop

Scream there are storm clouds
everywhere I turn
Screeeeeeeeeeeeeeam   scream
for love and death resides in the same
house
Scream for in their slow
dance of torture
eye to eye we will all die
vociferous noises sliding off
our tongues
our wailing shattering the sky

Scream   Screeeeeeeeeeeeeeam
I say scream   lest they come
in the morning to pick new flesh
off our sons' supple   bleeding backs.

•••

EUNICE KNIGHT-BOWENS

One Wing

for Etheridge

They took you
    from me

Like Vultures
    Laying claim
To the strength
    of your bones

Scavengers scent
    they wait
To pounce on
    Old dead Meat

There is no solace
    For those with Demon Eyes
Who claim
    strength from bones

With out your strength
    They have
only One Wing

And cannot fly   Until Tomorrow

•••

STUART McCARRELL
Paul Robeson

I was in the full bloom of life,
with my people's liberation
and Shakespeare flowing
through my heart and soul. But
strong as I was with twenty languages
and song, and history on my side—
the owners broke me—seized my passport
and would not let me perform at home. Now
they let cities name high schools for me.
But only because all that I ever stood for
will be denied, suppressed, lied about
in those very schools. Will the kids ever know
how 30,000 Canadian miners came to the border
to hear me sing about liberation? How in Spain
while their officers cursed
the Fascist soldiers stopped shooting, to overhear
my songs for the International Brigades.
Will the kids somehow discover
that I was battered, but never dishonored.
Never yielded one inch or gave
one name, or had any regrets
except that the people
were not yet ready to rise up
and free themselves.

•••

BECKY BILLIPS
Move!

Nine MOVE members were tried for the murder of a cop. The nine received a total of 3, 200 years.

How in the fuck can you sentence nine people for killing one cop? I'll never believe MOVE killed that cop in Philadelphia, anyway. Two MOVE members told me how badly they are harassed, how they were kept in the Restricted Housing Unit (RHU) for over three years. MOVE members incarcerated throughout the Commonwealth of Pennsylvania and else-where, both men and women, are brutally treated, not because they are troublemakers but because of their beliefs. This is the way of racist America, operating to control blacks in any vicious manner they can, trying to make us act, speak, and react the way they want us to.

I have the greatest respect for MOVE because they have unity. Come another Philadelphia Fire or another Noah's Flood, those women will stick together. When one member has a problem, it's everbody's problem. If one member is taken to "lock down," they all go to punishment.

Several inmates in the RHU related a story to me, which, to a certain extent, is quite humorous. As far as MOVE was concerned, though, it was not funny and understandably so. Several inmates were harassing MOVE members. One foolish inmate made the comment, "I saw John Africa in a shooting gallery." All the MOVE members were on DC (disciplinary custody)at this time. After this statement, you could hear a rat piss on cotton; for several minutes no one said a word. All of a sudden, in a very cool, controlled voice, you could hear MOVE members call out each and every one of their tormentors' names, adding, "When you come out for showers tomorrow, we're going to cut your hearts out!" They spoke very slowly and distinctly. Now that alone is enough to chill your blood, but those MOVE members are karate experts too. Those young ladies will make you a new asshole, if you are foolish enough to go up against them. The next day, the officers came around to give showers. All you could hear was, "No, thanks. I don't care for a shower today officer." "No, thank you!" "Maybe some other time." "I don't feel well today." "Thanks, officer, I'll skip today."

The inmates meant no harm. They were locked in a two-by-four cell and just had that urge to "fuck with somebody." Usually it's the police, but that day, they just wanted to harass MOVE members.

•••

SUSAN ROSENBERG
Some Ragings on AIDS

Doctors and nurses, who presumably have taken some sort of oath, look at a patient in respiratory arrest and then prescribe a cold pill? Is there a directive from higher ups not to send anyone outside the walls because of the security and expense involved? Is it that they are untrained and cannot recognize the difference between crisis and hypochondria? Is it that they are so biased against prisoners and women in particular that they simply don't care? Does medical ethics apply to HIV+ prisoners? No matter. Whatever the reason, the result is the same; the terrible and needless suffering of numerous women with HIV.

•

Conjure up this picture: You, a woman, wake up one day in Federal Prison looking at a 10 or 20 or 30 year sentence. Imagine (if you can) what your feelings might be: You have lost everything that up until that second was your life—your home, your children, your savings, your every worldly possession, your freedom, and, most likely, your friends. Then leap ahead a half year. You've just received the results of your blood work from three months ago; you are HIV+. Everything fades to gray. You can tell no one, neither cellmate nor family. Picture yourself one year later still. You are really sick. You sweat all night, wake up drenched, are losing weight, and have no energy. Imagine that your fever inexplicably spikes, and you are constantly breaking out with strange skin diseases. (You hope that no one starts wondering.) Imagine you have a full-time, back-breaking welding job making 44 cents an hour. Out of this $32.40 a month wage you must buy the vitamins the government medical department will not issue to you for free. If you are sick and go to sick call, you go at 6 A.M., wait on line 45 minutes to get an appointment, go back to work until you are scheduled; then go to see a health worker, and maybe then get an "idle," or maybe not.

Nonsensical rules regulate sick call, and they are strictly enforced. Only one complaint can be aired per visit. This iron-clad rule flies in the face of a disease like HIV. Anything remotely considered systemic is ignored. So, if you have migraines *and* a wasting disease as well, it is not possible to raise both problems. Or if you have asthma *and* some kind of painful gynecological infection, you cannot complain of both. At least not on the same day. You can mention it, but you won't be treated for both. So what if they are related problems? So what if you have several symptoms as a result of cancer? It might take months before someone here, a Physician's Assistant, makes a correct diagnosis. Then and only then will you be assigned to a doctor. That is, if the doctor is in, isn't too busy doing files, or feels well enough himself to deign to see you. Then, whatever the doctor says is law. Dare anyone, especially you, a prisoner, question the evaluation. And so it goes with sick call.

To get more specific, visualize this: You've been asking the medical department for the past six months why you have been cut-off anti-viral medication. Your last blood work was in April. Now it's September, and no one has explained the dramatic drop in your T-cell count. You also have what is known as the "HIV itch." A terrible nerve-related itch that grabs you from inside out and turns your eyes blood red, making you insane from itching. "What about my skin?" You are told it is nothing, merely a weakening of the immune system. "Take a Benedryl, or wash with calamine lotion," you are told. Maybe there is no real effective treatment for this itch. But what about ruling out dermatological infection, or fungi, or even lymphoma? Why not do a test to determine the cause? Even worse, your condition is complicated by asthma. There is nothing quite like it, not being able to breathe, and you need immediate medical intervention. With asthma it is not difficult to predict that HIV will attack the lungs, and that pneumonia will follow. Bactrum is prescribed, a proven prophylactic.

Fortunately, this nightmare scenario doesn't belong to you, but to a 40-year-old African American woman presently serving an eighteen-year sentence in federal prison; a woman diagnosed four years ago and now in a downward spiral. When this woman had her first bout with pneumonia did they give her Bactrum? No! They did not. This woman had three episodes. The third time around she was sitting on a chair in the hall, and she was in what appeared to be respiratory arrest. She was sweating and out of breath. More than out of breath she was gasping, and her yellowed eyes were glazed over. She was close to panic. Someone saw her and immediately said, "Let's go to medical."

"I've already been to medical—at 3 A.M. and 6 A.M.," she stammered.

"What happened?"

"They gave me a cold pill and told me not to sleep lying down."

The rattle and sloshing fluid in her lungs could be heard a few feet away. She started coughing and blood spewed everywhere, blood mixed with mucous and pus. Someone grabbed a coat and threw it over her. They walked very slowly to medical. An hour later she was in an outside hospital, where she stayed for two days. "PCP," the doctors said. In AIDS patients this is a common form of pneumonia, literally the breath of life is snatched away.

•

Prison is about loss. It's about loss of freedom, loss of control of any and all conditions of life, loss of family and friends. Prison is about punishment. Loss of freedom *is* the punishment. But that in and of itself is no longer enough. In a world where security always comes first we see, time and again, women dying right after diagnosis, because it is simply too late for decent care. We see women in chains, hauled off to the prison hospital only to languish in an isolated ward waiting for death.

The Bureau of Prisons (BOP) is mandated to conduct AIDS prevention education. They are allegedly mandated to subscribe to the standards of treatment as set forth by the Centers for Disease Control (CDC). In prison after prison they fail or are substandard in these areas. They are mandated to consider compassionate release. The majority of women who have been granted a type of compassionate release have died, while still in custody, waiting for the paperwork to be completed. As one AIDS activist said many years ago, "I do not want my epitaph to read, 'I died of red tape.'" Well, the reality is that hundreds of prisoners have died caught up in the red tape of chains and neglect.

•••

PAMELA SNEED
Rapunzel

Rapunzel was a sister.
You think I'm playing?
I said Rapunzel was a sister badder than your mama! That white woman with blonde hair, hanging out in a castle, pining for Prince Charming was a damn fairy tale!
Now, the Rapunzel I knew had dreadlocks longer than the Geechie River.
I'd say, "Rapunzel, Rapunzel!"
And she'd say, "What do you want now?"
I'd say, "Let down your hair."
And she'd let them dreadlocks (blonde from baking in the sun) fall reluctantly from beneath her red black and green cap so I could grab hold of one and climb up. We all know that fairy-tale-girl's hair was too slippery to hold anyone; and, anyway, Prince Charming should have left well enough alone, 'cause I found out the woman they said was a witch keeping 'Punzel prisoner was Rapunzel's lover, and that castle was the love they built.
Yeah, Rapunzel was a free woman, making her own choices, and did not need any rescuing.

•••

HETTIE JONES
Going to Jail

As a child I went to a summer camp run by a rabbi who worked as a prison chaplain. My family joked that his wife, unsure of her English, had once told a caller, "The rabbi's not home, he's in jail."

Though I found the joke cruel, I never thought I'd fill the rabbi's shoes.

I first saw Sing Sing's turreted walls at dusk. A sand castle on the Hudson. Coveted real estate, no doubt. I thought of Edith Wharton and the nineteenth-century landscape painters. Rockefellers lived nearby—but far, of course, from the men I later met. They called me the Prose Doc, one of them had won a PEN Award. I stayed six months, but the men were too hard. They resisted.

At Bedford, where the women are, I've lasted six years on the semipermanent gate list. It's dog-eared, in a looseleaf binder; you could be disappeared in an instant. Whoops—there goes the miscellaneous, creative writing teacher.

The other day a new student asked if I'd be coming back in the Spring. "Of course," a lifer answered. "She's here Spring, Fall—she's here forever."

I haven't made that decision.

But I've watched hair go gray, apple cheeks sink. Jail is an industry now, using and producing. I bear witness to its workings.

•••

RAYMOND M. BROWN
Epistle from Hell: A Review of
Live from Death Row

Death's shadow hangs over this book.

The Commonwealth of Pennsylvania wanted to execute its author on August 17, 1995.

An attempt to abort it by boycotting the publisher was launched in the Spring of 1995.

The volume includes commentaries that National Public Radio abruptly killed in May of 1994 after commissioning them earlier that year.

The dreaded book, *Live from Death Row,* is a collage of short essays, exposing both the tortured existence of prisoners anticipating termination and the shameful nexus between race and criminal justice. It climaxes with intriguing vignettes of the author's experience as a Black Panther and an admirer of MOVE founder John Africa.

The embattled author is Mumia Abu-Jamal, an award winning African-American journalist convicted of murdering a white Philadelphia policeman in 1981. His controversial trial and death sentence have galvanized supporters as diverse as Amnesty International, PEN, Ruby Dee, Ossie Davis, Alice Walker, and Ed Asner.

Abu-Jamal has not written a book about his case, but death's proximity has inspired his hand. While the courts weigh his fate he has hurled an incendiary missive over the wall.

John Edgar Wideman warns us in the Introduction that Abu-Jamal's voice is a "dangerous and subversive" one, which urges us to confront our "fear of the real problems caging us all." (p. xxx) The novelist applauds Abu-Jamal's message because,

> The facile notion of incarceration as a cure for social, economic, and political problems has usurped the current national discussion of these issues. [p. xxvii}

Abu-Jamal unmasks this nation's love affair with the death penalty, shining light on veiled conduct. For example, he reports that on Pennsylvania's death row every prisoner's words must run the gauntlet.

> Televisions are allowed but not typewriters: one's energies may be freely expended on entertainment, but a tool essential to one's liberation through judicial process is deemed a security risk. [p. 8]

He shares the struggle of one inmate "more interested in his life than entertainment" to convince prison authorities that the glass in his television set was more dangerous than typewriter parts. The response: Request for writing machine denied. It is easy to forget that public executions were abandoned in part to still the voices of the condemned.

In the capital prisoners' "nether world of despair" the mantra of security is invoked in gratuitously cruel ways. Abu-Jamal vividly describes his daughter's first visit to death row.

Denied physical contact with her father, the small girl with a "Minnie Mouse" voice banged on the transparent barrier separating her from her father. Her tiny fists pounded hopelessly on Plexiglas as she screamed "break it, break it." Relief came only when Abu-Jamal contrived a silly face to banish her pain briefly.

Abu-Jamal's prose tableau of isolation, mental deterioration, and humiliation among the voyagers on this "descent into hell" is not a jeremiad. It is a still life of death row as it strips its inhabitants of their humanity before extinguishing their lives.

Some cruelties stem from the whimsy of wardens while others are critical components of the machinery of death. The book's opening chapter, "Teetering on the brink between life and death," begins with a quote from Camus' famous essay on the death penalty,

> For there to be equivalence the death penalty would have to punish a criminal who had warned his victim of the date on which he would inflict a horrible death on him and who from that moment onward, had confined him at his mercy for months. Such a monster is not encountered in private life.

Ironically, federal courts have refused to rule that this macabre hiatus renders the death penalty unconstitutional.

Appropriately, death row denizens have come to view the courts more with hope than expectation. Abu-Jamal relates their sadness on receiving the "crushing news" of the resignation of Associate Supreme Court Justice William Brennan. Brennan's opinions are sacred texts for opponents of state sponsored death.

Abu-Jamal remembers that in 1987 in *McClesky v. Kemp* the death penalty was challenged on the basis of the disproportionate number of blacks executed in Georgia. (Nationally, African-Americans constitute 40% of the death row population.)

The Supreme Court majority in *McClesky v. Kemp* refused to entertain this claim because racial disparities in non-capital sentencing are equivalent to those in death cases. To prohibit them would undermine the entire criminal justice system. In one of the most eloquent dissents of this century, Brennan sharply chided the *McClesky* majority for its "fear of too much justice."

No such fear plagues Abu-Jamal. In the Afterward to his book his attorney Leornard Weinglass tells us that Abu-Jamal had an inexperienced, unprepared lawyer who was given only $150 for experts and investigators.

The judge, a notorious dispenser of death, permitted testimony about the defendant's youthful political ideas as well as those of his witness Sonia Sanchez. He also refused to make available an exculpatory police witness "on vacation" at the time of trial, a suspicious scenario considering Abu-Jamal's ardent criticism of the Philadelphia police.

Only a jury can decide innocence or guilt, but the record in this case reeks of race, politics and justice denied. Such miscarriages cannot be rectified after execution.

Abu-Jamal obtained no relief from the Supreme Courts of Pennsylvania or the United States. He now roams the desperate world of habeus corpus, seeking succor in an ancient writ now much disfavored.

Despite his peril Abu-Jamal writes with hope, insight, and occasional hints of humor noire. These flavor the final section of his book, a pilgrimage to the Panther pantheon. Huey P. Newton is lionized, David Hilliard's autobiography is criticized, and Abu-Jamal opines that Jesse Jackson "borrowed from the oratory and flair" (p. 154) of the martyred Fred Hampton.

More on Jesse?

In 1975 Jesse spoke to a PUSH convention in Philadelphia. Abu-Jamal covered the event for WHAT-AM. MOVE picketed and challenged the $25 per seat charge, arguing that, "John Africa teaches us that the truth is free like the air we breathe. It ain't to be sold." (p. 181) Jackson, interviewed by Abu-Jamal, retorted, "Who cares about a bunch of dirty unwashed niggas who don't comb their hair." (p. 184)

Deep, huh?

In another venue Abu-Jamal would be queried about his initial desire to be assisted by John Africa instead of skilled counsel!

He would be questioned about the compelling but eclectic structure of this book, combining elements of a prison notebook, a death penalty broadside, and a memoir. (Wideman favorably contrasts Abu-Jamal's defiant riffs with the biographic "crossover...fables" of O.J., Oprah, and Maya Angelou.) (pp. xxxi-xxxii)

Impending death moots these inquiries. Criticizing the defenseless is a fool's game.

Abu-Jamal sojourned among the living dead and lent them his voice and scorching pen.

The anti-Jamal forces, the slain officer's widow, Senator Robert Dole and the management of National Public Radio have no rationale for silencing him, simply saying that a convicted murderer should not be heard. One police union official opposed to the publication of *Live from Death Row* said, "The only thing I'm interested in Mr. Jamal saying is good-bye." How they fear the words of the damned!

Those who care about the poor and the unlettered, to whom America gives preference in the race for the death chamber need more of these words. Abu-Jamal is uniquely placed to supply them, but death's shadow hangs over his future works.

●●●

JELANI W. COBB
Review of Live from Death Row

Live from Death Row is a grim photo album, the soundbites from a penal netherworld where life vacillates "between the banal and the bizarre." The forty-one essays that comprise the volume were culled from Mumia Abu-Jamal's columns over the past eleven years and a series of commentaries commisioned by National Public Radio's *All Things Considered*. The commentaries, which were never aired due to pressure from police and civic associations, paint a vivid picture of the wretched of the earth, storehoused until the state sees fit to end it all. Death Row very nearly suffered its own public death sentence. Publisher Addison-Wesley was the target of the same type of boycott that police associations launched against Time-Warner in the wake of rapper Ice T's "Cop-Killer" fiasco.

Later, Maureen Faulkner, widow of the police officer whose death resulted in Mumia's death sentence, sued the publisher under the Son of Sam Law which prohibits criminals from profiting from their crimes. The suit garnered a near full-page spread in the *Washington Post*—neither Faulkner nor the *Post* mentioned the fact that, with the exception of an afterword from Mumia's lawyer, the Faulkner case is almost never mentioned in *Death Row's* 216 pages. This is a book about life—if it can be called that—in a penal abyss in Huntington, Pennsylvania.

Life on death row is an interminable suspense of waiting for the other shoe to drop, knowing that when it does, it spells the end. If the "mission" of this book can be telescoped down to a single goal, it is to highlight the flaws that make the death penalty fundamentally unworkable as a deterrent or punishment. Recently, *Washington Post* reporter David Von Drehle made this same point in his book *Among the Lowest of the Dead*—buttressing it with an impressive array of statistics and case citations. Mumia relies mainly upon a more humanistic approach. Von Drehle argues, in part, that the appeal system—which cannot be dispensed with if we are to maintain even a thin facade of justice—makes the death penalty not only ineffective, but more expensive than life imprisonment. *Death Row* tells the tales of prisoners who, driven insane by the infinite waiting, resort to hanging themselves or torching themselves to get the ordeal over with. Mumia Abu-Jamal doesn't ignore the "hard" data; he's penned a factual work. *Death Row's* strength lies in its ability to connect statistics and legal precedents to flesh-and-blood individuals.

While *Live from Death Row* is unquestionably a book with an agenda, it manages to steer clear of agitprop sermonizing in spite of the author's own visceral connection to his subject matter. He simply tells the stories of the men and the institution that surround him. If an inmate happens to slip into a coma and has grand mal seizures because the prison, without his knowledge, changed his epilepsy medication, so be it. The conclusions draw themselves. Mumia plays the role of biographer-journalist.

The book's tone vacillates between the reserve and that of the lyricism found in *Souls of Black Folk.* For instance, he observes in "Nightraiders meet rage":

> Prisoners are repositories of rage, islands of socially acceptable hatreds,
> where worlds collide like subatomic particles seeking psychic release.
> Like Chairman Mao's proverbial spark, it takes little to start the blazes
> blanked within repressive breasts.

He analyzes "Spirit death" offering the insight that:

> Prison is a second-by-second assault on the soul, a day-to-day degradation
> of the self, an oppressive steel and brick umbrella that transforms seconds
> into hours and hours into days... a person is locked away in distant nether-
> worlds, time seems to stand still; it doesn't.

The first section of the book, "Life on death row" examines just that. Its array of tales from the stark side provide the background and context for the second section, "Crime and punishment," in which the author makes his major arguments against the death penalty. The final section, "Musings, memories, and prophecies," is a compendium of columns, which reveal a more pensive Mumia reminiscing about blast-furnace summers in North Philly, the death of Black Panther comrade Huey P. Newton, the pay-per-view spectacle of Rodney King and the similarities between the Waco and MOVE bombings.

The narratives of "Life on death row" feature those who are driven insane by the day-to-day banality of waiting for death—one who's suicide borders upon being a mercy killing— and the tormenting tale of a six-year-old girl making her first visit to her father on death row.

These realities do not register in the public discourse. They are likely assigned the weight of a feather by a society so damaged by the specter of violent crime. Yet there remains some link between what happens on America's death rows and what happens in the society beyond the prison walls. Mumia calls into question the taxpayer-sub-sidized torture of prisoners and asks simply if this is the way a civilization addresses crime.

"Crime and punishment" opens with a flurry of factual essays, which focus more on the flawed structure of the criminal justice system, particularly as it relates to capital punishment. Exhibit A in Mumia Abu-Jamal's case against the death penalty is racial disparity in death sentencing. He points out early in the book that "You will not find a blacker world on death row than anywhere else. African Americans, a mere 11 percent of the national population, compose about 40 percent of the death row population." Pennsylvania's death rate is over 60 percent black. Not only are blacks more likely to receive the death penalty, in general, he observes, they are almost never sentenced to death for crimes against other blacks. It brings to mind the conventional wisdom of southern sheriffs during Jim Crow that "If a white kills a nigger, that's justifiable homicide. If a nigger kills a white, that's first degree murder. And if a nigger kills a nigger, why that's just one less nigger."

Circumstances and white supremacy almost ensure that most victims of black criminals are other blacks, so death row is a slaughterhouse for black souls who strayed to the other side, those who have transgressed white America. Mumia tells us the tale of William Henry Hance, a mentally retarded black man from Georgia whose jurors, eleven of whom were white, consistently referred to him as "the nigger" and theorized that a death sentence would leave "one less nigger to breed."

The racism doesn't stop at the prison door. Following a mandate that said that prisoners could not be kept locked up for the customary "twenty plus two" (two hours out of the cell, twenty-four locked in), Huntingdon Prison constructed outdoor recreation facilities—for whites. Black inmates, Mumia informs us, were locked in one-man outdoor cages. The central point in his argument, however, is the 1983 *Bladus Study*, which revealed the grossly racialized nature of capital punishment, and the Supreme Court decision in *McCleskey v. Kemp*. The study was cited as evidence in the McCleskey case and Justice Powell, while upholding the death sentence, observed, "McCleskey's claim, taken to its logical conclusions, throws into serious question the principles that underlie our entire criminal justice system." The decision, Mumia posits, was motivated far more by politics than by justice.

The final essays examine society at large. These are opinion pieces for the obvious reason of a hampered flow of information. From the vantage point of the prisoner, of course, it is far easier to critically analyze prison society than it is to do so for the world outside. The longest essay of the collection "Philly daze: an impressionistic memoir," covers the political, social, and personal terrain between Mumia's teenage Black Panther activities and the time of his arrest in 1981.

Because most of these essays are adopted from newspaper columns and the three-minute NPR commentaries, they are brief. The book often leaves you wishing for a fuller exploration of some of the lives and themes found on its pages.

The attack on the book by some media and many police associations served to generate a degree of interest in Mumia Abu-Jamal's case. But in the funhouse mirror that we know as reality, the trial of a millionaire ex-athlete (O.J. Simpson) garners the attention of the masses while community activists like Mumia languish in relative obscurity.

Is Mumia Abu-Jamal innocent? I do not know. I am sure, however, that nobody sitting on his jury knew either. His trial was rife with racist violations including a judge who deprived Mumia of his right to self-representation, without explanation, in the middle of his trial. White jurors, without informing the blacks, met to pre-deliberate and decide upon the terms they would follow when the "interracial" deliberation began. Robert Christgau wrote in the Village Voice that the feeling of interviewing someone who may very well die within a few months can only be compared to interviewing soldiers on the frontlines of a war. Mumia Abu-Jamal is in a war, but his is not the only life at stake.

•••

JEROME WASHINGTON
Stories from the Yard

The Soap Opera

All winter Dobbson sat in the South Yard watching his favorite TV soap opera. On the coldest days, Dobbson was there, bundled like an Eskimo, drinking hot coffee from his half-gallon thermos, clapping his mittened hands and stomping his feet to keep the blood flowing. Even when the snow blew in ten-foot drifts against the wall, Dobbson was there.

Many times Dobbson would be the only inmate out in the freezing yard and the shivering guard sergeant would plead for him to go inside. But Dobbson would just shake his head and say, "No good. This is my recreation and I'm going to enjoy myself." As long as Dobbson stayed in the yard, a full guard complement also had to stay out. The guards suffered, but Dobbson didn't. He watched his soap opera and forgot about the cold.

When spring came Dobbson was joined by other inmates. They were often loud and sometimes inconsiderate. They didn't really care for the soap opera and were only watching because they had no place else to be. But that didn't bother Dobbson. He was intent on his soap opera and paid them little attention. He had spent all winter with his soap opera and now that it was spring, he was in love and his world didn't include other inmates.

Dobbson's love wasn't the painful kind that people fall into and out of as if it were a container. It was a liberating love that offered a fantastic escape, and left him with a gratifying taste on his lips.

One sunny afternoon a couple of guys were high-jiving nearby, and one commented as he watched the female star of Dobbson's soap opera strut across the video screen, "Man," he said, "that there broad sure is a fine looking bitch."

Dobbson stiffened, but said nothing.

"Bet she can handle a joint like a flat-back whore at a cut-rate fire sale," the other guy said.

The first agreed. "A bitch like that," he said, "can cannibalize a swipe with one move."

Dobbson turned, looked at the two with cold eyes and said, "You men have got to show folks respect."

"Respect? Who? What?"

"The lady on TV," Dobbson said.

"Man, are you crazy?"

The other said, "That bitch is a thousand miles away and if she was right here, she wouldn't be worth my respect."

"You had better cool your roles," Dobbson warned. "Don't oversport your hands."

"I can always play my hand," one of the two wolfed, "and I know a two-bit bitch when I see one. And that there is one." He pointed to the soap opera's star.

"She ain't no bitch," Dobbson said. His eyes narrowed to a squint as he sized up the two men. "She my woman."

Both guys laughed, but Dobbson didn't crack a smile. This wasn't a laughing matter. He got up and quietly walked away.

When they saw Dobbson returning, they started to laugh again, but they didn't see the steel pipe that Dobbson carried low against his right hip. When they did see it, it was too late to run or even defend themselves. Dobbson struck. Blood, scalp and hair flew. Two bodies caved to the ground.

"Those guys have got to learn to respect another man's woman," Dobbson said as the guards rushed him away. "They have got to learn respect."

•

Saladine

When Saladine refused to take Thorazine, the guards said that he was rebelling. When Saladine tightened his fist against the pain of fifteen years in prison, the guards said that he had given the Black Power salute. When Saladine went to the parole board and asked to be released, the guards labeled him a "malcontent." When Saladine exploded and sent three fellow prisoners to the hospital, the guards relaxed and called Saladine a "well-adjusted prisoner."

•

Soul Strut

Chaka Kahn shakes her black booty in the warden's wife's face and the guards never understand why we relate to Aretha Franklin when she shouts, "Give me R-E-S-P-E-C-T."

Every time the warden sees us snapping our fingers, he smiles and prides himself for keeping us happy. What he doesn't realize is that we snap our fingers to keep our balance when strutting through his bleached out shit.

•

Sugar Ditch Pearl

Sugar Ditch Pearl and his lover, Rex, got married in the far corner of the exercise yard, and they spent their honey-moon lifting weights.

•

I used to have a large, nude pin-up on my cell wall. It was there, across from the bed, doing time just as I was, until I woke up from a wet dream and in the half light thought a naked woman was in the cell with me.

When fantasies become that real, it's time to give them up.

The next time I pin up a photgraph, it will be of something I can use–like helicopter.

•

"Rehabilitation is a hoax," Tripe, the guard sergeant, stated. "Don't waste your time on such trivia."

I was dumbfounded.

"A strong image is needed for rehabilitation to work," the sergeant said. "I am the strongest here, but I wouldn't want anyone remade in my image."

I nodded in agreement and received a seven-day disciplinary lockup for insulting an officer by assent.

•

The real horror of prison is not the torment of human flesh, but the system that tolerates it.

•••••

VIII. Breaking Prayers

ERNEST CRICHLOW, *"On Earth, Peace"*

(towards tomorrow)

DUDLEY RANDALL
Roses and Revolutions

Musing on roses and revolutions,
I saw night close down on the earth like a great dark wing,
and the lighted cities were like tapers in the night,
and I heard the lamentations of a million hearts
regretting life and crying for the grave,
and I saw the Negro lying in the swamp with his face blown off,
and in northern cities with his manhood maligned and felt the writhing
of his viscera like that of the hare hunted down or the bear at bay,
and I saw men working and taking no joy in their work
and embracing the hard-eyed whore with joyless excitement
and lying with wives and virgins in impotence.

And as I groped in darkness
and felt the pain of millions,
gradually, like day driving night across the continent,
I saw dawn upon them like the sun a vision
of a time when all men walk proudly through the earth
and the bombs and missiles lie at the bottom of the ocean
like the bones of dinosaurs buried under the shale of eras,
and men strive with each other not for power or the accumulation of paper
but in joy create for others the house, the poem, the game of athletic beauty.

Then washed in the brightness of this vision,
I saw how in its radiance would grow and be nourished and suddenly
burst into terrible and splendid bloom
the blood-red flower of revolution.

•••

ASSATA SHAKUR
Let Us Carry On Our Tradition, to Freedom!

The first time i heard a tape of one of Mumia's radio broadcasts, it was the first time i fully understood why the United States government was so intent on putting him to death. Mumia, the only African political prisoner on death row, didn't use any inflammatory rhetoric, what he said was so clear, so true, that i had to stop everything i was doing and concentrate on his message. Mumia Abu-Jamal—journalist, husband, grandfather, and African American—is not only articulate, he is brilliant. He has the ability to say what needs to be said, in the clearest, most vivid way. His language, his strength, and his intelligence reminds me of one man, El Hajj Malik Shabazz, otherwise known as Malcolm X. Mumia Abu-Jamal is a man who has truly carried on Malcolm's tradition, and the tradition of so many of our freedom fighters who have risked their lives for the freedom of their people. This year as i celebrated Malcolm's birthday, i couldn't stop thinking about Mumia. i couldn't stop thinking about the man who has spent thirteen years on death row, and remains strong, committed and beautiful. Mumia, political activist, revolutionary, and humanist has followed faithfully in Malcolm's footsteps. We can feel Malcolm's energy working through Mumia, we can feel Mumia's energy carrying on Malcolm's legacy. If Malcolm X were alive today, i know he would be fighting to save Mumia's life. If Malcolm X were alive today, i know he would be fighting to free all political prisoners. In the name of Malcolm X, i make a special appeal to you, Sisters and Brothers, to fight tooth and nail to save Mumia's life and to free him from the grips of his oppressors. As you honor our forefathers and foremothers i urge you all to honor our living heroes. When you honor the names of Nat Turner, Harriet Tubman, and Malcolm X, i urge you to honor the names of Geronimo Pratt, Sundiata Acoli, Mutulu Shakur, and Mumia Abu-Jamal. I urge you not to forget, and not to betray our living heroes. If we ignore their struggle, we are ignoring our own. If we betray our living history, then we are betraying ourselves. We could not save Malcolm X, but we can save Mumia. We can save him, and we must save him, because we love our Brother, and we need our Brother to help us fight for our freedom. Free Mumia Abu-Jamal! Free all political prisoners! Let us carry on our tradition to freedom!

N.B. Shakur is a former Black Liberation Army member and a former political prisoner now living in political exile in Havana, Cuba.

•••

MELBA JOYCE BOYD
Breaking Prayers

I.

despair hovers
with loneliness
in the shadows
of faint waiting.
i open empty
envelopes and
disappointment

slices like
a paper cut,
a crystal sliver
of insight
for whatever is
left longing.

perhaps,
bad dreams
or sorcery turned
your head in
the other direction.
even exchanges
against the odds
can catch
a blinking
eye.

II.

"what can we say to Che?"

what makes us
cut out our hearts
and sell them
to the clockmakers
is a cold
and sudden story.
when a dirge
hangs in the air
and follows
breathless words
far too long
for tenderness
to recover possibility,
we no longer
think about change.

we accept disaster
without wonder
and applaud the
removal of ruin

by clasping hands
in churches
for divine arousals
and devils are redressed
simply to satisfy strategies of denial.
are we really surprised
that the gulf growing
between intimacy
and youthful passion
to resist tyranny
disappears into fear?

what has happened
here, marking time,
goes forward
and sells us
at breakfast
before violet dawns
and the resurgence
of selfishness
or the horror
mocking our sorrow
and this pitiful case
of a nation broken.

what can we say
to Che?
holding our candle
in the heavens.
how can he
possibly believe
we were true
in the springtime
of the Great Revolution?

are we the
carriers of the
dream wheel, or
have our faces
given into grim retreats
and the lock-step
of clockmakers?

are we caught
in the gasping throats
of a survival
so bleak
our imaginations
can't lift even
a small stone
to cast into
the cave?
do we have
the courage
to stop time
at a funeral?
can we break
prayers and
end this
deafening peace?

•••

PIRI THOMAS
A Dialogue with Society

No longer can men, women and
children bend their backs and make
a cop-out to the freedom of dignity.

Heed us well, racists, segregationists, bigots,
multi-billion dollar murderers.
'Cause we're on our way.

Do you want to hate?
We'll put you all together
so you can waste yourselves.

Heed well world, my America.
Live by the precepts that this country
was supposedly founded on.

Do not build your golden gardens on the suffering
of your fellow human beings.
Do not buy toys for your children
bought at the price of other children, you have
sacrificed.

Set not a table spread with good food and comfort,
such as never been seen by the children of your
fellow human beings.

Sit not in churches and bend your knees in prayers.
Mouth not the words of Christ, of peace on earth,
and good will to all, while you know in your hearts
that you are truly lying.

For while you are smiling and living well,
black children, brown children, red children,
yellow children, white children, multi-colored children,
children, children,
because of your hypocrisy,
are dying,
physically,
mentally,
spiritually,
and secretly
in broad daylight.

I speak to myself as my mind rushes
back into time when I held in my hands
a beauty that was truly mine.

I was a child
running through dark ghetto streets
I let the seas of hatred wash over me.
I was too young to know.
Momma had filled my eyes with the wondrous
city and its pearly gates.

If I could have the power, I'd wipe out all bad
memories.
But, since I don't, I'll give you a piece of advice,
cool-breeze, cut like a piece of ice.

Share! Let our children share.
Stop teaching them the petty stinking hates.
Children know love from the git-go.
And you who are without love have taught
them hate up to the very ending.

We are tired of demigods and tyrants
bred by a mother and father who leave
their marks on earth a death-chant
a mountain of sufferings, a dirge.

It is time for new bells to toll.
It is time for new trumpets to blare.
It is time for a new language to be heard.
For from the very beginning of time to
this time, we should have learned by now,
we should have learned how,
We should have learned
to love.

•••

DENNIS BRUTUS

Sequence for Mumia Abu-Jamal

I:

Some voices must be silenced
they threaten the structures
of seemingly safe respectable lives
their clear vibrations
may shatter the crystalline shelters
that encase us from reality
shielding us from unbearable truths

but some may choose not to be deaf
they beat with broken palms
against the smooth impenetrable glass
of lies and comfort and power
and beg to hear the piteous cries
rising from the smoke and fire:
some voices must not be silenced.

II:

The smooth impenetrable glass
of indifference and uncaring
is cool and pleasant to the touch
like the stone heart of power
that conceals the rottenness within.

III:

In the night
anger burns like fire
along the veins
in the brain
and at the core
of the anguished
unavailing heart.

IV:

Red and orange and saffron
the fiery ghosts
rise in the night
to sear the dreaming brain
and blast the wakeful eyeballs
staring into the dark:
images of terror.

V:

Red, bright red as blood
luminous with life
anger runs through the brain
anger against injustice
anger against pain
anger against impotence

And red, red as a rose
red as soft red velvet
red as a deep red rose
with shadows dark to black
red as poppies in sunlight
red as massed salvia

red as the blood of children
in the dust of Soweto
(come see the blood of children
in the streets of Soweto)
red as poppies in sunlight
with their fragile beauty
with their indestructible beauty
steadfast under battering rain
so strong, so red our courage:
we will not bow down
we will not submit to defeat
our courage will endure
our truth will survive.

VI: Postscript

When the blight of stillness advances
when songs and speech are silenced
when a light of life and laughter is gone,
the spirit still speaks and endures
like sparks that flash from silica—
tough stardust, common dust of the world.

•••

AMIRI BARAKA

For Mumia: Revolutionary Culture at the Side of the People

The following essay is an edited excerpt of a speech given by Amiri Baraka in July 1995, in Johannesburg, South Africa. The speech primarily deals with forming an international writer's union to help chip away at the yoke of cultural imperialism, which places a wedge between artists and artists, artists and country, artists and their right to survive off of their art, and artists and their responsibility to tell the truth. Towards the end of Baraka's piece, he brings in the case of Mumia Abu-Jamal, which he submits, along with petitions, to ex-political prisoner President Nelson Mandela for his endorsement.

Today we witness what W.E.B. Du Bois called "The Sisyphus Syndrome," where like the ill-fated Sisyphus we are doomed to forever roll the rock of liberty up the mountain, only to have cruel "gods" roll it back down on us, as a penalty for our refusing to die!

Yes, and just yesterday, twenty-five years after we brought the Afro-American petty bourgeoisie into electoral hegemony in the revolutionary era of the U.S., they have allowed the peoples' enemies to return, having long ago, to paraphrase James Weldon Johnson, "sold their heritage for a mess of pottage."

My point is that we must make certain our leaders are actually working class leaders and not followers of the bourgeoisie (in mufti). That is, they must be part of the great majority of workers and farmers. And not be fighting merely to get into the ruler clique. And, alas, that is often true of the middle class, that they are not struggling to end oppression so much as merely trying to get the same status as the oppressors.

It is the same of writers and intellectuals. If we are not serious representatives of the people, we will wind up on the side of our enemies. And no matter the piles of glittering resources a society might have, remember the people are its most precious resource.

Our false leaders and turncoat artists don't understand this. They believe being Beggars is the utmost dignity—just as our Kneeling Negroes in Newark. For instance, isn't it obvious that if we are going to fight illiteracy and push mass education that the arts are one of the best ways to do this? And that there can be no real anti-illiteracy program without mounting a massive arts program? A writers' union must be in the leadership of this.

It should be equally obvious that the old use of society's institutions is inadequate. We must eliminate the Beggar Mode of social life and call for and help implement the self-reliant mode. Toward this end even government and other public agencies must be moved to self-reliance. Schools, for instance, if understood correctly, are natural economic producers. The combining of the arts with education at these facilities, decentralizing the programmatic functions of arts and mass education, gives more venues and ends the strictly Bureaucratic/Beggar concept of funding public institutions.

Just as the writers' union itself, if understood correctly, we must be collective and self-reliant. Small capitalism can't compete with imperialism. But selfreliant collectives can provide alternative circuits for resources providing an aggregation of resources that can be naturally expanded with the development of enterprises—our focus being on providing more service, more employment, more anti-illiteracy and mass education programs in which the target groups are central to their functioning.

If we can implement this collective and self-reliant mode of operation and eschew complete submission to begging our enemies and the friends of our enemies, we will develop. If not, we won't.

And it must be said for the Pan African people, not just U.S.A./U.S.A. And eventually it must be said for all the people. For us in the U.S., our national priority must proceed always with an eye to expansion throughout the whole of Pan America, i.e., the Western Hemisphere. And like Africa, we must also be constantly in touch with like-minded comrades throughout the Third World. Because they are hardest hit by imperialism. But we must always be open to revolutionary and progressive peoples' internationally.

Where are our Arts Festivals in the great capitals of the world? Our writers' union could do this. Why do we wait for SONY or JVC or IBM? Goree, Elmina, Johannesburg, New Orleans, Havana, Beijing, for starters. What a circuit! Why should we wait for "Budweiser?" It would be much wiser if the Bud were our own. Where our people are, where sympathetic people are, these are our venues, and they must be networked without being dominated by capital. Our union would take the lead in setting up international programs to proliferate collective solutions and self-reliance. It is the petty bourgeois beggar mentality of these governments supposedly sympathetic to the people that has prevented them from doing these things.

No more complaining that Big Capital won't let our writing or other art undermine them sufficiently. That *they* won't publish our books, which tell them to die, or produce our plays, exhibit our paintings, which show ways Big Capital can be destroyed. It is we who are fools if we don't understand why. Not them!

And Now's The Time! as Charlie Parker said. In the flush of newly won democracy in South Africa, we must move. In the other U.S.A., we are in the backward, downhill mode. Sisyphus' rock has come tumbling down the mountain, once again. We are beset with confederate maniacs, new Hitlers, and younger Goebbels. Negro propagandists for white supremacy and Hanging Judges, Tom Ass Clarences abound, and Colored Colons to connect the large and small intestine of capital to the "wreck them!"

The Civil Rights Movement, like the nineteenth century reconstruction has been underminded and all but murdered. It will happen here [in South Africa], for the same reasons, if we let it. In the U.S., the government murderers are trying to murder another one of us, the writer Mumia Abu-Jamal! It is the most spectacular frameup of recent years.

The would-be murderers want us to believe that the struggle for democracy and self-determination is over, and that democracy and self-determination themselves have been defeated. And that these Doles and Gingrichs, these Hêlms and Klan militia lynchers have won. And one of the purposes of my visit, aside from the conference, is to present a package on Mumia to President Mandela for his intervention. It would be a powerful act, just as millions of us throughout the world swore and acted to see that he would not be executed when Apartheid so mandated!

The ANC, through Cyril Ramaphosa, has already spoken out against this state lynching. Even South Africa has banned the Death Penalty. Only the U.S., of the industrial states, maintains the Death Penalty, restored to emphasize, in Blood, Sisyphus' rock rolled down the mountain again.

But the Death Penalty itself must be banned. You know what it takes to do that. A collective Self-Reliant effort. I hope I can get everyone here to sign a petition calling for the end of the legal state murders. And, of course, you must understand that like the old Apartheid government, these legal lynchings are aimed in the main at black people!

So let our call for the freeing of Mumia Abu-Jamal and the end of the death penalty mark the beginning of a new dispensation. The coming together of the artists and intellectuals internationally to struggle against imperialism and its stifling imposition of the beggar mentality on us. To consistently provide a presence that is unified to struggle at the side of the people to end the old social relations of slavery, colonialism, and neo-colonialism and spawn a new era of collective growth based on Self-Reliance and Self-Determination. We will do it!

•••

ARTHUR AMAKER

After the March
Philadelphia, PA Mumia Abu-Jamal Protest

Here
On this day
of outrage
At this hour
of protest

After the last
wearied speech
After the last
shout against
the vicious
machinations of
the state
The banners
waved
now torn
The placards
risen
now dropped
An army of
streetsweepers coming
to sweep the
last footprints left
from the march
away
with the dust

A father holds
up his babies
laughing
infant lips
kissing the wind
riddled with the
blood and breath of
the people

Brother and sister
play
dance and sing in
the circle of
the sights of
ever present
riflemen
Aloof to this
line of fire
Unaware of such
a petty thing as
repression

Even in the center
of struggle
there is peace
Even in the midst
of death
There is
life

•••

OLORI *

In Praise of Spirit

They tell me
things are symbols and to always look behind
They teach me
there are no dead things
just things that move and don't
that vision is layered
like touch of skin & feel of spirit

You see
my mouth like my life
is not my own
We are all shared things
whether we give or not

I see a line of people
ancestors standing in front
standing behind in front
a part of the continuum
recreated recreating
lesson after lesson after lesson

I feel my ancestors
like a rockin' a rockin'
cradling me pass public injuries
and personal crucifixions

chanting, chanting
you are the son of Wind & Word
Oya, Esu
and we give you voice to sing our praise
Amen

•••

LINDA WASSON*

Truth, can we save you before it's too late?

Another black man in a white man's court...
take a moment to pause on this absurdity
take a look at the twentieth century
(that is, how the white man measures time)

white men in robes and black men in chains
white children going to school
black kids joining gangs

when historians open this moment of time
will the quest for Truth be a waste of time
because it was buried by
insanity and corruption beneath the search for better interest rates?

Mumia spoke the Truth
and he has been victimized
just as *if* I speak the Truth,
I am ostracized because I don't give two shits on a rat's ass about
    capital gains tax debates

it is time to say, enough is enough
we must have peace, everyone, not just some
everyone deserves peace of mind, peace of heart, and a piece of the
    pie

it is time to say no more hospitals in white neighborhoods
when the poor have no health care but they should
and no more banks, anywhere,
until all the poor eat every day not just on Christian holidays

this greed is madness
this insane thirst for power is lunacy
this insatiable desire to destroy this planet in the name of profit
is not the way I raised my son

It is not what people should live for
and it is not what Mumia Abu-Jamal should die for

Mumia is leading the fight against this insanity
making the people's voices heard and stopping the filthy voracity
his inspiration has taken people to the streets,
challenging this oppression as the lethal cancer that it is,
taking back our dignity, facing down the police

We must stop this killing of our leaders who protect the Truth
Mumia has put his life on the line for the people's liberty
don't we, the people, owe him the same courtesy?
the government laws protect police
we, the people, must make laws, now, here, today, to protect the least
    of us
who the police seek to intimidate

for this government means not to protect the free
do you not see that
it is set only to annihilate any who would disagree

we all want our children to be free yet how can that possibly be
when even the animals are possessions of white man's greed
triumphs only of a flaccid penis
whether as heads on a wall, ivory implements or behind electric
    fences in a zoo-prison,
for the ignorant masses to come and stare
emblemized eternally as symbols of terror

the Truth is there it asks simply why
we killed your elephant mothers and your gorilla fathers
now you must entertain us until you, too, die
here in our beautiful cages we have built for you
and the Truth is the price of ivory is higher than gold

white man says we must save a few
so we can hide the Truth about third world's mortality
dark-skinned people, mostly
swept under the white man's rug, hidden from the people's eyes
covered up by Beverly Hills 90210 on weeknight TV

our dear beloved planet is reeling from the toxins and poisons we
    continue to excrete
ideals of nature are twisted and torn, broken and bent by
    government's lack of discrete
desire to show the Truth about ecological destruction awaiting our
    fate
should we continue this course of apathy and hate

this killing must stop of our leaders who would only make the world
    a better place
but not just the killing, we must put a stop once and for all of
this whole idea of white as a master race

I will weep no tears for that destruction,
for the old who show hatred and ignorance as the only instruction to
    their young
No tears for the woman who raised the child to pick up a gun
no mercy for the police who had a choice, and chose to lie, to shoot,
    and take a life
no mercy for the corporate bastard whose desire for profit was
    greater than making love to his wife
so he built the factory that spits tainted and venomous air in the
    poorer part of town
his year end bonuses go up and the people's standard of living only
    goes down
no mercy, either, for the rich white bitch
she made life miserable for the immigrant housekeeper,
who needed a job to feed her family but found herself serving time
    in a hell hole household
where the family dog got more respect
Today let truth state that the line has been drawn

it's time to choose what side that you're on
the people have spoken—hear what they say:
judge sabo, tom ridge, this is YOUR judgment day
don't think for a moment we'll just sit idly by
and allow Mumia Abu-Jamal to innocently die.

the time for tears is past, mercy no longer
the time for change is now, the quest for equal justice is coming
let Truth speak loud and clear
the PEOPLE have decided the revolution is here.

•••

GRAHAM RAYMAN

Cyber-Organizing for Mumia— The Progressive Use of the Worldwide Web

It's ironic that a method of communication largely developed by the government has become such an effective means of organizing protests against the government. Before the advent of the internet and the Worldwide Web, an individual with a cause to promote often had to stand on a street corner, passing out leaflets.

These days, the same person with similar resources can transmit his or her views across the country and around the world. As imperfect as they are, the internet and the web are great equalizers.

In what are quickly becoming the old days, an organizer would have to rely entirely on paper mail and the telephone to coordinate a demonstration. Now he or she may send detailed instructions to organizers without having to suffer the postal service. And instead of holding just one demonstration in one place, it is now much easier to coordinate demonstrations on the same issue in many places at once.

The ability to do this translates almost directly to more coverage and more influence. Reporters now take it as a matter of course to note what kind of activity has developed around an issue on the internet. This wasn't the case even a year ago.

Supporters of Mumia Abu-Jamal are recently not the first activists to benefit from this technology, but they are the first to use it so effectively on an issue unrelated to computers. This past summer, for example, dozens of demonstrations occurred around Abu-Jamal's petition for a new trial. Via the internet and electronic mail (and the fax as well), Abu-Jamal's supporters were able to organize protests of various types in the United States, Europe, and elsewhere, often at the same time.

It was, in part, through this communications technology that so many influential people felt compelled to get involved. And it was no small victory for activists–and testimony to the effectiveness of the campaign–that the judge on the case, Albert Sabo, felt enough pressure to respond from the bench.

All of this was done, by the way, without the millions of dollars, and the thousands of hours of television coverage devoted to the O.J. Simpson trial.

As the demonstrations went on, other groups employed their web sites to collect information and agitate on Abu-Jamal's behalf. Among the dozens of webites to follow the case, Solidarity Group Political Prisoners kept a running file of articles, press releases, and newspaper accounts on the case, continually updating the site as news developed.

Refuse and Resist published, among other things, the full text of Judge Sabo's decision to stay the execution. It was a brief document, but important because it opened up the opportunity for the defense to appeal beyond Sabo to the Pennsylvania Supreme Court and the federal courts. These groups and others could never have reached such a large audience without web access. Printing and distribution costs on the same scale would have been too high.

Particularly in July and August, as Abu-Jamal's attorneys were making their case for a new trial, the activity on the web and on the internet was astonishing. In one five-day period this summer, according to published reports, more than 200 entries in the internet news groups (soc.culture.african american, alt.politics.equality, etc.) helped speed extensive information about the case across the country. Imagine trying to do that in the days of the telegraph or even with a telephone.

The postings focused not only on news about the demonstration, but they carried detailed, often emotional dialogues about Abu-Jamal's guilt or innocence, whether he received a fair trial, what the case says about the American system of criminal justice, and other topics.

In writing an account of the events surrounding the night of December 9, 1981, for the web magazine, *Word*, I found that sites and postings were a primary source of information on both the case and the protests.

As a relative neophyte to the web, I was amazed that so much information–outside the normal print and television media–was so easily available. Much of the information wasn't carried on television or in the newspaper. *The New York Times* itself, for example, didn't really start following the case until this summer.

In the past (without access to a newspaper research department), I would have had to go to a well-stocked library and then contact the activist organizations, the defense, and the prosecution to learn about the case. Yet, with web access, I was able to assemble a list of players both in an out of court and to learn about the issues in an afternoon.

One by-product of the technology is that the space constraints of magazines and newspapers and the time constraints of television are irrelevant on the web. You can write as long as you want. You can use video, audio, graphics, and text to tell your story. By the same token, a person with interest in the case can read in as much detail as they want and sample all kinds of views before taking a position.

The medium certainly has its imperfections. The cost of computers prohibits people in lower income groups from home web access. Most web users are still upscale whites. Journalism on the web is still scarce compared to the large amount of advocacy that exists. Dialogues within the internet news groups often degenerate into name-calling. Fancy graphics take too long to download for people with slow modems.

But still, it says a lot about the power of this new medium that regular folks hundreds and thousands of miles apart were able to discuss the Abu-Jamal case and arrive at their own conclusions, rather than being forced to watch passively as television talk shows and newspaper columnists dominated (or ignored) the issue. It took a healthy chunk of the initiative and the control over public opinion and put it in the hands of the public.

•••

ANGELA JACKSON
Fannie (of Fannie Lou Hamer)

Fannie sang in jailhouse cells.
Don't you know her songs
swung the bars
high in the window
back and forth between snot
hard tears and stars.

Fannie Hamer sang about climbing
Jacob's ladder
        rung
             by
             rung
that cottony voice rose
             above smoke
and robes and swamps, dust
roads, lynch ropes, and water
hoses, dogs, badges, and mud
weary beaten bones and bullets.

Miz Fannie sang about climbing
Jacob's ladder, wrestling
angels, climbing
swinging rung by rung, from crying
                     to shining
bringing one by one,   from crying
                     to shining
           as far as the heart can
see,
           as far as the back can
carry.

Fannie sang in jailhouse cells.
Don't you know her songs?

Have you ever seen a Queen Spider dance?
She seems to be kneeling, but is not.
She is always getting up.

Have you ever seen a Queen   Spider dance?
Some of them have wings.

•••

NZADI ZIMELE KEITA

pass the word

our history is our whole lives
the swallowed sea
of all we have done and undone

from word to song to sanity
we scour the earth,
dragging riverbeds for lies

wrinkles and dimples and uncreased brows
bring the story forward
on the first morning after death
molding new ancestors from rust

our history walks in our talk,
living in language we made
living every voice

in crooning swamps
in rasping dust,
in corporate valleys

a story, creasing the Atlantic,
curls between the many islands
of our blood
this chain, this river
of what we do
lives in our breath

we tell, and tell, and tell
so we can look tomorrow down
with a conquering eye

•••

SANDRA MARÍA ESTEVES *

Till the Cows Come Home

for Mumia Abu-Jamal and political prisoners who are Voices of the Voiceless

Sing when your heart moves you/ sing when you need to/ sing
when the sun comes up/ sing in the day to carry you thru the
chaos in view/ sing to reclaim the inner part of you/ sing
cause you want to whenever the song comes to you/ sing
quietly inside in sync to your inner mind/ sing to voice
your choice/ sing out loud when you feel beautiful and
proud/ sing cause you care/ sing to feel good/ sing to be
healed from being misunderstood/ sing to find your note in
harmony with the grand concerto/ sing in your own sweet
rhythm and blues tunes/ sing in whatever music you are
moved/ sing cause it pleases you/ sing to be alive and full
in this moment that is you/ sing at high noon when the sun
shines bright and clear/ sing to bring down the rain/ sing
to let out pain/ sing to release them crazy feelings/ sing
to feel sane/ sing when you're dry and there's nothin to
drink/ sing to hear the music in your mind, to find the beat
where you're moved to think about who you are and why we are
here/ sing till it comes clear/ and if you can sing great
and loud, sing and send your vibrations out and around, from
within your house and down the steps, across the street and
over the river, ridin on the tracks and speedin thru the
expressway, past the toll booths and police blockades, thru
the arsenals and penitentiaries/ sing to knock them monsters
down/ sing the beast to sleep/ sing because the world is
round and green/ sing because you love your mother/ sing to
your mother/ sing to the wind in your face/ sing to the
stars who guide the night/ sing to call us together, to pray,
to play, to gather us from our long and tedious sleep/
sing to wake up/ sing to rise up/ sing to fly up/ sing to
walk, to run, to march/ sing to dance and overcome/ sing to
war, to overrun/ sing to struggle, to grow, to love/ sing to
discover reasons for being/ sing to find it, align with it,
open your mind to it/ sing and don't stop/ sing on and on in
peace and love/ sing in unity and struggle/ sing to free your
soul/ sing to free Mumia/ sing to free one another/ sing/
sing, and don't stop/ keep singing.

•••

Who Says I Can't

Who says I can't scream if I must, complain
about the way I live till my voice is gone

Who says I can't be who I am and speak my language
in my rhythm dance all the way to the moon
create pictures if it's how I feel

Who says I can't take a stand, defiantly question
clean the poison from my street living in my children's veins
or tear down the walls that imprison my flesh
play my drums any time of the day
carry my stick   live in any neighborhood   walk where I choose
this is my land paid for in blood
who says I can't be where I am

Who can tell me how to comb my hair
what silken gardenia to place by my ear
what words to speak from my tongue

Who says I can't save my earth from its dying last breath
scientific pollution is not the solution
I reserve my right to protest !!!

Who says I can't kill away my pain
cause the clouds to rain and wash away the smell of old abuse
believe in the gods I choose
dream in ideals
lay foundations that orbit the power giving sun
and movement of stars
Who says I can't shine inside and speak my words
like darts aimed at target
like relief for a headache
like warm bath to soothe aching feet

Who says I must be   ...sweet   ...soft   ...barefoot   ...& helpless
when stepped upon I will scream
be hard and cold   break bottles and windows
RAGE!!! with revenge
Who says we can't?

•••

VICKI GARVIN
Step Up the Offensive Today for Victory!

The Civil War never ended for us, with the Emancipation Proclamation and other edicts, captured African people, enslaved in the U.S. for centuries.

The U.S. Constitution and subsequent amendments have remained, in effect, paper documents, never truly enforced for our people.

Recall what happened during (and after) the brief "Reconstruction" years. Civil Rights legislation, won through prolonged struggle, not benevolently bestowed, did produce some gains. Now even they are being systematically wiped out.

The siren song of our integration and assimilation in the proclaimed "melting pot" is increasingly becoming a lament and nightmare for the masses of our people, as Malcolm correctly described this white supremacist, exploitative society decades ago.

Witness what is happening to us today in education, healthcare, housing, employment, and social services, not to mention the judicial system. Our belated and limited breakthrough in the political arena as elected officials in various levels of government is in serious jeopardy.

The U.S. power structure has openly declared that we are expendable, genetically mentally inferior, deadbeats, criminals, and brutal savages. Our masses are no longer needed in the labor market in the high-tech economy. Cheap labor is abundant in the "Third World."

All forms of the mainstream media have carried this pronouncement throughout this country and to worldwide populations. We are now at total war for survival—all classes of us—as racism increases and the economy decreases. Racial cleansing of people of color is underway in the U.S. also.

Our middle class, substantially in the public, not private, sector, albeit now enjoying higher income, more material possessions, professional and other fancy titles, is at grave risk. The white middle class is screaming about its declining status and benefits. Where is our economic base and political clout? In the suburbs, the inner cities? If we had vigorously fought for justice for attorney Alton Maddox, is it possible he could have been on the team handling Mumia's case?

Many of our people are waging a battle for our just demands on many issues and this should be continued. We know that many of them have and are being attacked, paying a personal price.

Why was so little known about Mumia's and others' plight, history, and contributions after all their years on death row? Maybe we haven't clearly defined who is a political prisoner, why and how charges are concocted against them? How do we analyze their alleged crimes as compared with others who are arrested and brought to trial?

Mumia's fight for life and justice is not just another personal one. He is not the first, only, or last one facing death as a political activist. We cannot permit such victims to be assigned to oblivion once a court rules they should be incarcerated.

Upon what criteria do we assess the role of today's dedicated freedom fighters, those who dare to carry on the legacy of their heroic forebears—men and women—who endured severe persecution and died in struggle?

As we know, the media is the leading vehicle through which most information is disseminated to influence public opinion in preparation for subsequent action. No comment on how the mainstream media distorts, portrays, or omits news about us!

It is obvious that we, as a people, have very few outlets and limited access to radio and television stations to present our message. No comments on the handful of some black faces and voices airing the prepared scripts of their bosses.

What is the role of the black press? I believe we should learn from the focus on exposure, agitation, and advocacy of David Walker, Frederick Douglass, John Brown Russwurm, Dr. W.E.B. Du Bois, Ida B. Wells, Carlotta Bass, and many others who struggled—in a period far more oppressive than the current one—in which we have but a toehold and sometimes bask in "democratic progress." Happily, there has been some progress in our media in recent years, but much more needs to be done.

In New York City, for example, we have quite a few Black newspapers competing with each other for circulation and advertisements. How many can (or will) our people buy?
I submit we desperately need one good daily paper with a common orientation to keep us accurately informed on current developments—locally and internationally—our just demands, initiatives, history, and achievements (along with sections on sports, entertainment, cultural events, religious, and social news.) In this respect, I personally salute New York City's, *The Daily Challenge*, especially. With combined resources, talented, experienced reporters, investigative journalists, scholars, authors, cartoonists, and others, we can fulfill this mission. It would be possible to extend sources of national and international news beyond that of the dominant wire services, and provide daily, timely editorials on a variety of subjects.

Mergers in the corporate, media, and other arenas, to consolidate their power, are the trend. Should we be fragmented in the information field, as we are in other entrepreneurial endeavors? I can dream, can't I, as we attempt to promote unity and effectiveness among us on this and other fronts. There are, of course, many differences of opinion, priorities, etc., in our ranks as is true of all peoples, but as a long-standing oppressed segment of society, we can agree on some basic goals.

We welcome the positive response from thousands of people and their elected spokespersons speaking and demonstrating on behalf of our Mumia Abu-Jamal. In this vast country there should be many thousands more, including some we label liberal and progressive. Some expressions of support may be due to timely, but delayed information, obviously omitted from the mainstream media. So the responsibility rests on our shoulders to agitate, educate, and organize.

The clock is ticking rapidly, but we still can win, and free Mumia to continue his revolutionary work among us.

Queen Mother Moore is one of my role models. She has been the main torchbearer for long-denied reparations for our abuse and unpaid labor, and a true Pan-Africanist.

Obviously, I am in the twilight of my life and will be 80 in December. I've been able to survive and sustain my spirit and hope because of the struggles and sacrifices of countless others.

Count on me and many other elders to remain in the ranks of our ongoing battle for justice, genuine equality, and full liberation. We cannot settle for condolences, editorials, or even a street named in honor of Mumia Abu-Jamal if he is condemned to death or to prolonged incarceration.

Step up the offensive today for victory!

•••

SONIA SANCHEZ
For Sweet Honey

I'm gonna stay on the battlefield
I'm gonna stay on the battlefield
I'm gonna stay on the battlefield til I die.

I'm gonna stay on the battlefield
I'm gonna stay on the battlefield
I'm gonna stay on the battlefield til I die.

i had come into the city carrying life in my eyes
amid rumors of death,
calling out to everyone who would listen
it is time to move us all into another century
time for freedom and racial and sexual justice
time for women and children and men time for hands unbound
i had come into the city wearing peaceful breasts
and the spaces between us smiled,
i had come into the city carrying life in my eyes.
i had come into the city carrying life in my eyes.

And they followed us in their cars with their computers
and their tongues crawled with caterpillars
and they bumped us off the road turned over our cars,
and they bombed our buildings killed our babies,
and they shot our doctors maintaining our bodies,
and their courts changed into confessionals
but we kept on organizing we kept on teaching believing
loving doing what was holy moving to a higher ground
even though our hands were full of slaughtered teeth
but we held out our eyes delirious with grace.
but we held out our eyes delirious with grace.

I'm gonna treat everybody right
I'm gonna treat everybody right
I'm gonna treat everybody right til I die.

I'm gonna treat everybody right
I'm gonna treat everybody right
I'm gonna treat everybody right til I die.

come. i say come, you sitting still in domestic bacteria
come. i say come, you standing still in double breasted mornings
come. i say come, and return to the fight.
this fight for the earth

this fight for our children
this fight for our life
we need your hurricane voices
we need your sacred hands

i say. come, sister, brother to the battlefield
come into the rain forests
come into the hood
come into the barrio
come into the schools
come into the abortion clinics
come into the prisons
come and caress our spines

i say come, wrap your feet around justice
i say come, wrap your tongues around truth
i say come, wrap your hands with deeds and prayer
you brown ones
you yellow ones
you black ones
you gay ones
you white ones
you lesbian ones

Comecomecomecomecome to this battlefield
called life, called life, called life.....

I'm gonna stay on the battlefield
I'm gonna stay on the battlefield
I'm gonna stay on the battlefield til I die.

I'm gonna stay on the battlefield
I'm gonna stay on the battlefield
I'm gonna stay on the battlefield til I die.

•••

MIKE FARRELL

Why I Joined Mumia's Ranks

All of the hoopla, hucksterism, media manipulation and name-calling associated with the campaign to kill Mumia Abu-Jamal seems clearly intended to drown out any rational discussion of the facts of the case. After all, the man has been tried, convicted and sentenced to death. A new governor is committed to carrying out the death penalty. The die, it would seem, has been cast.

So whence comes all the hair-tearing and hand-wringing? Is it simply bloodlust? Is it wrong to question the validity of a death sentence handed down by a jury manipulated by a prosecutor who played on their fear of the defendant's ten-year-old political statements?

Is it wrong to question a verdict of premeditated murder when a man happens on his brother being brutally beaten by a police officer and attempts to intervene? (And this is only if one accepts the prosecution's theory.)

Is it wrong to question the theory on which a capital conviction is based when ballistic evidence—the path of the bullet through Mumia's body–contradicts it?

Is it wrong to question why none of the testimony when other witnesses tell of being threatened, bribed and intimidated by police?

Is it wrong to question why none of the testimony indicating another individual running from the scene of the crime, corroborated by three people who did not know each other, was ever followed up?

Is it wrong to question the conviction of yet another African American defendant in a racially charged and polarized situation, to demand that the process stand up to rigorous scrutiny? And when that scrutiny reveals serious defiencies, is it wrong to demand another proceeding where all witnesses can be heard, where the racial makeup of the jury reflects the community in which it is held and where inflammatory racial and political statements by the prosecution are not allowed?

Given the retrograde tone of the campaign being waged—and signed onto by too many normally responsible journals—one understands why so many of the disenfranchised find themselves willing to believe the powers-that-be are once again conspiring to remove from their midst an articulate and passionate voice who offers an alternative vision.

If people believe in justice, they must be willing to pay the price, to stand up to the scrutiny, to encourage questions and supply objective, rational, truthful answers.

•••

NAOMI LONG MADGETT

Tree of Heaven
(Ailanthus Altissima)

I will live.
The ax's angry edge against my trunk
Cannot deny me. Though I thunder down
To lie prostrate among exalted grasses
That do not mourn me,
I will rise.

I will grow:
Persistent roots deep-burrowed in the earth
Avenge my fall. Tentacles will shoot out swiftly
In all directions, stubborn leaves explode their
                  force
Into the sun.
I will thrive.

Curse of the orchard.
Blemish on the land's fair countenance,
I have grown strong for strength denied, for
                  struggle
In hostile woods. I keep alive by being the
                  troublesome,
Indestructable
Stinkweed of truth.

•••

LOUIS REYES RIVERA *

the blacklit face of Mumia

celebrai-brai-brai-brai-bray
celebrai-brai-brai-brai-bray
Celebrate even the dreds of Mumia
rooted in the mind of curled & braided
fluffed and plucked blacklit crown
haloed around the stomping ground
of freedom wanting liberation

JOHN ABNER

locked inside the mortared gates of brick & stone
like the ancient pens of forgotten castles
or the makeshift barracoons of grief & greed
holding kidnapped children stained & chained
to the latch & hatch of whips & ships
the dreds of a dreadless voice in a sandbarred cell
stand & state how seasons changing bring & ring
the reasons ranging at the bottom of a well
that brinks on the edge of struggle

celebrai-brai-brai-brai-bray
celebrai-brai-brai-brai-bray
Celebrate even the look of Mumia
Afrocentered stolen stalk
taken from savannahs of birth & worth
then raised amid these slanted slabs of stars & bars
the klux klan crew of rust & bust
to try & fry this branching baobab
for the killing of a bounty hunting cop
or the wanton slaughter of a bastard lie

caught & brought before the black robes of white hoods
that prey & weigh upon the quilt & guilt of innocence
hovering over the whelps & wounds that mark the bark
of tree trunk transplants like Mumia
flourishing against cracked corridors of submissive steps
where cutstone chiseled condescending stairs
pave the slave to dungeon heap & death row chairs
as the watchful glare of riot guns & rifle fire
do not scare this transplant branch
from refusing to simply sit & stare at walls & halls
mulling over the final moment of execution
I said, say celebrai-brai-brai-brai-bray
celebrai-brai-brai-brai-bray
Celebrate even the song of Mumia
written on a page of rage now
echoing a modulated riff of mighty chants that rant
& stomp the streets throughout this planet

breaking out & springing up
the stalking roots of rasta fari
marching toward the halls of hell
where the cracked bell at independence mall
drops its chime of dimes telling on themselves
while prongs of tongues replanted in the soil of our souls
raise up lots & crops of stalwart anger lingering
with selfembracing glints of light
that stand against the arrogance of spit
that spits in the blacklit face of a man like Mumia
who sings against the scalding singe of
philly's finest stormtroop binge
dragged out & drugged in
from another shift of beating men with branding irons
& brandished cuffs that break the breath of flesh arrested
where even Marcus Garvey in his grave
returns to overturn the stench of burns
& stays the order to have Mumia killed

so celebrai-brai-brai-brai-bray
celebrai-brai-brai-brai-bray
celebrai-brai-brai-brai-bray...

•••

JAN CAREW

If We Let Him Go Quietly We, Too, Will Bleed

People get trial and prison ... (and death) while governments get hearings and re-elections.
—**Mumia Abu-Jamal**, July 12, 1995

Listen, my friends,
Brother Mumia Abu-Jamal says quietly
"Look and you'll see a widening politics of DEATH?"
And MALCOLM'S mesmeric voice
echoes across three decades, cautioning,
"WHEN YOU BEGIN TO THINK, YOU FRIGHTEN THEM."
Mumia had the "malice" to discover truths
hard and glittering like agate
and capturing thoughts
in a crucible of anguish
he closed the ocean span
between crystalline beliefs and action.
With mind and pen and eloquence of tongue
he trumpeted wakeup calls
that burst like stardust
deep inside our skulls.
That's why Inquisitors
in robes and wigs, and terminator's vines
are hawking death on the installment plan
trying to amortize, kill, calcify
the human self that's him,
proxying Hitler's Parisian victory jig
when that stealer of numberless lives,
metaphorically speaking,
danced on the graves of innocents.
Beware!
This is burgeoning jail cell time
mushrooming Death Row time,
chain gang time
death watch time
reclaiming the streets time,
EUPHEMISMS FOR LEGAL MURDER
"...tuff on crime unless it's their own"
Brother Jamal said quietly,
"People get trial and prison... (and death)

while governments get hearings and re-elections."
Murder flea-marketed at the hustlings
A sly in-justice system
spawning blood-seeds
coated with rhetoric of Kali the Destroyer
chorusing Kill, kill, kill!
The death penalty song
is number one
on a doomsday hit parade
in the White House
State Capitols
Mayors' Mansions
obscene Court Houses
the nation's Parliament of Greed
Kill, kill, kill!
warehouse the souls of Blacks, Latinos
and, of course, the rainbow-colored poor,
perform spin-doctors' rites in a media for hire
weave tangled webs of racist fantasies
But, in particular,
silence Mumia Abu-Jamal
a five-to-midnight man with an enchanted tongue
a truth-teller
defying the sowers of death.

Who sings of life
and mornings when sunrise burnishes
awakening eyes.
We're tied to him with a blood-knot
flesh and sinew, bones and dreams
whirlpool inside
the same cauldron
of pain and hope
the same invincible bonding
of ancestral longings.
Let him live
for if we let him go quietly
to his long night
to satisfy
the blood-lust of new Grand Inquisitors
we, too, will bleed.

•••

LAMER BELLE STEPTOE (AGE 10)

Mumia

We won't let them murder you
like they did Malcolm,
Martin, Medgar
and many others.

Mumia,
if they kill you
City Hall will be in flames!
America will be enraged
Sabo, Judge Sabo
will be embalmed in a coffin too.

We'll fight for freedom 'til we die.

•••

Afterword

S.E. ANDERSON and TONY MEDINA

While we want you to enjoy the artistry embracing these pages, we also want you to act on behalf of Mumia Abu-Jamal's struggle for a speedy and fair trial.

• First: Stay informed by calling the Mumia Hotline (212) 330-8029 for the latest news regarding trial and informational activities around the country and the world. You may leave a message, and a coalition member will get in touch with you.
• Second: Set up speaking engagements wherever you are, i.e., community centers, schools, universities, labor unions, spiritual centers.... A representative from the Free Mumia Abu-Jamal Coalition might be available to speak and/run a workshop or lead a teach-in.
• Third: Hold fundraisers to benefit the Mumia Abu-Jamal Legal Defense Fund and/or for organizing work. It takes serious financial resources to obtain justice.
• Fourth: Help distribute information in your area on the case and on what needs to be done.
• Fifth: Donate pre-paid phone cards to help the Coalition with long-distance phone calls.
• Sixth: Call or write U.S. Attorney General Janet Reno, asking her to order a special investigation into Mumia's case.

Department of Justice
10th & Constitution Ave, N.W.
Washington, D.C. 20530
(202) 514-2001

•We must save Mumia's Life! Mail tax-deductible donations
  to Legal Defense Fund:

The Mumia Abu-Jamal
Black United Fund/Maj Account
419 S. 15th Street
Philadelphia, PA 19146
(215)732-9266

Contributors

John Abner is a young artist who lives and works in Philadelphia, Pennsylvania. As a cultural worker, Abner has worked in prisons such as Pennsylvania's Holmesburg Prison where he conducted workshops and art classes. This experience is documented in the book *Notes of Testimony: Art from Holmesburg Prison,* a product of the Arts and Humanities Program of the Pennsylvania Prison Society.

Mumia Abu-Jamal is, as you know by now, a political prisoner on deathrow in the state of Pennsylvania. As a teenager, Abu-Jamal was a member of the Black Panther Party who went on to become an award–winning political journalist supporting John Africa and the MOVE organization and exposing corrupt and criminal behavior within the Philadelphia Police Department. While on deathrow, Abu-Jamal was not only writing, but served as a jailhouse lawyer to fellow inmates, created political comic strips, and dispatched his writings across radio waves. His first book, a collection of essays, *Live from Death Row,* was released from Addison-Wesley in 1995.

Ammiel Alcalay chairs the Department of Classical and Oriental Languages at Queens College. His latest book, *Keys to the Garden: New Israeli Writing,* is being published by City Lights. His other books include the cairo notebooks and *After Jews and Arabs: Remaking Levantine Culture.* He edited *For/Za Sarajevo* and has also translated widely from Bosnian.

Shawn Alexander is a Brooklyn-born artist now attending the School of Art at the Cooper Union, New York. As a painter in Cro-Maat Communication, he is a contributor to the most recent issue of *NOBO: A Journal of African American Dialogues, Black Prison Movements U.S.A.* (Africa World Press, 1995) and to *The Black Holocaust For Beginners* (Writers and Readers, 1995).

Samuel Allen was born in Columbus, Ohio in 1917. He attended Fisk University and while there, studied creative writing under James Weldon Johnson. He continued his education at Harvard, New York University, and the Sorbonne in Paris. As a poet he was "discovered" by the novelist Richard Wright, who published Allen's poems under his pseudonym, "Paul Vesey," in the classic journal, *Présence Africaine.* As a soldier in the army in Europe, a limited edition of his book *Elfenbein Zähne (Ivory Tusks)* was published both in German and English in 1956, out of Heidelberg, Germany. His poetry is widely anthologized and appears in such books as *Beyond the Blues, American Negro Poetry, New Negro Poets U.S.A., Kaleidoscope, In Search of Color Everywhere.* Mr. Allen is also a lawyer, who lives and works in Boston, Massachusetts. His most recent book is *Every Round* (Lotus Press, 1987).

Arthur Amaker is a graduate of Morehouse College. His work will appear in an upcoming volume of the literary magazine, *Long Shot*. A founding member of Oyster Knife Collective (based in Atlanta, Georgia), he is at work co-editing an anthology of black male poets. Currently, he is completing his master's degree in education at Columbia University's overseas program in Benin, Africa, where he is at work as an English teacher. He is also doing research for a historical novel.

Sam Anderson, a veteran activist/educator, has been involved in the Black Liberation Movement on many levels. He is a mathematics professor, a Senior Editor of *NOBO: Journal of African American Dialogue*, a founding member of the Network of Black Organizers and of The African Heritage Studies Association, an essayist, and the author of *The Black Holocaust for Beginners* (Writers and Readers, 1995). Sam lives in his native New York City.

Zöe Angelsey is from Oregon. She is the editor of *Stone on Stone/Piedra Sobre Piedra*. She teaches and lives in Brooklyn, New York, where she grows, in the summer, grapes, kale, mint, basil, peppers, tomatoes, squash, melons, arugula, and flowers, in her rented backyard.

asha bandele, born in New York City in 1966, is a poet and political activist who divides her time between New York and California. As an activist and member of Hunter College's legendary B.S.U. (Black Student Union), bandele has been (and still is) heavily involved in the student, political prioner, and youth movements, as well as having a strong presence on the cultural front. A co-founder of Black Star Express (with tenets in New York City and Oakland), her work appears in the anthologies *In The Tradition: An Anthology of Young Black Writers* (Harlem River Press, 1992) and *Aloud: Voices from the Nuyorican Poets Cafe* (Henry Holt, 1994). She has also co-authored a book of poetry with poet/educator Lorena Craighead entitled *A Wo/man's Voice Must Be Heard*.

* **Amina Baraka**—painter, dancer, actress, poet—was born in 1942 in Charlotte, North Carolina. Married to poet, playwright, and political activist Amiri Baraka, she is the mother of seven children, including Ras Baraka. The author of the poetry collection, *Songs for the Masses*, Ms. Baraka co-authored, with Amiri Baraka, *Confirmation: An Anthology of Afro-American Women Writers* (Quill, 1983) and *The Music: Reflections on Jazz and Blues* (William Morrow, 1987).

* **Amiri Baraka**, cultural architect who helped define and shape the Black Arts Movement of the 1960s, has produced over twenty plays, three jazz operas, seven books of non-fiction, a novel, *The System of Dante's Hell*, and thirteen volumes of poetry. He is a professor of Africana Studies. His most recent books are: *The Amiri Baraka/LeRoi Jones Reader* (Thunder's Mouth Press, 1991) and the epic poem *Wise Whys Y's* (Third World Press, 1995).

---

* One of the thirty-nine poets who read at the public poetry reading dedicated to Mumia Abu-Jamal at the Schomburg Center for the Study of Black Culture, in Harlem, August 11, 1995, hosted and coordinated by Tony Medina and Sam Anderson.

* **Ras Baraka** co-edited, with Kevin Powell, the anthology *In The Tradition: An Anthology of Young Black Writers* (Harlem River Press, 1992). He teaches junior high school in the public school system of Newark, N.J. A community activist, he is a founding member of Black Nia F.O.R.C.E. He ran for mayor of Newark, N.J. in 1994. Ras is a graduate of Howard University, where he helped to orchestrate the Howard University Protest '89 that helped get rid of republican leader Harvey Lee Atwater. His upcoming book of poetry is *Big Cities, Hometowns, Ghettoes.*

Paul Beatty was born in L.A. and currently lives in New York City. The author of *Big Bank Take Little Bank* (Nuyorican Poets Cafe Press, 1991) and *Joker Joker Deuce* (Penguin, 1994), his work appears in *In The Tradition: An Anthology of Young Black Writers* (Harlem River Press, 1992) and *Aloud: Voices from the Nuyorican Poets Cafe* (Henry Holt, 1994).

Gregory Benton is an artist whose illustrations have appeared in *The New York Times*, the *Village Voice* and *The Stranger*. His comix credits include: *World War 3, Nozone* and *Instant Piano*. He is currently working on his graphic novel, *Hummingbird*, due out from Slave Labor Graphics in June of 1996.

Becky Billips is a legal assistant at the Center for Constitutional Rights. She is a former Navy and Army personnel. During her tour of duty she was employed in the Pentagon Security Department. She was also employed by Franklin Williams, co-founder of the Peace Corp. and former ambassador to Uganda, as a legal secretary for the New York State Judicial Commission. Miss Billips is also an ex-offender and is very active doing volunteer work on behalf of inmates and prisoner's rights.

Kraig Blue was born January 31, 1968 in New York City's South Bronx to L. & L. Blue. A graduate of Fashion Institute of Technology in New York City, he's been drawing since the age of twelve. His work appears in *NOBO: Black Prison Movements U.S.A.* (Africa World Press, 1995), *Freedom Rag, The Black Holocaust for Beginners* (Writers and Readers, 1995). His work has also been displayed at the Neighborhood Defenders of Harlem and was recently contracted to create a series of hip–hop greeting cards for Black Heritage Greeting Cards.

Herb Boyd is an award-winning author and journalist who has taught Black Studies at the college level for over thirty years. He is the co-editor of *Brotherman: The Odyssey of Black Men in America–An Anthology* (One World, 1995), which was the recipient of the American Book Award in 1995. His history book, *Down the Glory Road*, has received wide acclaim. He is also the author of *African History for Beginners* and *The Black Panthers for Beginners*, both from Writers and Readers. Boyd is a prolific journalist whose articles, essays, and reviews can be found in more than a dozen publications, including *Black Scholar, Black Enterprise, The Crisis, Class, The Amsterdam News, Detroit Metro Times,* and *The City Sun*. He is currently an instructor of African American History at the College of New Rochelle in Manhattan and the New York City Technical College in Brooklyn.

Melba Joyce Boyd is an associate professor in the Department of Africana Studies at Wayne State University and an adjunct associate professor at the Center for Afro-American and African Studies at the University of Michigan, where she received her Doctor of Arts degree. She is the author of *The Inventory of Black Roses* and three other books of poetry. Her most recent work is *Discarded Legacy*, a critical biography on the life and political work of poet/activist Frances E.W. Harper. Ms. Boyd is the director and producer of the film and video *Black Unicorn*, a documentary on the life and work of the legendary Detroit poet and publisher Dudley Randall.

Jill Witherspoon Boyer is a poet whose book, *Breaking Camp*, was published by Lotus Press in 1984.

Keelyn Bradley, 22, was born and raised in Warren, Ohio. He was educated at Swarthmore College and now lives in Philadelphia, Pennsylvania, as a poet, performing artist, and activist-screaming loud and off-key.

Gwendolyn Brooks, the first African American to win a Pulitzer Prize, was born in Topeka, Kansas, and has lived in Chicago, Illinois since infancy. She is a graduate of Chicago's Wilson Junior College and has been awarded over 50 honorary degrees. She has taught at the University of Wisconsin (Madison), City College of New York, Columbia College of Chicago, Northeastern Illinois University, and Elmhurst College. She has published 16 books including poetry, children's verse, writing manuals, one novel, and an autobiography. In 1985, she became the 29th appointee as Consultant in Poetry to the Library of Congress. She is a member of the American Academy of Arts and Letters. Among her awards are the American Academy of Arts and Letters Award, the Shelley Memorial Award, the Anisfield-Wolf Award, the Kuumba Liberation Award, and two Guggenheim Fellowships. Ms. Brooks holds the Gwendolyn Brooks Chair in Black Literature and Creative Writing at Chicago State University.

Lesley-Ann Brown was born and raised in Brooklyn, New York. She has a B.A. in Writing Literature from The New School for Social Research. She is currently working on her novel, *The Mothers of Memory*. Aside from being contributing/assistant art editor for *One World* magazine, she is an associate at Marie Brown Associates.

Raymond M. Brown is a trial lawyer in New Jersey who writes when he can. He is an opponent of the death penalty.

Dennis Brutus was born in Zimbabwe but educated in South Africa. He became a schoolmaster and vigorous opponent of Apartheid. He was banned in 1961, arrested in 1963, shot in the back while trying to escape, and imprisoned on Robben Island. He went into exile in 1966 and successfully campaigned abroad for South Africa's exclusion from the Olympic Games. Since 1970 he has taught at Northwestern University, Swarthmore College, and the University of Pittsburgh. His books include *Sirens, Knuckles, Boots; Letters to Martha and Other Poems from a South African Prison; A Simple Lust; Poems from Algiers; Stubborn Hope; Strains; China Poems; Salutes and Censors; Airs & Tributes;* and *Still The Sirens.* He was the recipient of the Langston Hughes Award in 1987 and the first annual Paul Robeson Award in 1989.

Marilyn Buck is a North American anti-imperialist political prisoner currently serving 80 years on conspiracy charges stemming from supposedly bombing government buildings, committing armed robberies, and allegedly aiding in the 1979 prison escape of Assata Shakur. Captured in 1985, Marilyn has little chance of parole. She is currently working with various Prison Rights projects, as well as prison artists and writers.

> Marilyn Buck #00482-285
> FCI Dublin
> Pleasanton, CA 94558

Safiya Bukhari is a former political prisoner and Black Panther Party member. She served eight years in prison for refusing to testify to the Grand Jury against the Black Liberation Army. She is currently the chairperson of the New York Coalition to Free Mumia Abu-Jamal.

Richard Cammarieri is a poet and community organizer. A life-long resident of Newark, New Jersey, Cammarieri is a board member of the Newark Coalition for Neighborhoods.

Steve Cannon, long-time Lower East Side legendary figure and literary guru, has been involved in changing the face of American literature for some thirty years. A member of the influential and pioneering Umbra group, he has conspired with Ishmael Reed to found the publishing house, Reed, Cannon and Johnson. A prolific playwright, Mr. Cannon's plays have been widely produced. His first novel, *Groove, Bang and Jive Around* was published in 1966 and is set to be re-issued. Currently retired from his teaching position at Medgar Evers College, Mr. Cannon's writers workshop, The Stoop, is responsible for releasing to the public many of the poets down with The Nuyorican Poets Live tour. His home acts as an art gallery, which features the work of artists from all backgrounds, and his literary journal, *Tribes*, sets the pace for the diverse, multi-media, multi-cultural publications to come.

Jan Carew was born in 1920. He is a novelist, poet, playwright, journalist, critic, and historian. Currently the director of the Center for the Comparative Study of Humanities at Lincoln University, he taught at Northwestern University for fifteen years, where he is now Emeritus Professor of African American and Third World Studies. He taught previously at Princeton, Rutgers, and George Mason universities. Carew, whose first novel, *Black Midas*, was a landmark in Caribbean literature, has been an adviser to heads of state in Africa and the Caribbean. A member of the board of the international journal, *Race and Class*, his essay entitled "The Caribbean Writer and Exile" was awarded the 1979-1980 Pushcart Prize. His most recent books are *Fulcrums of Change* (1988) and *Ghosts in Our Blood: With Malcolm X in Africa, England, and the Caribbean* (Lawrence Hill Books, 1994).

Frank M. Chipasula is an associate professor of Black Literature at the University of Nebraska at Omaha and is the author of *Visions and Reflections, O Earth Wait for Me, Nightwatcher, Nightsong, When My Brothers Come Home: Poems from Central and Southern Africa* , and *Whispers in the Wings*.

Ernest Crichlow was born on June 19, 1914 in Brooklyn, New York. Crichlow was trained in art at Hoaren High school in Brooklyn and at the Commercial Illustration School of Art. The recipient of many honors and awards, he has taught at the College of the City of New York, the State University of New York at New Paltz, and the Art Students League in New York. Along with the artists Romare Bearden and Norman Lewis, Crichlow founded the Cinque Gallery in New York City's Soho area.

Clairesa Clay lives in Brooklyn, New York. She is a graduate of Baruch College. She teaches English at Long Island University and in the New York Public School system. Currently she is at work co-editing a book of poetry with poet Tony Medina.

Lucille Clifton was born in Dewpe, New York, and educated at the State University of New York at Fredonia and at Howard University. She has taught at Coppin State College, Goucher College, and the American University in Washington, D.C. Her other teaching experiences have included appointments as Elliston Poet at the University of Cincinnati, Jenny Moore Visiting Lecturer in Creative Writing at George Washington University, and Woodrow Wilson Scholar at Fisk University, Trinity College, and other universities. She currently teaches at the University of California at Santa Cruz. Clifton's awards and distinctions as a poet and fiction writer include the University of Massachusetts Press' Juniper Prize for poetry, a nomination for the Pulitzer Prize in poetry, an Emmy Award from the American Academy of Television Arts and Sciences, creative writing fellowships from the National Endowment for the Arts, and Poet Laureate of the State of Maryland.

Jelani W. Cobb, a graduate of Howard University, was involved in that school's student protests in the late 80s, which brought about the formation of Black Nia F.O.R.C.E. (an organization of young community organizers). A freelance writer, Mr. Cobb's work appears in such publications as *Third World Viewpoint* and *Quarterly Black Review.*

Kecia Élan Cole received her B.S. degree in journalism from Kent State. She has worked as a community organizer since 1991 and is a freelance writer and musician. Her work has appeared in such publications as *Emerge* magazine and *Freedom Rag.* She is currently pursuing a Masters of Science degree in teaching at the New School for Social Research in New York City.

Jayne Cortez lives in New York City. She is the author of nine books and producer of six recordings of poetry. Her poems have been translated into twenty-eight languages and published in journals, magazines, and anthologies such as *Daughters of Africa, Post Modern American Poetry, The Jazz Poetry Anthology, Moment's Notice, Women on War, Free Spirits, Black Scholar, Sulfur* and *UNESCO Courier.* She has lectured and read her poetry with and without music throughout the United States, Africa, Asia, Europe, Latin America, Canada, and the Caribbean. Her most recent books are *Poetic Magnetic and Fragments,* and her latest CD recording, *Cheerful & Optimistic,* with her band the Firespitters has been released.

Renaldo Imani Davidson, influenced by the Black Power Movement and hip–hop music, is a young artist who lives and works in New York City. His work appeared on the cover of *Emerge* magazine and *See* (Whirlwind Press, 1991).

E.L. Doctorow is the other of the novels: *The Book of Daniel* (1991), *Ragtime* (1975), *Loon Lake* (1988), *Lives of the Poets* (1984), *World's Fair* (1986), and *The Water Works* (1994). He has also published a volume of selected essays, *Jack London, Hemingway, & The Constitution,* and a play, *Drinks Before Dinner,* which was produced by the New York Shakespeare Festival. He has won the National Book Critics Circle Award (twice), the National Book Award, the Pen/Faulkner Award, and the William Dean Howells medal of the American Academy of Arts and Letters. He lives and works in New York City.

Eric Drooker was born in 1958 in New York City. He is a poster artist who uses the streets of Lower Manhattan as his gallery. His work appears regularly in *The New York Times, The New Yorker, The Village Voice,* and *Wold War 3 Illustrated.* He's the author of the award-winning book, a novel in pictures, *FLOOD* (Four Walls Eight Windows, 1992). His latest work *ILLUMINATED POEMS*, a collaboration with Allen Ginsberg, will appear in the Spring of 1996 by Four Walls Eight Windows.

Cornelius Eady was born in Rochester, New York, in 1954 and attended Empire State College and the MFA program for writers at Warren Wilson College. He is the author of five books of poetry: *Kartunes* (1980); *Victims of the Latest Dance Craze* (1986), winner of the 1985 Lamont Prize from the academy of American Poets; *The Gathering of My Name* (1991), nominated for the 1992 Pulitzer in poetry; *You Don't Miss Your Water* (1995); and *The Autobiography of a Jukebox* (1996). He is the recipient of an NEA Fellowship in Literature (1985); a John Simon Guggenheim Fellowship in Poetry (1993); a Lila Wallace-Readers Digest Traveling Scholarship to Tougaloo College in Mississippi (1992-1993), and a Rockefeller Foundation Fellowship to Bellagio, Italy (1993). His work appears in many journals and magazines and was featured on National Public Radio's "Morning Edition." He has taught poetry at New York University, The College of William and Mary, and the 92nd Street Y, and he is currently associate professor of English and director of the Poetry Center at SUNY Stony Brook.

Mel Edwards was born in 1937 in Houston, Texas. He lives in New York City; works and teaches in New Jersey at Rutgers University, Mason Gross School of the Arts. His work has been included in major exhibitions since 1970. His primary medium is welded steel, although he has created installations, prints, and drawings. His work is in many public collections and he has completed several large commissions, in addition to receiving many honors, awards, and fellowships. Widely traveled, in Africa, Asia, Central America, the Caribbean and Europe, Edwards began extensive research on the African Diaspora 25 years ago. In 1993, the Neuberger Museum honored Edwards' art by organizing a 30-year retrospective that traveled.

Martín Espada was born in Brooklyn, New York in 1957. Before becoming an assistant professor of English at the University of Massachusetts at Amherst, he worked as a housing lawyer with Su Clínica Legal, a legal services program for low-income tenants in Chelsea,

Massachusetts. The author of *Rebellion Is the Circle of a Lover's Hands*, *Trumpets from the Islands of Their Eviction*, *The Immigrant Iceboy's Bolero*, and *City of Coughing and Dead Radiators*, Espada has also translated *The Blood That Keeps Singing: Selected Poems of Clemente Soto Vélez* (with Camilo Pérez-Bustillo and edited *Poetry Like Bread* (Curbstone Press).

* **Sandra María Esteves**, one of the original Nuyorican Poets, first burst upon the scene in that movement's primary anthology, *Nuyorican Poetry*. Since then she has gone on to become a cultural worker, activist, and a prime member of the Latino literary culture. Her work is published widely in many magazines, journals, and anthologies, including *Puerto Rican Poets at Home in the U.S.* and *Aloud: Voices From The Nuyorican Cafe*. Her books include *Yerba Buena* and *Bluestown Mockingbird Mambo*.

Mari Evans, educator, writer, musician, activist, resides in Indianapolis. Formerly distinguished writer and assistant professor, Africana Studies and Research Center, Cornell University, she has taught at Indiana University, Purdue University, Northwestern University, Washington University in St. Louis, SUNY at Albany, the University of Miami at Coral Gables, and Spelman College in Atlanta. She is the author of *Where Is All the Music* (1968), Nightstar (1981), and *Black Women Writers (1950-1980): A Critical Evaluation*, among other books. She is the recipient of a National Endowment for the Arts Creative Writing Award, a John Hay Whitney Fellowship, and the Hazel Joan Bryant Award from the Midwest Afrikan American Theatre Alliance. Her most recent collection of poetry is *A Dark & Splendid Mass* (Harlem River Press, 1992).

Robert Farr grows hot peppers and listens to jazz outside of Washington, D.C. He's is in the process of trying to start an organic farm. He has recently begun a marketing writing business. His work has appeared in the journals and anthologies *Lictuca*, *Negative Capability* (*African American Anthology*) and *Our Ancestors Speak*. He's currently working on a collection of poems.

Mike Farrell, the actor, is co-chair, with Ossie Davis, of the Committee to Save Mumia Abu-Jamal. He is president of Death Penalty Focus of California and a director/member of the National Coalition to Abolish the Death Penalty. He starred in the television series M*A*S*H.

Tom Feelings has focused on African culture and the Black American experience throughout his distinguished career. *Soul Looks Back in Wonder* (Dial), whose award-winning art was exhibited at the Schomburg Center for Black Culture in New York City, has original poems by Maya Angelou and Margaret Walker, among others, as well as a previously unpublished poem by Langston Hughes. Mr. Feelings collaborated with Maya Angelou on *Now Sheba Sings the Song*. His cartoon series is published in the award-winning book *Tommy Traveler in the World of Black History* (Black Butterfly Children's Books, 1991). His most recent work is *The Middle Passage: White Ships / Black Cargo* (Dial, 1995). Born and raised in Brooklyn, New York, he attended the School of Visual Arts and later lived in Ghana, West Africa and Guyana, South America. He is the recipient of a grant from the National Endowment for the Arts, and is currently a professor of art at the University of South Carolina in Columbia, South Carolina.

Larvester Gaither is the publisher and editor of *The Gaither Reporter*, a monthly letter/journal out of Houston, Texas, designed to enhance awareness of African American ideological developments in the cultural, political, and literary field.

Vicki Garvin is a veteran community activist and political organizer.

Maria Mazziotti Gillan, born and raised in Paterson, New Jersey, is the founder and director of the Poetry Center at Passaic County Community College in Paterson, New Jersey, and editor of *Footwork*. Her writing has been collected in several books, and with her daughter, Jennifer, she edited an anthology of new American poetry entitled *Unsettling America* (Penguin, 1994). Her most recent collection of poetry is *Where I Come From* (Guernica Editions, Toronto).

Allen Ginsberg was born in 1926 in Newark, New Jersey, a son of Naomi Ginsberg and lyric poet, Louis Ginsberg. In 1956, he published his signal poem *Howl*, which overcame censorship trials to become one of the most widely read poems of the century. Ginsberg's most recent books include *Collected Poems: 1947-1980*; the annotated *Howl*, *White Shroud: Poems 1980-1985*, and *Cosmopolitan Greetings: Poems 1986-1992*. A member of the American Institute of Arts and Letters, awarded the medal of Chevalier de l'Orde des Arts et Lettres by the French Minister of Culture in 1993, and co-founder of the Jack Kerouac School of Disembodied Poetics at the Naropa Institute, the first accredited Buddhist college in the western world, Ginsberg lives on New York's Lower East Side.

* **Suheir Hammad**, a child of Palestinian refugee parents, grew up in Brooklyn. She was the co-recipient of the Audre Lorde Poetry Award at Hunter College, CUNY. As an activist, Ms. Hammad has been involved in the student movement as well as The Mumia Coalition Out-Reach Committee. A collection of poems and a memoir by Hammad will be published in Fall 1996.

Abdul Haqq is a political prisoner in the U.S.A.

Theodore A. Harris was born in New York City in 1966 and grew up in Philadelphia, Pennsylvania. From 1983 through 1993 he's painted murals throughout the city of Philadelphia for the Philadelphia Anti-Graffiti Network. He was a poetry coordinator for the West Philadelphia Cultural Alliance, a cultural conduit for the public school system. His work has appeared in *Real News, North Philly Matters*, and in the anthology *Voices: How Our Ancestor's Speak*.

David Henderson was born in Harlem and lives in New York City. A widely anthologized poet, he is the author of *Felix of the Silent Forest, De Mayor of Harlem, The Low East*, and *'Scuse Me While I Kiss the Sky: The Life of Jimi Hendrix*.

Safiya Henderson-Holmes is an assistant professor at the Graduate Creative Writing Program at Syracuse University. She has been published in numerous newsletters, periodicals, and anthologies. Her first collection of poetry entitled, *Madness and A Bit of Hope* (Harlem River Press) won the 1990 William Carlos Williams Award. Her latest collection, *daily bread*, was published in 1994 by Harlem River Press.

Nat Hentoff, journalist, novelist, jazz critic, social critic has been a long-standing columnist for New York City's *The Village Voice.*

Diana Hernandez is a multi-media artist, painter, print maker, poet, jazz singer, and song writer. A bona fide Nuyorican, she is a self-taught artist born in San Juan, and living on the Lower East Side.

Victor Hernández Cruz was born in Puerto Rico in 1949. His highly acclaimed first book, *Snaps*, was published the year he turned nineteen. His books include *Mainland; Tropicalization; By Lingual Wholes; Rhythm, Content and Flavor,* and *Red Beans.* He has received numerous awards, including a National Endowment for the Arts Fellowship, and a Creative Artists Program Service (CAPS) grant. His legendary dynamic reading ability has led to his being twice crowned as the World Heavyweight Poetry Champion in Taos.

Fred Ho lives in Brooklyn, New York. A former member of the Black Panther Party, Ho is a Chinese American baritone saxophonist, composer, leader of the Afro-Asian Music Ensemble, and the Monkey Orchestra; and revolutionary socialist activist. His recordings include *Bamboo That Snaps Back* and *The Underground Railroad to My Heart.*

* **Rashidah Ishmaili** is a lecturer in Africana Literature, and Black Psychology at Rutgers University, and also works as an associate director of an academic support program for minority students at Pratt Institute of Arts and Sciences in Brooklyn, New York. Her work appears in such anthologies as *Confirmation* and *For Sarajevo,* and her books include: *Oniybo and Other Poems* (Shamal Books), and *Missing in Action and Presumed Dead* (Africa World Press).

Angela Jackson was born in Greenville, Mississippi, raised on Chicago's South Side, and educated at Northwestern University and the University of Chicago. The author of four earlier, smaller collections: *Voo Doo/Love Magic, The Greenville Club, Solo in the Boxcar Third Floor E,* and *The Man with the White Liver,* Jackson's latest collection is *Dark Legs and Silk Kisses: The Beatitudes of the Spinners* (Triquarterly Books/Northwestern University Press, 1993). She lives in Chicago and is at work on a novel.

* **Bethany Johnson** was born August 21, 1978. She was raised in East Orange, New Jersey. She plans to go to college and major in English literature. She spends her time trying to write poetry and short stories.

Hettie Jones is a poet and a prose writer. She is the author of the memoir *How I Became Hettie Jones.*

June Jordan is a political activist and an award-winning poet and essayist. She is the recipient of the 1995 Lila Wallace-Reader's Digest Writer's Award. She is the author of over twenty books, including *Civil Wars, Technical Difficulties, Haruko/Love Poems,* and the libretto *I Was Looking at the Ceiling and Then I Saw the Sky.* A frequent contributor to *The Progressive,* Jordan is professor of African American Studies at the University of California-Berkley.

Eliot Katz is a poet and political activist from New Brunswick, New Jersey. He has published two books of poetry: *Space and Other Poems for Love, Laughs, and Social Transformation* (Orono,

ME: Northern Lights, 1990) and *Les voleurs au travail* (Paris: Messidor Press, 1992). A co-founder of *Long Shot* literary magazine, his poems are included in the recent anthologies, *Aloud: Voices from the Nuyorican Poets Cafe* (Henry Holt, 1994) and *Blue Stones and Salt Hay: An Anthology of Contemporary New Jersey Poets.*

Rick Kearns is a freelance journalist, poet, activist, teacher, and musician operating out of Harrisburg, Pennsylvania. His poems have been published in *Chicago Review, Drumvoices Revue, The Blue Guitar, The Painted Bride Quarterly* and the anthology, *Aloud: Voices from the Nuyorican Poets Cafe.* He is currently a part-time lecturer at Rutgers University, where he teaches a class "The Poetry of Protest " in Latin America. His first book of poems, *Street of Knives,* was published by Warm Springs Press (1993). He also published a chapbook called *The Intime Poems* (1984).

Nzadi Zimele Keita, the proud mother of two sons, is a poet who lives and works in Philadelphia, Pennsylvania. She was a student of poet Sonia Sanchez and affiliated with Seshet Poetry Circle. The recipient of a Pennsylvania Council Literature Fellowship, Keita's work is featured in the anthology *Confirmation.* Her most recent book is *Birthmark,* published by Nightshade Press (1993).

Diedra Harris-Kelley is an award-winning fine artist and art instructor at New York University. Her works have been widely published and exhibited nationally and internationally.

Eunice Knight-Bowens is the founder of the Etheridge Knight Festival for the Arts in Indianapolis, Indiana. A poet and playwright, Knight-Bowens is the sister of the late poet Etheridge Knight.

KRS-One is the most revolutionary hip hop artist there is. He has been in the forefront of using his music and poetry to advance the struggle against American capitalism since 1986. Since that time, he has been prolific, as well as innovative. His recordings include: *Criminal Minded* (1987), *By All Means Necessary* (1988), *Ghetto Music* (1989), *Edutainment* (1990), *BDP Live Hardcore* (1991), *Sex and Violence* (1992), and most recently, *KRS-One* (1995). KRS-One has also lead the Stop the Violence Movement in hip hop and has lectured at universities such as Harvard, Yale, Vassar, Columbia, New York University, and Stanford.

William Kunstler devoted his entire career to defending the disenfranchised. He won such groundbreaking cases as *Dombrowski v. Pfister,* where the Court halted the prosecution and harassment of Civil Rights workers in Louisiana and the South, under state subversion laws. In 1967, he convinced the District Court to desegregate Washington, D.C.'s public schools (in *Hobson v. Hansen).* The cases that brought Kunstler the most notoriety were his defense of the Chicago Seven in 1968, and of prisoners in the Attica Rebellion. In 1986, he successfully represented Larry Davis, who was accused of trying to kill nine New York City policemen. He also got acquitted El Sayyid Nosair, who had been charged with the murder of Meir Kahane. In 1995, William Kunstler died of heart failure.

* **Michael C. Ladd**, born in 1970 in Boston, Massachusetts, received a B.A. degree in African American Travel Writing in the Nineteenth Century from Hampshire College in 1993. He's been published in several magazines including *Freedom Rag, Forehead,* and *Black History.* His work also appears in the anthology, *Aloud: Voices from the Nuyorican Poets Cafe and in the book Swing Low: Black Men Writing.* Currently he teaches at Long Island University and lives in Brooklyn, New York.

Peter Linebaugh teaches history at the University of Toledo and is the author of *The London Hanged: Crime and Civil Society in the Eighteenth Century* (Cambridge).

Julia López is a South Bronx-born poet and performance artist. She has performed for the Painted Bride Arts Center, Taller Puerto Riqueño, Inc. Homer Jackson's Spirits in the Dark Festival in Philadelphia. She has also performed and read extensively in the Philadelphia area at colleges, prisons, and for community organizations. She studied at the Eugene O'Neil Theater Institute and received a B.A. in Theater at Weslyan University in Connecticut. She presently lives in Philadelphia and is producing two video documentaries with women inmates, *From My Body...* (at Camden County Jail) and *Portraits/Retatos* (at the Philadelphia Institute Correctional Facility).

Naomi Long Madgett, poet and publisher of Lotus Press, was born in Norfolk, Virginia. She received an M.A. from Wayne University and lives and works in Detroit. A widely published poet, her work has appeared in June Jordan's *Soulscript,* among other anthologies. She is also the author of *Songs to a Phantom Nightingale, The One and The Many, Star by Star,* and *Octavia and Other Poems.*

Manning Marable is a professor of history and director of the Institute for Research in African-American Studies, Columbia University, New York City. His syndicated column, "Along the Color Line," appears in 300 newspapers and journals and is broadcast by over 80 radio stations worldwide. Dr. Marable's publications include *From the Grassroots, Blackwater: Historical Studies in Race, Class Consciousness and Revolution, How Capitalism Underdeveloped Black America,* and *Race, Reform and Rebellion: The Second Reconstruction in Black America, 1945-1982.*

* **Bahíyyih Maroon** is a 22-year-old native of New York, by way of a dozen different cultures. Her work has appeared in Firewater Poetics, *The Fuse—A Journal of the Nuyorican Poets Cafe, The New York Times,* and several small New York literary journals and 'zines. She's currently at work on a non-fiction book and a poetic mythogography. As a Black woman, mother of a small child, wife of one, her work is an effort to explore and explode the boundaries and fiction that surround her.

Jorge Matos Valldejuli born in 1969, is originally from Rio Piedras, Puerto Rico, but was raised in Virginia near Washington, D.C. He moved to New York City in 1991. He is currently a student at Hunter College and works at the Center for Puerto Rican Studies. A performance poet, most of his work is in Spanish and deals with race, class, and colonialism in Puerto Rico and Latin America.

Stuart McCarrell is a Chicago playwright and poet. His cycle of plays on Goethe's life include: *LILI; Charlotte; Chritiane;* and *Bettina.* His play *Faust* is a re-creation of Goethe's *Faust in Modern Terms.* Besides *New York Visions Struggles Voices,* his books of poems in print include: *Voices Insistent Voices* and *A Wild Serenity.* His poems have appeared in many magazines and in three anthologies.

Mac McGill is an artist whose illustrations have appeared in many progressive publications. He is currently illustrating *Toni Morrison For Beginners* for Writers and Readers.

Rosemari Mealy is a poet, essayist, radio producer, and freelance journalist who lived in Cuba in 1985-87. She has written for both national and international news agencies, and her work has appeared in numerous literary journals and anthologies. She is the author of *Lift these shadows from our eyes* (West End Press) and *Fidel and Malcolm X* (Ocean). Mealy serves on the executive committee of the National Venceremos Brigade and is an NGO representative for the National Alliance of Third World Journalists at the United Nations. Currently, she is working on a law degree and lives in New York City with her husband Sam Anderson.

* **Tony Medina** teaches English at Long Island University's Brooklyn campus. He is the Literature Editor of *NOBO: A Journal of African American Dialogue.* The author of *Emerge & See* (Whirlwind Press, 1991), *Arrest the I.R.S.!!!* (Ban Dung Books, 1994), and *No Noose Is Good Noose* (Harlem River Press, 1996), his work is featured in the anthologies *In the Tradition* (Harlem River Press), *Aloud: Voices from the Nuyorican Poets Cafe, Soulfires,* and *Spirit & Flame,* as well as many literary and popular culture publications. He lives in New York City.

* **Nancy Mercado** is an editor of the classic underground literary journal *Long Shot,* which comes out of Hoboken, New Jersey. Her work has appeared in several magazines and journals, as well as the anthologies *Aloud: Voices from the Nuyorican Poets Cafe* and *U.S. Poems of Protest,* to be published in France. Mercado, who teaches creative writing to children and young adults, is also an activist and the author of five plays... has collaborated with legendary poet Pedro Pietri on Alicia in Project Land, and directed "Pietri's" *Let There Be Children* performed by New Jersey youth. Currently, Mercado is the director of the Lola Rodriguez de Tio Cultural Institute of the Puerto Rican Organization for Community Education and Economic Development, Inc. (P.R.O.C.E.E.D), in Elizabeth, New Jersey.

David Mills, a graduate of New York University's M.F.A. program, lives in Langston Hughes' house. He writes for *QBR* (Quarterly Black Review). His play *The Serpent and the Dove* (based on the life of Dr. Martin Luther King, Jr.) was produced January 1995 at Julliard. His work has been published in magazines such as *Vibe* and *The Source* magazines. His poetry appears in the anthologies *In The Tradition: An Anthology of Young Black Writers* (Harlem River Press, 1992) and *Aloud: Voices from the Nuyorican Poets Cafe* (Henry Holt, 1994).

Lenard D. Moore, a native of Jacksonville, North Carolina, received a B.A., magna cum laude, from Shaw University and attended Coastal Carolina Community College, University of Maryland, and North Carolina State University. His poems have appeared in numerous magazines and anthologies including *Callaloo, Xavier Review, African American Review, Obsidian II, Pembroke Magazine, Essence Magazine, The Greenfield Review, Midwest Quarterly Review, In Search of Color Everywhere, I Hear A Symphony, Kansas Quarterly, The Hailu Anthology, Southern Exposure, Haiku Moment, Steppingstones, Okike,* and *The Langston Hughes Review.* He was twice awarded The Haiku Museum of Tokyo Award. He is the recipient of a 1989 Emerging Artist Grant. He is the author of *Desert Storm: A Brief History* and *Forever Home.* He is the founder and executive director of the North Carolina African American Writers' Collective. He is a former writer-in-residence for the United Arts Council of Raleigh and Wake County, the chairman of North Carolina Haiku Society, and recently taught English at William G. Enloe High School in Raleigh.

Lenina Morales Nadal, Puerto Rican poet born in Brooklyn to Nuyorican activists, was raised in Long Beach, Long Island, and has been published in *The Olive Tree Review,* a Hunter College literary magazine. She is currently a student activist at Hunter College, pursuing a degree in Media Studies and Political Science.

Tracie Morris is a published essayist, poet, songwriter, and performer. Her work is featured in the anthology *Aloud: Voices from the Nuyorican Poets Cafe* (Henry Holt, 1994), and she is the author of a collection of poetry, *Chap-T-her One* and a collection of poetry and essays, *Rhyme Scheme.*

Toni Morrison is Robert F. Goheen Professor in the Council of the Humanities at Princeton University. Author of *The Bluest Eye, Sula, Song of Solomon, Tar Baby, Beloved, Jazz,* and *Playing in the Dark: Whiteness and the Literary Imagination,* and editor of the anthology, *Race-ing Justice, En-gendering Power.* Morrison is the recipient of both the Pulitzer Prize for Literature and the Nobel Prize in Literature (1993).

MOVE, founded by John Africa, is a revolutionary, deeply religious organization, galvanized to free all life from exploitation and enslavement.

Wangechi Mutu, born in Kenya, was educated in Nairobi and finished off her last two years of high school at The United World College of the Atlantic in Wales. She currently attends Cooper Union School of Art in New York City. She is part of Cromaat Communication, a collective of young artists and designers, the illustrators of *The Black Holocaust For Beginners.*

Gaston Neal, poet, community activist, teacher, has been a force in Washington's cultural and political life for three decades. He was a passionate civil rights warrior in the struggles of the 1960s and 1970s. His commitment to equality and justice is just as strong now, although he currently focuses on the myriad of devastating public health issues that beset the District. A nationally known poet and lecturer, Neal's work is highlighted in several anthologies, including *Black Fire, Black Power Revolt,* and *Voices of Struggle.* In addition, his work has been published in many literary journals, and he has lectured in over 100 universities and countless community and national forums.

* **Ngô Thanh Nhàn** is a Vietnamese poet who lives in New York City.

Sally O'Brien is an activist and journalist who works for WBAI public radio in New York City.

* **Olori** (aka **Linley Alison Smith**) is a healer, a warrior, and an artist whose underground written works span two decades.

Abiodun Oyewole, a founding member of The Last Poets, is also a consultant for the New York Board of Education.

Jesus Papoleto Meléndez was born and raised in El Barrio, New York City. His work is widely published in magazines, journals, and many anthologies, including *Nuyorican Poetry, Paper Dance*, and *Unsettling America*. His books include: *Casting Long Shadows, Have You Seen Liberation, Street Poetry & Other Poems*, and *Concertos on Market Street*.

Raymond R. Patterson was born in Harlem, New York, and studied at Lincoln University, Pennsylvania, and New York University. His poetry is represented in numerous anthologies and has been translated into several languages. He is the author of *26 Ways of Looking at a Black Man and Other Poems* and an unpublished book-length poem, *Dearest Phillis*, on the life of Phillis Wheatley. Awards for his poetry include a New York State CAPS Fellowship and an NEA grant. He has given readings at schools and colleges around the country, at the Library of Congress, and recently at the Stugra Poetry Evening in Macedonia, Yugoslavia. He is professor emeritus at the City College of the City University of New York and is a member of PEN. He is also the author of *Elemental Blues*.

Leonard Peltier is in Leavenworth Prison, serving two life sentences for allegedly shooting an FBI agent at the siege of Wounded Knee in the early 1970s. In prison for approximately twenty years, he is under maximum security. His first parole was set for twenty years. The Leonard Peltier Defense Committee has been campaigning to free Leonard Peltier who, like Mumia and many other political prisoners, was framed and did not receive a fair trial. He is an artist.

* **Willie Perdomo** lives in East Harlem, New York. His work can be found in the anthologies, *In The Tradition; Aloud: Voices from the Nuyorican Poets Cafe*; and *Boricuas*. He is touring across the country with the Nuyorican Poets Live! Perdomo can be seen on several video programs, including Alive From Off Center's *Words in Your Face* and PBS's *The United States of Poetry*. His first collection of poetry, *Where a Nickel Costs a Dime* was released by W.W. Norton in January 1996.

* **Carolyn Peyser** is the director of public relations at Poets House in New York City. Her poetry and essays have been published in several magazines and journals. She is also featured in the anthology, *Aloud: Voices from the Nuyorican Poets Cafe* (Henry Holt, 1994) and in the CD recording, *Nuyorican Symphony-Poetry Live at the Knitting Factory*, which she co-produced.

Pedro Pietri is a poet and playwright who has published seven books of poetry and an anthology of his plays, published by the University of Puerto Rico Press. *Puerto Rican Obituary* is Pietri's most renowned book of poems, which has become a classic in Puerto Rican literature and has been translated into thirteen languages. Most recently, an anthology of his poetry was published in Italian in Milan. Pietri's plays have been produced at the Public Theatre, La Mama, and the Nuyorican Poets Cafe, among others. He has received grants from CAPS and the National Endowment for the Arts, as well as being an alumni of the New Dramatists and serving as a member of the governing board of the Poetry Society of America from 1984 until 1989.

Deborah Pohl is a visual artist and teacher from Central Jersey. Her work has been shown at Trenton City Museum, City Without Walls Gallery (Newark), Womenmade Gallery (Chicago), AIR Gallery (New York City), and Rutgers University, (Piscataway).

Katha Pollitt is an associate editor at *The Nation*.

Kevin Powell is a staff writer at the New York-based *Vibe* magazine, a contributing editor to *Eyeball*, a literary arts journal; co-editor of *In The Tradition: An Anthology of Young Black Writers*, with Ras Baraka, and the author of the newly-released poetry collection, *recognize* (both published by Harlem River Press). His memoir, *homeboy alone*, is forthcoming.

Dudley Randall is the legendary founder and publisher of Broadside Press, circa 1965, one of the most significant presses to come out of the Black Arts Movement of the 1960s and 1970s, responsible for first publishing the works of such poets as Nikki Giovanni, Don L. Lee (Haki Madhubuti), Audre Lorde, Sonia Sanchez, and Etheridge Knight. He was born in Washington, D.C. in 1917. He received his B.A. in English from Wayne University in 1949 and an M.L.S. from the University of Michigan in 1951. He is co-author, with Margaret Danner, of *Poem Counterpoem*; co-editor with Gwendolyn Brooks, Haki R. Madhubuti, and Keorapetse Kgositsile of *A Capsule Course in Black Poetry Writing* and *The Burning Cities*. His anthology *For Malcolm* is the precursor of this volume dedicated to Mumia.

Margaret Randall lives and writes in Albuquerque, New Mexico, after successfully battling the U.S. Immigration and Naturalization Service that ordered her deported in 1985. She won her case in 1989. Recent books are: *Gathering Rage: The Failure of Twentieth Century Revolutions to Develop a Feminist Agenda* (Monthly Review Press, 1992), *Sandino's Daughters Revisited* (Rutgers University Press, 1994), and *Our Voices/Our Lives: Stories of Women from Central America and the Caribbean* (Common Courage Press, 1995). Forthcoming from Routledge is *The Price We Pay: The Hidden Cost of Women's Relationship to Money*.

Graham Rayman is a senior editor for *Word*, a magazine published on the world wide web. Previously, Rayman was a reporter and editor at *New York Newsday*. He has written for *The New York Times*, *The San Francisco Chronicle*, *Entertainment Weekly*, *US*, and other publications. He holds an M.S. from Columbia University Graduate School of Journalism, class of 1993.

* **Eugene B. Redmond** is poet laureate of his native East St. Louis, founding editor of *Drumvoices Revue*, and associate publisher/editor of *Literati Internationale* and *The Original Chicago Blues Annual*. A professor of English at SIUE, he won a 1993 American Book Award from the Before Columbus Foundation for *The Eye in the Ceiling: Selected Poems* (Harlem River Press, 1991).

* **Louis Reyes Rivera**, a native of Brooklyn, New York, is the author of *Who Pays The Cost*, 1977; *This One For You, 1983;YO!, 1990* (a recording), and *Three by One*, was a professor of literature and history in Africana Studies at SUNY at Stony Brook. Publisher of Shamal Books, Rivera's most recent collection is *Scattered Scripture*.

Staci Rodriguez, a 25-year-old black poet, was born and raised in Brooklyn, New York. She received a B.A. in philosophy from SUNY at Binghamton. She currently attends City College CUNY, where she is pursuing an M.A. in literature, focusing on Black feminist thought in poetry. Her work has also appeared in *NOBO: A Journal of African American Dialogue*.

Susan Rosenberg is a North American political prisoner serving 58 years on conspiracy charges stemming from alleged bombings, weapons and explosive possession, and false identifications. She is to have no parole possibility unless she renounces her revolutionary political beliefs. Susan runs an AIDS program for women prisioners and is the recipent of two PEN Writers Awards.

> Susan Rosenberg #03684-016
> FCI Danbury
> Pembroke Station
> Danbury, CT 06811

Kalamu ya Salaam is a professional writer/editor and producer/arts administrator. For thirteen years, he edited *Black Collegian*, and now he organizes Black arts festivals. He has completed two anthologies: *Word Up/Black Poetry of the 80s from the Deep South* and *Black New Orleans*. His most recent book of poetry and prose is *What Is Life?: Reclaiming the Black Blues Self* (Third World Press, 1995).

Raul Salinas, poet, teacher, and community activist, spent years in four of the most notorious prisons in this country: Soledad, Huntsville, Leavenworth, and Marion. He also participated in the Leavenworth/Marion prison rebellions of the late 60s and early 70s and has worked extensively in the are of prisoner's rights with the American Indian Movement, International Indian Treaty Council, and the Leonard Peltier Defense Committee. Salinas now owns and operates Resistencia Bookstore, Casa de Red Salmon Press, and is working with the National Commission on Gang Violence and the Prisoner's Rights Support Network. The author of four books of poetry—*Viaje/Trip, Un Trip Through the Mind, East of the Freeway*, and *Indio Trails*– "Salinas" has been included in numerous anthologies throughout the country, including, most recently, *Aloud: Voices from the Nuyorican Poets Cafe* (Henry Holt, 1994).

Juan Sánchez, born in Brooklyn, New York in 1954, is a painter, photographer, and writer who lives and works in New York City. He teaches at Hunter College of the City University of New York. Sánchez has been involved with several artist/activist collaborative groups. He has had numerous exhibitions in the United States, Central and South America, the West Indies, and Europe, and has won various awards and fellowships. He has also written, lectured, and curated exhibitions and has taught widely.

Sonia Sanchez—poet, activist, scholar—is Laura Carnell Professor of English and Women's Studies at Temple University and a national lecturer. She is the author of thirteen books and recipient of many awards and honors, including a National Endowment for the Arts grant and the Peace and Freedom Award from Women's International League for Peace and Freedom. Her most recent book is *Wounded in the House of a Friend*, published by Beacon Press.

Trinidad Sanchez, Jr. originates from Pontiac, El Michoacan del Norte, Michigan. He is the ninth of ten children born to Sofia Huerta and the late poet Trinidad V. Sanchez. He has been recognized for his activism on behalf of those in the penal system and his involvement in peace and justice issues with the Dr. Martin Luther King Keep The Dream Alive Award. His essays, literary reviews, and poetry have been published in several anthologies and alternative press publications. His most recent works include *Authentic Chicano Food Is Hot!*, *Compartiendo De La Nada, Why Am I So Brown?*, and two volumes of poetry with his father, *Poems by Trinidad V. Sanchez and Trinidad Sanchez, Jr.*

Moe Seager was born in Pittsburgh, Pennsylvania in 1952. Currently, he lives in self-imposed exile in Paris, France, and works on behalf of international political prisoners. He is a poet, an award-winning journalist, activist, and playwright. The father of four children, his work has appeared in such publications as *Z* magazine and *In Pittsburgh*, as well as many other publication. Seager, is also the founder of the White Panther Party in Pittsburgh, Pennsylvania. He is the author of *Fishermen and Pool Sharks*.

Assata Shakur, as a member of the Black Panther Party, was a target of J. Edgar Hoover's campaign to defame, infiltrate, and criminalize black nationalist organizations and their leaders, known as COINTELPRO. In 1973, she was involved in a shoot-out on the New Jersey Turnpike in which a state trooper was killed, and she was shot. Ms. Shakur was subsequently convicted, and two years later escaped from prison. She was given political asylum by Cuba, where she now resides. Her life story is told in the classic *Assata: An Autobiography*.

Danny Shot, publisher and editor of the underground literary journal *Long Shot*, was born in the Bronx, New York, where he now teaches English at a junior high school.

Daniel Simmons is president of Rush Philanthropic Arts Foundation, which provides artistic and educational opportunities to artists of diverse cultural backgrounds whose work and talent, though socially relevant and timely, would otherwise not be promoted through mainstream venues. He's a surreal and abstract artist. The art of Daniel Simmons not only depicts the woes of society, but offers the viewer the belief in the resiliency of the human spirit and hope for the future. The cover painting for *In Defense of Mumia*, "The Black Male in Contemporary Society," was created in response to the Black Male exhibit at the Whitney Museum in New York City in 1995, which, to Simmons, was not an accurate representation of the black male in American society.

* **Shariff Simmons** was born on Long Island, New York, in 1969. A poet, musician, and songwriter, he has a band called *"Speaking Seeds."* His work is featured in *African Voices* magazine, and he made a cameo appearance in the film *Panthers* in which he read his poetry. Currently, Simmons is at work on his first volume of poetry titled, *Fast Citites and Objects that Burn*. He lives in Brooklyn, New York, with his wife and their infant son.

George 'Geo' R. Smith is an artist whose primary medium is the collage. He was educated at New York Phoenix School of Design and the School of Visual Arts, in New York City. Throughout the 1980s and 1990s his work has been featured in group exhibitions in the New York and New Jersey area. His solo exhibits were featured at the Grinnel Gallery and the Cinque Gallery, both in New York City.

Pamela Sneed is a New York-based poet, actress and solo performer who's read her work in the U.S. and abroad. She has been featured in *The New York Times, Vibe* and *Reflex* magazine. Her work appears in numerous publications as well as *Aloud: Voices from the Nuyorican Poets Cafe* (Henry Holt, 1994) and in *The New Fuck You: An Anthology of Lesbian Performance Text*. Sneed also is the featured dancer in the Digable Planet's video/song tribute to Marvin Gaye.

Standing Deer is an Oneida/Choctaw prisoner presently incarcerated in Texas, where he continues to struggle for Native American spiritual rights in addition to monitoring prison abuses from within. Standing Deer was instrumental in exposing the U.S. government's plot to assassinate Leonard Peltier.

> Standing Deer a.k.a. Robert H. Wilson
> Ellis 1 #640289
> Huntsville, Texas 77343.

LaMer Belle Steptoe began writing at the age of six. Born in Philadelphia, Pennsylvania in 1985, she has traveled throughout the United States, Europe, and the Caribbean. Besides writing poetry, Steptoe enjoys photography and painting. Currently she is working on her first book of poetry, entitled *What in the Poet Are You Writing?*

Lamont B. Steptoe, poet, photographer, publisher, father, and Vietnam Veteran, was born and reared in Pittsburgh, Pennsylvania, and is the author of seven books of poetry, including *Crimson River, American Morning/Mourning, Mad Minute, Uncle South China Sea Blue Nightmare,* and *Dusty Road*. Recently, Steptoe was nominated for the Pushcart Prize. His work has also appeared in the following anthologies: *Brother-Two-Brother, In Search of Color Everywhere, Unsettling America*, and *Aloud: Voices from the Nuyorican Poets Cafe* (Henry Holt, 1994). Steptoe has read at the Library of Congress, the National Library of Nicaragua, the Geraldine R. Dodge Poetry Festival, and Shakespeare & Company in Paris, France.

Halim Suliman is an activist poet. A member of the jazz/poetry group Blue Ark led by Amiri Baraka, he is the author of a book of poems, *Swift Soft Slashes*.

* **Cheryl Boyce Taylor**, born in Trinidad, is a poet, actor, director, and visual artist. Her photo/poetry exhibit of Goree Island (which depicts the slave house and surrounding area of Goree Island Senegal, West Africa) was installed at CB's 313 Gallery in New York City and Common Boundaries Gallery in Jersey City, New Jersey. Her work is featured in *Aloud: Voices from the Nuyorican Poets Cafe* (Henry Holt, 1994), *Cayenne, Catalyst, The Maryland Poetry Review, Caprice, Excursus* (to be published), and *The Zenith of Desire*, an anthology (Crown, 1996).

Ngùgì wa Thiong'o, has published many books, among them *Petals of Blood* and *Devil on the Cross* (novels); *Barrel of a Pen; Decolonizing the Mind; Writers in Politics;* and *Writing Against Neocolonialism* (essays); *This Time Tomorrow* and *The Black Hermit* (plays); he has also co-authored the plays *I Will Marry When I Want* (with Ngugi wa Mirii) and *The Trial of Dedan Kimathi* (with Micere Mugo); *Njamba Nene and the Flying Bus* and *Njamba Nene's Pistol* (children's stories translated from the original Gikuyu by Wangui wa Goro); *Detained: A Writer's Prison Diary*, which is his account of being imprisoned without trial by Kenyan authorities for his anti-imperialist and anti-colonialist writings. Ngugi is also the creator of a 20-minute feature film, *Bloodgrapes and Black Diamonds*.

Piri Thomas, author of *Savior, Savior Hold My Hand; Seven Long Times; Stories from El Barrio* and the classic *Down These Mean Streets* has influenced generations of Puerto Rican and African American writers. His most recent work, *Sounds of the Streets*, is a tape and CD of his reading poetry over a background of Afro-Latin jazz music featuring the great Patato Valdez.

Seth Tobocman is a founding editor of *World War 3-Illustrated*, a radical comic book that features cartoons by Mumia Abu-Jamal and others. Tobocman's first book *You Don't Have to Fuck People to Survive* was published in 1990. He is working on a second book, *War in the Neighborhood*, a graphic novel about riots and housing struggles on New York's Lower East Side.

Lance Tooks is a New York-based writer and illustrator. He worked as an assistant editor at Marvel Comics, animated nearly one hundred commercials, films and videos and created comics for *Shade* and *Vibe* magazines, among other projects. His comic strip, "Baby Ranks," which appears in the children's newspaper *Zuzu*, is being developed into a children's book.

Askia M. Touré, poet, essayist, editor, and political activist, is an architect and leading voice of the Black Arts Movement. He is a former editor of the *Journal of Black Poetry, Black Dialogue & Black Star*, and staff writer for *Liberator* magazine, organs of the Black Power Revolt. Touré is widely published in a host of anthologies in the United States and abroad. He is author of *JuJu, Songhai!*, and *From the Pyramids to the Projects*, volumes of verse, and co-author of *Samory Touré*, a political biography.

Brenda Walcott is a poet, playwright, educator and cultural worker who lives and works in Cambridge, Massachusetts. A prolific playwright, Walcott's recent play *Tongues of Fire* has been produced at the African American Museum in Boston and at the Black Arts Festival in Atlanta, Georgia.

Jerome Washington is the survivor of sixteen years and three months incarceration in New York State's maximum security prison system. He is an award-winning journalist and playwright, a teacher, performance poet, lecturer and the author of *Iron House* (QED Press), for which he received a Western States Arts Federation Book Award. His business card reads: *Jerome Washington / Optimist.*

* **Linda Wasson** has been writing poetry for 30 years but has never been compelled to go public until she was inspired by the urgency of Mumia's case. She is from West Texas and is part Choctaw. A long-time supporter of A.I.M. (American Indian Movement), she's been a feminist and activist for all of her life. She is a member of the Leonard Peltier Defense Committee and is also a member of the Save Mumia Abu-Jamal Coalition.

Michael S. Weaver was born and raised in Baltimore, Maryland. He's a tenured professor at Rutger's University (in Camden), where he teaches English. His books include: *Water Song, My Father's Geography, Timbre and Prayer.* Also a playwright, Weaver's play *Rosa* received its world premiere at Venture Theater in Philadelphia, Pennsylvania. At present he lives in Philadelphia.

Cornel West has taught at Yale University, Union Theological Seminary, and Princeton University, as well as at Harvard University and the University of Paris. He is the author of *Prophecy Deliverance! An Afro-American Revolutionary Christianity; Prophetic Fragments; The American Evasion of Philosophy; The Ethical Dimensions of Marxist Thought; Breaking Bread: Insurgent Black Intellectual Life; Keeping Faith; Race Matters;* and co-editor of *Post-Analytic Philosophy; Out There: Marginalization and Contemporary Cultures;* and most recently *Jews and Blacks: Let the Healing Begin* with Michael Lerner.

John Edgar Wideman, Phi Beta Kappa and All-Ivy Basketball at the University of Pennsylvania, Rhodes Scholar at Oxford, PEN/Faulkner Award winner and National Book Critics Circle Award nominee, is the author of several books, including *Philadelphia Fire; Fever; Brothers and Keepers; Reuben; The Lynchers; Hiding Place; Sent For You Yesterday; Hurry Home; Damballah;* and *A Glance Away.*

Ian Williams wrote a column on the United Nations for the weekly *New York Observer,* which gained a wide readership because of its irreverent but accurate coverage of areas of the U.N. that diplomats and bureaucrats would prefer to keep under cover. He is the author of *The Alms Trade* (1989) and a contributor to *The Nation* and the *New Statesman.* He is also the author of *The U.N. For Beginners* (Writers and Readers, 1995). In 1995 he became President of the U.N. Correspondents Association.

Patricia J. Williams, a professor at Columbia Law School, is the author of *The Alchemy of Race and Rights* (Harvard) and *The Rooster's Egg* (Harvard, 1995).

Saul Williams, twenty-three, has been relentlessly preparing himself for a career in the theater for most of his life. He has been acting on the stage since the age of five and began training at the age of thirteen. Williams began writing (as an aspiring rapper) at the age of twelve and, thus, poetry. He is a founding member of the Red Clay Collective, which publishes *Red Clay Magazine* out of Atlanta, Georgia. Williams received his B.A. in Drama and Philosophy from Morehouse College and is currently pursuing an M.F.A. in acting at New York University.

Ted Wilson grew up in Harlem, New York. For many years, active in community organizing, Wilson was an editor of *Pride* magazine and on the staff of Liberator magazine. Once a frequent contributer to the Associated Negro Press, Wilson's poetry has appeared in the anthology *Black Fire: An Anthology of Afro-American Writing*, edited by LeRoi Jones (Amiri Baraka) and Larry Neal (1968) and, most recently, in *Callalloo*.

Marvin X is a legendary poet-playwright-journalist whose writings appeared in many publications throughout the years: *Muhammad Speaks, Black World, Jet, Black Scholar, Black Nation, Oakland Tribune, Journal of Black Poetry, Black Theater, New Bay Review, California Voice*, and elsewhere.

Xochipielli wishes to remain anonymous.

Daisy Zamora, poet, painter and psychologist, was a combatant of the National Sandinista Liberation Front and served as vice minister of culture after the 1979 revolution. She currently lives in Nicaragua where she is an activist with groups concerned with women's issues. She is the author of *Riverbed of Memory* (City Lights) and *Clean Slate: New and Selected Poems* (Curbstone).

•••••

Credits

Sam Allen, "I Saw The Executioner" from *Every Round*. Copyright Lotus Press. Reprinted by permission of the author.

Ammiel Alcalay, "A Stitch in Time" first appeared in *For Palestine*, edited by Jay Murphy. Copyright 1993, Writers and Readers Publishing. It is reprinted here by permission of Ammiel Alcalay.

Herb Boyd, "Award-winning Journalist Denounces NABJ." Copyright 1995, *The Daily Challenge*. Reprinted by permission of the author.

Jill Witherspoon Boyer, "George Jackson," from *Breaking Camp*. Copyright 1984, Lotus Press. Reprinted by permission of the author and Lotus Press.

Gwendolyn Brooks, "To The Prisoners," from *to disembark*. Copyright 1981, Third World Press. Reprinted by permission of the author.

Raymond M. Brown, "Epistle from Hell: A Review of *Live from Death Row*." Copyright 1995, *QBR: The Black Book Review*. Reprinted by permission of *QBR: The Black Book Review*, Vol. 3, No. 1.

Jan Carew, "Tribute to Andrew Salkey," from *Third World Viewpoint* (Summer 1995). Copyright 1995, Third World Viewpoint. Reprinted by permission of *Third World Viewpoint*.

Frank M. Chipasula, "We Must Crush the Parasite" from *Whispers in the Wings*. Copyright 1991, Heinemann. Reprinted by permission of the author.

Lucille Clifton, "move" and "samson predicts from gaza the philadelphia fire," from *The Book of Light*. Copyright 1993, Copper Canyon Press. Reprinted by permission of Canyon Press.

Jelani W. Cobb, "Review of *Live from Death Row*," from *Third World Viewpoint* (Summer, 1995). Copyright 1995, *Third World Viewpoint*. Reprinted by permission of *Third World Viewpoint*.

Jayne Cortez, "What's Happening," from *Poetic Magnetic*. Copyright 1991, Bola Press. Reprinted by permission of the author.

Naomi Long Madgett, "Images," from *Octavia and Other Poems*. Copyright 1988, Third World Press. Reprinted by permission. "Tree of Heaven," from *Star by Star*. Copyright 1965, 1970, Naomi Long Madgett. Reprinted by permission of the author.

Jesus Papoleto Meléndez, "San Diego/Southern African Night," from *Concertos on Market Street*. Copyright 1993 Kimetic Images. Reprinted by permission of the author.

Toni Morrison, "Racism and Fascism" from *The Nation* (May 29). Copyright 1995, *The Nation*. Reprinted by permission of the author.

Abiodun Oyewole of The Last Poets, "Political Prisoners." Copyright 1995, Abiodun of The Last Poets. Reprinted by permission of the author.

Willie Perdomo, "Dreaming, I Was Only Dreaming" from *Where a Nickle Costs a Dime*. Copyright 1996, W.W. Norton. Reprinted by permission of the author.

Katha Pollitt, "Subject to Debate" from *The Nation* (September 11). Copyright 1995, *The Nation*. Reprinted by permission of *The Nation*.

Kevin Powell, "altar for four" from *recognize*. Copyright 1995, Harlem River Press. Reprinted by permission of the author.

Dudley Randall, "Roses and Revolutions" from *The Black Poets*. Copyright 1971. Reprinted by permission of the author.

Louis Reyes Rivera, "the blacklit face of Mumia" Copyright *Scattered Scripture*. Reprinted by permission of the author.

Lamont B. Steptoe, "Osage" from *American Mourning/Morning*. Copyright 1990 Whirlwind Press. Reprinted by permission of the author.

Piri Thomas, "A Dialogue with Society" first appeared in *Long Shot*. Copyright 1993. Reprinted by permission of the author.

Ngugi wa Thiong'o, "Prison Without Trial" from *Detained: A Writer's Prison Diary*. Copyright 1981, Heinemann. Reprinted by permission of the author.

Jerome Washington, "Soap Opera" and other pieces on pages from 17, 55, 73, 86, 101, and 126 of *Iron House: Stories from the Yard*. Copyright 1994, QED Press. Reprinted by permission of the author and the publisher.

Ted Wilson, "Take It Again" first appeared in *Callalloo*. It is reprinted here by permission of